ANDREW LYCETT is author of an acclaimed biography of Rudyard Kipling. As a former foreign correspondent, he has travelled widely and worked in most parts of the world written about by Kipling. His other books include highly regarded lives of Ian Fleming, Dylan Thomas and Sir Arthur Conan Doyle. He is a member of the Council of the Kipling Society and a Fellow of the Royal Geographical Society.

Press reaction to Andrew Lycett's *Rudyard Kipling* when it was first published by Weidenfeld & Nicolson, 1999

'Andrew Lycett's biography is very good . . . especially good in his analysis of the marriage with Carrie.'
Allan Massie, *Daily Telegraph*

'Andrew Lycett's fascinating new biography . . . is another valuable step to restoring most of Kipling's art, and much of his character, to comply with today's more severe standards of respect.' Craig Brown, *Mail on Sunday*

'The best book on a misunderstood man for 20 years, and a sound guide to the India of his early life.'
Miranda Seymour, *Sunday Times*

'Charts Kipling's picaresque progress through India, Vermont, Capetown and Sussex with admirable even-handedness. The book is neither an apologia nor a polemic; there is no feebly disingenuous attempt to excuse Kipling's racist ravings, or to maintain, as others have done, that his more odious political doctrines have simply been misunderstood.'
Terry Eagleton, *Independent on Sunday*
(who chose it as his 'International Book of the Year'
in *Times Literary Supplement*)

'Lycett has looked at Kipling warts and all, and conducts us through his life and times with authority, dispassion and clarity. This is an excellent biography, with everything in its place.' Lawrence James, *Literary Review*

'Lycett . . . succeeds in getting to grips with his chosen subject, showing Kipling in all his colours: raging Imperialist, unhappy spouse and grieving father.' Mark Sanderson, *Time Out*

'This richly detailed biography . . . will still be read long after the latest psycho-histories and literary deconstructions have deconstructed one another to bits. Exploring the complexity of his life and opinions, it allows us to see the almost child-like simplicity of the man.' Noel Malcolm, *Sunday Telegraph*

'RUDYARD KIPLING

KIPLING ABROAD

Traffics and Discoveries from Burma to Brazil

INTRODUCED AND EDITED BY

ANDREW LYCETT

I.B. TAURIS

LONDON · NEW YORK

Published in 2010 by I.B.Tauris & Co Ltd
6 Salem Road, London W2 4BU
175 Fifth Avenue, New York NY 10010
www.ibtauris.com

Distributed in the United States and Canada Exclusively by Palgrave
Macmillan,
175 Fifth Avenue, New York NY 10010

ISBN 978 1 84885 072 9

A full CIP record for this book is available from the British Library
A full CIP record is available from the Library of Congress

Library of Congress Catalog Card Number: available

Typeset by JCS Publishing Services Ltd, www.jcs-publishing.co.uk
Printed and bound in India by Thomson Press India Ltd

CONTENTS

ACKNOWLEDGEMENTS

I would like to acknowledge the help and advice of Professor Thomas Pinney, whose magisterial six-volume edition of Kipling's letters was an invaluable resource. I am also very grateful to many others who offered useful support at different stages, including David Page, John Radcliffe and John Walker.

INTRODUCTION

'I can't keep still,' declares Jimmy Pitt in P.G. Wodehouse's early novel, *A Gentleman of Leisure*, published in 1910. 'I've got the go-fever, like that man in Kipling's book.'

Not to worry: all travellers should show symptoms of 'go-fever'. If the phrase wasn't actually coined by Rudyard Kipling (the dictionaries are inconclusive), it should have been. For it epitomises the mania for travel that followed the extraordinary opening up of the world towards the end of the nineteenth century – a mania which Kipling, a quirky Englishman born in India, observed, promoted and brilliantly conveyed in his writings.

The book Wodehouse had in mind was *The Light That Failed*, an under-rated novel that Kipling wrote in 1891/2 while trying to advance his literary career in London. He hated the dampness and darkness of the British capital and longed to get away, preferably to the warmth of his native India, scene of his success as a writer over the previous decade. His neurotic desire for escape took fleshly form in Dick Heldar, the war correspondent-turned-artist at the heart of *The Light That Failed*. On one occasion, after hearing stirring stories of sea voyages, Heldar speaks of a go-fever 'which is more real than many doctors' diseases', and wants 'to go away and taste the old hot, unregenerate life again – to scuffle, swear, gamble, and love light loves with his fellows; to take ship and know the sea once more, and by her beget pictures; to talk to Binat among the sands of Port Said while Yellow Tina mixed the drinks. . . .'

The hyperbole harks back to a more romantic era of travel. It reminds us that Kipling was writing during a transitional period when old-fashioned notions of travel as a form of heroic endeavour were giving way to a more realistic approach that accepted that, as result of mass transportation, the world was getting smaller and most places were now accessible.

Kipling was an ideal person to chronicle this change. As a young journalist, he had worked for what we might now describe as the emerging mass media. Apart from this professional training, he had the gift of observation in his genes, being the son of an architectural sculptor and nephew of the pre-Raphaelite painter Sir Edward Burne-Jones.

Kipling quickly grasped some of the basics of modern travel, such as its commercial underpinnings. This stemmed partly from his father's friendship with John Mason Cook, scion of the Thomas Cook travel firm, who had visited Lahore to discuss shipping arrangements for the hajj. Kipling also understood travel's close reliance on empire. Typically he poked light-hearted fun at this in his poem 'The Exiles' Line', which celebrated the P&O (Peninsula and Orient) company's role in ferrying servants of the Raj between Britain and India.

Even as he moved around India, he came across a new species he disparagingly called 'the Globe-trotter', who breezed through countries, hurriedly visiting sites such as the Taj Mahal, failing to take much in, only intent on the goal of being 'home by Christmas'. When he ventured outside the land of his birth to the Far East and North America, Kipling encountered different aspects of mass travel, but was seldom impressed. Coming across several 'excursion parties' at Yellowstone National Park, he commented,

> A brake-load of Cook's Continental tourists trapezing through Paris (I've seen 'em) are angels of light compared to [them]. It is not the ghastly vulgarity, the oozing, rampant Bessemer-steel self-sufficiency and ignorance of the men that revolts me, so much as the display of these same qualities in the women-folk.

When, after living in Vermont, he moved back to Sussex, he was alarmed to find that he himself had become a tourist attraction. Trippers regularly drove up to his house in Rottingdean and tried to catch sight of him.

These experiences did not deter him from becoming an enthusiastic tourist himself, particularly in middle age, when he and his family regularly took the Union Castle Line to South Africa, which, in the bleak British winter, provided an acceptable warm weather substitute for India.

Hand in hand with his sense of the business of travel came an appreciation of its logistics. In India this meant Kipling was a devotee of the railway system that features in so many of his stories. In 'The Man Who Would Be King', for example, 'The beginning of everything was in a railway train upon the road from Mhow to Ajmir.' There the narrator meets 'a wanderer and a vagabond like myself [. . .] He told tales of things he had seen and done, of out-of-the-way corners of Empire in which he had penetrated, and of adventures in which he risked his life for a few days' food.'

If Kipling had had to choose, he would have admitted a greater passion for ships than for railways. Trains were fine for covering long distances in India, North America and even Europe, but ships were more challenging and indicative of character. Essentially, they were more romantic. So he waxed lyrical about all aspects of seafaring in both poetry and prose. Specific vessels such as the *Bolivar*, *Clampherdown* and *Mary Gloster* were celebrated in ballads, while more generic groups were also feted – ocean-going craft in 'Big Steamers' and 'The Liner She's a Lady', warships in 'Cruisers' and 'Tin Fish' (the submarines which 'move[d] in the belly of death' during the First World War), and even 'the Mother and Father of all ships' in 'The Junk and the Dhow'.

For every reference to shipping and the sea in verse, there was another in fiction, from 'Judson and the Empire', which came to him as a result of a meeting in the Navy Club at Simon's Town, South Africa, in 1891, through the Pyecroft stories, which drew on Kipling's cruises with the Channel Squadron in HMS *Pelorus* in 1897 and 1898 (also recorded in 'A Fleet in Being'), to later tales, including 'The Manner of Men', which used his knowledge of the Mediterranean to evoke the ways of seafarers during the time of St Paul.

In keeping with his life-long fascination with the men who

made things function – in particular, the administrators, builders and soldiers of empire, Kipling made a special study of ships' engineers – men such as the eponym in 'McAndrew's Hymn', who enthuses about the music of his vessel's engines. When asked whether steam spoils romance at sea, McAndrew retorts:

> Damned ijjit! I'd been doon that morn to see what ailed the throws,
> Manholin', on my back – the cranks three inches off my nose.

He wants a poet

> like Robbie Burns to sing the Song o'Steam!
> To match wi' Scotia's noblest speech yon orchestra sublime
> Whaurto – uplifted like the Just – the tail-rods mark the time.
> The crank-throws give the double-bass, the feed-pump sobs an' heaves,
> An' now the main eccentrics start their quarrel on the sheaves:
> [. . .]
> Now a' together, hear them lift their lesson – theirs an' mine:
> 'Law, Orrder, Duty, an' Restraint, Obedience, Discipline!'

As he entered the last phase of his life, after the First World War, Kipling's empathy with the ordinary sailor became more marked. He contributed an epitaph to the war memorial for merchant seamen, he enrolled as a master mariner and he was instrumental in suggesting the name for the National Maritime Museum, to which institution he donated a large number of his nautical books.

Among his close friends were the chairmen of two large shipping lines: Sir Donald Currie of Union Castle and Sir Percy Bates of Cunard. Kipling even suggested the name Magnalia for Cunard's *Queen Mary*, launched in 1934. He told a friend around this time that one of his two unrealised ambitions in life was to buy a 400-ton brig and sail round the world (the other was to participate in an archaeological dig).

After he returned to live permanently in Britain in 1896, the motorcar became Kipling's preferred means of domestic transport. He was happy to use the train to travel between London and Etchingham – the station nearest 'Bateman's', his home in

Sussex – but he drove everywhere else. His first car, acquired in 1900, was a 'Victoria-hooded, carriage-sprung, carriage-braked, single-cylinder, belt-drive, fixed ignition Embryo which, at times, could cover eight miles an hour'. He then moved through several exotic marques, including a Locomobile and an unreliable Lanchester, which he called Jane Cakebread (after a notorious London prostitute with ninety-three convictions to her name), before settling on a Rolls Royce, which he updated for the rest of his life, always calling the current model 'the Duchess'.

His love of motoring took many forms – his friendship with Claude Johnson, manager of Rolls Royce; his membership of the (Royal) Automobile Club; his motoring diaries, meticulously detailing the mileage and road conditions on the many occasions when he took his beloved Duchess of the moment on trips to France (and further afield, to Spain and even Algeria). Not surprisingly, he wrote effusively about cars, particularly in the Edwardian era before the First World War. In 1904 he contributed a selection of verse parodies, 'The Muse Among the Motors', to the *Daily Mail* (which was trying to promote motoring as a new pastime). His version of Wordsworth sets the tone, with its opening stanza:

> He wandered down the mountain grade
> Beyond the speed assigned –
> A youth whom Justice often stayed
> And generally fined.

In later years his motoring verses were more practical, such as 'A Song of the French Roads', his paean to the simplicity and user friendliness of the Napoleonic road system.

In short stories, such as 'Steam Tactics', he liked to satirise the antics of early motorists, but he left no doubt of the importance of cars in his personal life. He wrote to his friend Filson Young:

> the chief end of my car [. . .] is the discovery of England. To me it is a land full of stupefying marvels and mysteries; and a day in the car in an English county is a day in some fairy museum where all the exhibits are alive and real and yet none the less delightfully mixed up with books.

More prosaically, he claimed that cars helped promote both temperance and education, since drivers had to remain sober and to read road signs.

Such observations, which strike us as faintly ludicrous today, underline the thoughtfulness of Kipling's approach to travel. As well as revelling in its details, he had a strong sense of its abstract qualities, as he brought out in 'Aspects of Travel', his lecture to the Royal Geographical Society in February 1914. There, among characteristic disquisitions on the importance of smells for wayfarers and on the qualities of successful expedition leaders, he addressed the question of the world's fast-diminishing boundaries:

> Month by month the Earth shrinks actually, and, what is more important, in imagination. We know it by the slide and crash of unstable material all around us. For the moment, but only for the moment, the new machines are outstripping mankind. We have cut down enormously – we shall cut down inconceivably – the world-conception of time and space, which is the big flywheel of the world's progress. What wonder that the great world-engine, which we call Civilisation, should race and heat a little; or that the onlookers who see it take charge should be a little excited, and, therefore, inclined to scold?

Given the date, he was clearly forecasting the onset of the First World War, and pointing to the speed of travel as a cause for it. He took up this theme in an oblique manner in two stories about air travel. While not a great flyer himself, he took a writerly interest in aircraft as a novel means of covering long distances. In 'With the Night Mail, A Tale of 2000 AD' (1905), about vast airships circumnavigating the globe, he introduces the Aerial Board of Control, a shadowy oligarchy that oversees the world's air traffic and has, as a result, assumed quasi-dictatorial powers. In 'As Easy as ABC' (1912) this international quango, with its motto 'Transport is Civilisation', realises its sinister potential when it intervenes from the air to quell social unrest in Chicago.

For all the illumination Kipling brought to bear on the more philosophical aspects of travel, however, his forte – and the main matter of this book – was his ability to conjure up the colour and feel of a particular spot on the globe for his travel-hungry readers. His skills can be traced back to his memories of being wheeled round Bombay (modern Mumbai) in his pram by his ayah. Included in this selection is a passage from his autobiography *Something of Myself*, where he recalls his early impressions of the vividness of India's light and colours.

Before long, this outward environment changed:

> Then those days of strong light and darkness passed, and there was a time in a ship with an immense semi-circle blocking all vision on each side of her. (She must have been the old paddle-wheel P&O *Ripon*.) There was a train across a desert (the Suez Canal was not yet opened) and a halt in it, and a small girl wrapped in a shawl on the seat opposite me, whose face stands out still. There was next a dark land, and a darker room full of cold, in one wall of which a white woman made naked fire, and I cried aloud with dread, for I had never before seen a grate.

Kipling was recalling snatches (including a brief encounter with Egypt – later reprised in *The Light That Failed*) of his first trip to a dank England. Even at the age of 2, he was aware of the startling contrast with his native India. However, this was to stand him in good stead in his later career as a writer. His experience of both East and West had helped give him 'two sides to my head' – as he put it in some epigrammatic verses for *Kim*. This enabled him to see the world with unusual objectivity – the subject of his charming poem 'We and They', which ends:

> All good people agree,
> And all good people say,
> All nice people, like Us, are We
> And everyone else is They:
> But if you cross over the sea,
> Instead of over the way,
> You may end by (think of it!) looking on We
> As only a sort of They!

His mother, Alice, was an inspiration in this respect, feeding

him the line that he took up in his poem 'The English Flag': 'And
what should they know of England, who only England know?'

As a pupil at the United Services College in Westward Ho!,
Devon, he began to write about the English countryside. Then,
in 1878 his father, on leave from India, took him to Paris – the
start of a life-long passion for France.

Since his parents could not afford to send him to university,
Kipling returned to Lahore, aged not quite 17, to join a newspaper, the *Civil and Military Gazette*. His 'seven years' hard' as a
journalist allowed him to get out and write about India – around
Lahore, but also further afield in the Punjab and in the hills at
the Raj's summer capital, Simla. After moving to the *Pioneer* in
Allahabad, he was able to roam in Rajasthan and Bengal – the
subject matter of his collection *Letters of Marque*.

Having decided that his literary future lay in England, he took
an easterly route to Europe, via Burma, Malaya, Singapore, Hong
Kong, China, Japan and the United States – all of which provided
excellent copy for travel pieces. When London did not live up to
expectations, he succumbed to his 'go-fever' and travelled, via
South Africa, to Australia and New Zealand, where he appreciatively described the southern city of Auckland in 'The Song of
the Cities' as 'Last, loneliest, loveliest, exquisite, apart'. He had
hoped to continue to Samoa to visit Robert Louis Stevenson, a
literary hero. But his schedule did not allow this, so he returned
to England, via his parents in Lahore. (On this occasion he wrote
his superb account, reproduced here, of his railway journey up
India from Tuticorin.) While enjoying his return to the subcontinent, he received news of the death of his close friend, Wolcott
Balestier, a London-based American publisher, in late 1891.

He rushed home and, shortly afterwards, married Balestier's
sister, Caroline. As a result, he moved to the United States and
went to live in her home state, Vermont, where he built a house,
'Naulakha', just outside Brattleboro'. On their honeymoon the
couple travelled through Canada to Japan, which fascinated
him. Once again he hoped to make his way to Samoa, but he lost
the then significant sum of £2,000 when the New Oriental Bank
Corporation collapsed and the Kiplings were forced to return to
their new home in America.

He never settled, however, and, after four years, returned to England, where in 1902 he put down roots at 'Bateman's' in Burwash, Sussex, from where, for the remainder of his life, he ventured out regularly on trips abroad. Both before and after the Boer War, Kipling enjoyed winter sojourns in South Africa, where his friend Cecil Rhodes lent him a house, 'The Woolsack'. In 1907, he travelled across Canada in a special Pullman car as the guest of the railway company, Canadian Pacific. At around this time he took to motoring and, with the assistance always of a chauffeur, began venturing in his car across the Channel to France. He also visited Italy, Sweden (to receive the Nobel Prize in 1907) and Switzerland, where he liked to spend a few weeks with his family during the winter. In 1913 he journeyed to Egypt, which, as recorded in his book *Egypt of the Magicians*, excited him as the gateway to the East.

After the start of a conflict with Germany that he had long anticipated, he wrote for Britain's Propaganda Bureau, a role that again took him to France and Italy, where his account of the war in the mountains conveyed a strong sense of the physicality of the Alps.

The loss of his son John at the Battle of Loos curtailed his appetite for overseas forays for a while. His involvement with war graves in northern France and Belgium helped him through his period of mourning, however, and gradually drew him back to Europe, taking him to France on many occasions, and also to Spain and Czechoslovakia (in August 1935, a few months before his death). He also travelled further afield – to Algeria (1921), Brazil (1927), Egypt and Palestine (1929), Jamaica and Bermuda (1930) – though he published only one more series of travel articles, *Brazilian Sketches*.

At each stage in his life, Kipling reacted enthusiastically to his surroundings – in articles, verse, letters, diaries and descriptive passages that formed part of his fiction. In this selection I have tried to strike a balance between these genres – showing how he sometimes expanded a piece of journalism in a poem or a story.

Although he romanticised the lives of certain voyagers, particularly sailors, Kipling's travel writing has stood the test of time because it is vivid and practical, as if part of a conversation between him and his readers about the world, its attractions and its problems. In this respect it anticipates the work of a more recent Nobel Prize winner, V.S. Naipaul. There is another reason for Kipling's continuing readability: throughout his wanderings, he was always interested in people. As an imperialist, he may have held unyielding opinions about political systems, but as a writer in touch with the two sides of his head, he was much more flexible in his attitudes to individuals. He liked to understand what made them tick, and scrutinised them in the context of their jobs, beliefs and environments.

One finds this quality in his novel *Kim*. The book abounds with detailed descriptions of places from Lahore to the Himalayas. But Kipling is careful to populate them with credible human beings. 'Look!' exclaims an old soldier familiar with the Grand Trunk Road, 'Brahmins and chumars, bankers and tinkers, barbers and bunnias, pilgrims and potters – all the world going and coming.' Kipling had an enviable ability to evoke that sense of bustle and purpose – the 'go-fever' – in any situation. 'And truly the Grand Trunk Road is a wonderful spectacle,' comments the narrator in *Kim*. In Kipling's writing the entire world becomes a wonderful spectacle.

INDIA

From the Plains to the Hills

Bombay (Mumbai) – Patiala – Lahore – Peshawar – North-West Frontier – Umballa – Simla – Taj Mahal and 'the Globe-trotter' – Jaipur – Amber – Chitor – Jodhpur – Jamalpur – Ghazipur – Calcutta (Kolkata) – Indian Railways – To Lahore by Train.

Rudyard Kipling spent little more than a decade of his life in India. He never went back after he was 26. Nevertheless it is impossible to think of him apart from the subcontinent. It was there that he learned to observe people and places and to become a writer, initially as a small child living in Bombay (modern Mumbai), the city of his birth (on 30 December 1865), and later, following a break for schooling in England, as a young journalist in Lahore and Allahabad (from 1882 to 1889).

The two pieces here about Bombay demonstrate Kipling's range – how he could summon up situations in different styles, according to his mood or intent. The first, from his autobiography, shows him in old age reflecting on his enduring memories of the light, colour and sensations of his native city. The second, a poem from his middle years, is more rhetorical – a piece of high-flown verse expressing the genuine pride he felt for his cosmopolitan birthplace and its position at the hub of international commerce.

Kipling returned to India after school in England and took a job on the *Civil and Military Gazette* (CMG) in Lahore, where his parents lived. This proved an ideal apprenticeship for a writer with a keen eye for what was happening around him. After a short but intensive period as an in-house subeditor, he was encouraged to explore further afield – initially as a 'special correspondent' in the princely state of Patiala, in the Eastern Punjab.

Before long he was given a domestic beat, with a regular feature, 'A Week in Lahore'. Along with run-of-the-mill articles about municipal elections and public health, he wrote descriptive pieces about the old city, with its exotic peoples and cultures. In his autobiography he recorded how 'the night got into [his] head,' and he 'would wander till dawn in all manner of places – liquor-shops, gambling and opium dens, which are not a bit mysterious, wayside entertainments such as puppet-shows, native dances; or in and about the narrow gullies under the Mosque of Wazir Khan for the sheer sake of looking'. In this context, 'The City of Dreadful Night', an early, dramatic report on nocturnal Lahore, appeared in the *CMG* in September 1885 and was later reprinted in *Life's Handicap* (1891). Moving easily between genres, he also fictionalised aspects of the Old City in stories such as 'The Gate of the Hundred Sorrows', which is sampled here.

A similar link between reportage and fiction occurred when Kipling tackled other subjects that interested him, such as native festivals. Like any good writer, he was prepared to recycle any decent material he came across. For the *CMG*, he reported on the Mohurrum, a Muslim commemoration of the deaths of the Prophet's grandsons, the Imams Hasan and Hussein. The *tazias* he refers to are the ceremonial floats representing the imams' tombs, which are carried in procession. In Kipling's day this festival often sparked communal violence, which provides the backdrop to 'On the City Wall', a subtle and energetic story about the conflict between fanaticism and civilisation.

In another article for the *CMG*, he reported on the Mela Chiraghan, a festival commemorating the death of the Punjabi poet and Sufi saint Shah Hussain (1538–99), who was born in Lahore and whose tomb and shrine are at Baghbanpura (Begumpora today), adjacent to the Shalimar Gardens, a short distance outside the city. These Mughal-built gardens are one of the physical delights of the Lahore area – a haven of sparkling fountains and panoramic terraces, much frequented by picnickers and day-trippers.

Having proved his journalistic credentials, Kipling was sent west to Rawalpindi in March/April 1885 to report on the Durbar (or ceremonial court) arranged by the new Viceroy Lord Dufferin for the Afghan Amir, Abdur Rahman. This event was essentially a diplomatic spectacle designed to shore up the Amir's support during a fraught period of the 'Great Game' (with the Russians) for control of India. Kipling used the occasion to journey up to the Khyber Pass on the Afghan frontier. He contributed a number of pieces to his newspaper about both the event and his travels. The most interesting came from Peshawar, where he made no secret of his trepidation when confronted by a host of swarthy tribesmen (Pathans and others).

That same year (1885) Kipling started visiting Simla, the Himalayan hill station that was the summer seat of the imperial government. The journey was not easy, as his piece on the bumpy grind from Umballa shows. As the CMG's special correspondent, he would stay there with his family during the hot summer months when living in Lahore became intolerable.

In November 1886 he began translating his experiences into a series of short stories. Originally published as 'turn-overs', denoting that they moved from one page to another, these often biting satires about Raj social life made Kipling's name when they appeared in book form as *Plain Tales from the Hills*, first published in India by Thacker, Spink in 1888. He also wrote more conventional pieces about Simla for his paper, such as his exuberant account of the local monkeys, which is included here. Among his other stories about the place was 'The Phantom Rickshaw', which incorporates landmarks, such as Peliti's Grand Hotel, into a ghost tale, originally published in *Quartette*, the CMG's 'Christmas annual' in 1885 – an issue written entirely by the Kipling family.

In late 1887, Kipling resigned from the CMG and went to work on a sister paper, the *Pioneer*, in Allahabad. One of his first assignments was in Rajasthan, which he described to his cousin Margaret Burne-Jones as 'the home of a hundred thousand legends and the great fighting pen of India'. His reports, collected in the volume *Letters of Marque*, first published by A.H. Wheeler in Allahabad in 1891, started at the Taj Mahal in Agra, where he had trenchant views about not only the great monument but also the new breed of sightseer or 'globe-trotter' who came to visit it. His travels in Rajasthan also took him to Jaipur, Amber, Chitor and Jodphur (among other places). Apart from observing cities now firmly on the tourist trail, his output was notable for his description of his revulsion at visiting the Gau-Mukh shrine in Chitor.

With Allahabad as his base, Kipling was able to roam among the more easterly states of the Raj, visiting Jamalpur, the East India Railway's headquarters and workshop, in modern Bihar, and Ghazipur, the country's largest opium factory, in Uttar Pradesh.

He also made his way to Calcutta (modern Kolkata), which provided copy for articles for the *Pioneer* and its sister papers from February 1888. He collected these pieces in *The City of Dreadful Night and Other Places* (1891), a title he had already used of Lahore, and one that looked back to James Thomson's bleak poem of the same name.

Having enjoyed some success, not only with his articles, but with books such as *Plain Tales from the Hills*, Kipling decided in 1889 to seek his literary fortune in London. His journey to Britain took him eastwards by ship through South-East Asia to Japan and across the Pacific, then mostly by train through the United States, before boarding a transatlantic liner for the final stretch to Liverpool and London. As always, he kept readers of the *Pioneer* informed of his travels – a process that started in March 1889 with an update of his views on Calcutta. They had not changed much. He still purported to dislike the place – and its smell.

By now a seasoned traveller on the subcontinent, Kipling was acutely aware of the importance of railways to daily existence – a theme of the short extract here from his story 'The Man Who Would Be King'. More specifically, when he returned briefly to India en route back from Australia in late 1891, he wrote a vivid account of his train trip up the length of the country – from the tip of the southern coast to Lahore in the far north.

BOMBAY (MUMBAI)

M̦Y FIRST IMPRESSION IS of daybreak, light and colour and golden and purple fruits at the level of my shoulder. This would be the memory of early morning walks to the Bombay fruit market with my *ayah* and later with my sister in her perambulator, and of our returns with our purchases piled high on the bows of it. Our *ayah* was a Portuguese Roman Catholic who would pray – I beside her – at a wayside Cross. Meeta, my Hindu bearer, would sometimes go into little Hindu temples where, being below the age of caste, I held his hand and looked at the dimly-seen, friendly Gods.

Our evening walks were by the sea in the shadow of palm-groves which, I think, were called the Mahim Woods. When the wind blew the great nuts would tumble, and we fled – my *ayah*, and my sister in her perambulator – to the safety of the open. I have always felt the menacing darkness of tropical eventides, as I have loved the voices of night-winds through palm or banana leaves, and the song of the tree-frogs.

There were far-going Arab dhows on the pearly waters, and gaily dressed Parsees wading out to worship the sunset. Of their creed I knew nothing, nor did I know that near our little house on the Bombay Esplanade were the Towers of Silence, where their Dead are exposed to the waiting vultures on the rim of the towers, who scuffle and spread wings when they see the bearers of the Dead below. I did not understand my Mother's distress when she found 'a child's hand' in our garden, and said I was not to ask questions about it. I wanted to see that child's hand. But my *ayah* told me.

[*Something of Myself*]

THE CITIES ARE FULL of pride,
    Challenging each to each –
This from her mountain-side,
    That from her burthened beach.

They count their ships full tale –
    Their corn and oil and wine,
Derrick and loom and bale,
    And rampart's gun-flecked line;
City by City they hail:
    'Hast aught to match with mine?'

And the men that breed from them
    They traffic up and down,
But cling to their cities' hem
    As a child to the mother's gown.

When they talk with the stranger bands,
    Dazed and newly alone;
When they walk in the stranger lands,
    By roaring streets unknown;
Blessing her where she stands
    For strength above their own.

(On high to hold her fame
    That stands all fame beyond,
By oath to back the same,
    Most faithful-foolish-fond;
Making her mere-breathed name
    Their bond upon their bond.)

So thank I God my birth
    Fell not in isles aside –
Waste headlands of the earth,
    Or warring tribes untried –
But that she lent me worth
    And gave me right to pride.

Surely in toil or fray
   Under an alien sky,
Comfort it is to say:
   'Of no mean city am I!'

(Neither by service nor fee
   Come I to mine estate –
Mother of Cities to me,
   For I was born in her gate,
Between the palms and the sea,
   Where the world-end steamers wait.)

Now for this debt I owe,
   And for her far-borne cheer
Must I make haste and go
   With tribute to her pier.

And she shall touch and remit
   After the use of kings
(Orderly, ancient, fit)
   My deep-sea plunderings,
And purchase in all lands.
   And this we do for a sign
Her power is over mine,
   And mine I hold at her hands!

['To the City of Bombay', *The Seven Seas*]

✠ ✠ ✠

PATIALA

ASCENDING MANY STAIRS WE come to another department of the Museum. When His Highness bought any thing he did it wholesale, and everything is repeated many times over. I counted a hundred and fifty penknives, twenty or thirty nail-brushes of various patterns, and then gave it up as a hopeless task. At the risk of being tedious I will give a list of a few of the more prominent features of the department. Bolts, nuts, and screws in assorted cases, sheets of lead; wire net-work, zinc and tin, ten or twenty of each; albums in Russia leather, malachite, ivory, mother-of-pearl, silver, onyx and agate, piled anywhere and any-how; dressing bags in scores; liqueur stands, riding whips, sausage-machines, champagne-tweezers, candlesticks, and chimney-piece ornaments more than I could count; pictures of all kinds, piled face to the wall; twenty-seven brass parrot cages, and fourteen courier bags; an assortment of cigar and card-cases in tortoise-shell and gold; several telescopes and binoculars, dozens of glove cases in agate and onyx; then musical boxes as big as small organs, stereoscopes, patent medicines, patent inks, and a flock of India-rubber decoy ducks, flattened and dusty, butcher's scales, spring balances, and Bramah locks and children's toys, all of the newest and most expensive kinds. This is not a tenth part of the contents of that room, and it was a little depressing to see how everything was gradually being spoilt with neglect.

As I was leaving, an official asked me if I would care to see His Highness's dressing cases. I had seen nearly a hundred, and explained that it was all very grand, but a trifle monotonous. Then the official told me that the dressing cases he referred to had cost half-a-lakh each, and I changed my mind. Each case stood four feet high and was mounted in solid silver with the Maharajah's monograph 'M.S.S.' in silver half-a-foot long, on the outside. Inside was a complete service for dressing, dining, and writing, surgical instruments, and cheroot cases, all in silver with the Maharajah's monogram in blue and white enamel on each article. A complete set of plate in silver, and a whole stand of liqueur bottles made up the contents, which numbered over two hundred and fifty articles, all embedded in purple velvet. When I say that the toilet service was silver, I would be understood in the most literal sense. Every bottle and case was of solid silver throughout. Unfortunately the Maharajah died before the dressing cases reached him from England – for which he is a good deal to be pitied.

They must be worth every rupee of the hundred thousand spent on them, and, however much I might write about them, I should fail to give any idea of their appearance. It would be worthwhile to visit Patiala to see those dressing cases alone. In common with all the other things, they are sadly neglected, and one is so warped that the lock is hampered and will not open. Further exploration of the Palace led to some curious discoveries. I had been close upon two hours in the building, and was only on the outskirts of it. Ten minutes' wandering across huge silent squares, baking in the sunlight, and through innumerable dark passages, brought me out to a second and smaller edition of the wonders I had left behind. More chandeliers, more statues and knicknacks, but all of a much older date, and covered with the dust of years. Two or three natives, who looked as if they had grown grey in the guarding of these treasures, salaamed wearily as I entered, and were good enough to leave me alone. Beyond these aged servitors not a soul was visible, though, all round the square, (it was the third I had entered) I could hear steps and the sounds of far off voices, and, now and then, the noise of suppressed laughter.

[*CMG*, 22 March 1884]

✠ ✠ ✠

LAHORE

THE DENSE WET HEAT that hung over the face of land, like a blanket, prevented all hope of sleep in the first instance. The cicalas helped the heat, and the yelling jackals the cicalas. It was impossible to sit still in the dark, empty, echoing house and watch the punkah beat the dead air. So, at ten o'clock of the night, I set my walking-stick on end in the middle of the garden, and waited to see how it would fall. It pointed directly down the moonlit road that leads to the City of Dreadful Night. The sound of its fall disturbed a hare. She limped from her form and ran across to a disused Mahomedan burial-ground, where the jawless skulls and rough-butted shank-bones, heartlessly exposed by the July rains, glimmered like mother o' pearl on the rain-channelled soil. The heated air and the heavy earth had driven the very dead upward for coolness' sake. The hare limped on; snuffed curiously at a fragment of a smoke-stained lamp-shard, and died out, in the shadow of a clump of tamarisk trees.

The mat-weaver's hut under the lee of the Hindu temple was full of sleeping men who lay like sheeted corpses. Overhead blazed the unwinking eye of the Moon. Darkness gives at least a false impression of coolness. It was hard not to believe that the flood of light from above was warm. Not so hot as the Sun, but still sickly warm, and heating the heavy air beyond what was our due. Straight as a bar of polished steel ran the road to the City of Dreadful Night; and on either side of the road lay corpses disposed on beds in fantastic attitudes – one hundred and seventy bodies of men. Some shrouded all in white with bound-up mouths; some naked and black as ebony in the strong light; and one – that lay face upwards with dropped jaw, far away from the others – silvery white and ashen gray.

'A leper asleep; and the remainder wearied coolies, servants, small shopkeepers, and drivers from the hack-stand hard by. The scene – a main approach to Lahore city, and the night a warm one in August.' This was all that there was to be seen; but by no means all that one could see. The witchery of the moonlight was everywhere; and the world was horribly changed. The long line of the naked dead, flanked by the rigid silver statue, was not pleasant to look upon. It was made up of men alone. Were the women-kind, then, forced to sleep in the shelter of the stifling mud-huts as best they might? The fretful wail of a child from a low mud-roof answered the question. Where the children are the mothers must be also to look after them. They need care on these sweltering nights. A black little bullet-head peeped over the coping, and a thin – a painfully thin – brown leg was slid over on to the gutter pipe. There was a sharp clink of glass bracelets; a woman's arm showed for an instant above the parapet, twined itself round the lean little neck, and the child was dragged back, protesting, to the shelter of the bedstead. His thin, high-pitched shriek died out in the thick air almost as soon as it was raised; for even the children of the soil found it too hot to weep.

More corpses; more stretches of moonlit, white road; a string of sleeping camels at rest by the wayside; a vision of scudding

jackals; ekka ponies asleep – the harness still on their backs, and
the brass-studded country carts, winking in the moonlight – and
again more corpses. Wherever a grain cart atilt, a tree trunk, a
sawn log, a couple of bamboos and a few handfuls of thatch cast
a shadow, the ground is covered with them. They lie – some face
downwards, arms folded, in the dust; some with clasped hands
flung up above their heads; some curled up dog-wise; some
thrown like limp gunny-bags over the side of the grain carts;
and some bowed with their brows on their knees in the full glare
of the Moon. It would be a comfort if they were only given to
snoring; but they are not, and the likeness to corpses is unbroken
in all respects save one. The lean dogs snuff at them and turn
away. Here and there a tiny child lies on his father's bedstead,
and a protecting arm is thrown round it in every instance. But,
for the most part, the children sleep with their mothers on the
housetops. Yellow-skinned white-toothed pariahs are not to be
trusted within reach of brown bodies.

A stifling hot blast from the mouth of the Delhi Gate nearly
ends my resolution of entering the City of Dreadful Night
at this hour. It is a compound of all evil savours, animal and
vegetable, that a walled city can brew in a day and a night.
The temperature within the motionless groves of plantain and
orange-trees outside the city walls seems chilly by comparison.
Heaven help all sick persons and young children within the city
tonight! The high house-walls are still radiating heat savagely,
and from obscure side gullies fetid breezes eddy that ought to
poison a buffalo. But the buffaloes do not heed. A drove of them
are parading the vacant main street; stopping now and then to
lay their ponderous muzzles against the closed shutters of a
grain-dealer's shop, and to blow thereon like grampuses.

Then silence follows – the silence that is full of the night
noises of a great city. A stringed instrument of some kind is just,
and only just audible. High over head someone throws open
a window, and the rattle of the woodwork echoes down the
empty street. On one of the roofs a hookah is in full blast; and
the men are talking softly as the pipe gutters. A little farther on
the noise of conversation is more distinct. A slit of light shows
itself between the sliding shutters of a shop. Inside, a stubble-

bearded, weary-eyed trader is balancing his account-books among the bales of cotton prints that surround him. Three sheeted figures bear him company, and throw in a remark from time to time. First he makes an entry, then a remark; then passes the back of his hand across his streaming forehead. The heat in the built-in street is fearful. Inside the shops it must be almost unendurable. But the work goes on steadily; entry, guttural growl, and uplifted hand-stroke succeeding each other with the precision of clock-work.

A policeman – turbanless and fast asleep – lies across the road on the way to the Mosque of Wazir Khan. A bar of moonlight falls across the forehead and eyes of the sleeper, but he never stirs. It is close upon midnight, and the heat seems to be increasing. The open square in front of the Mosque is crowded with corpses; and a man must pick his way carefully for fear of treading on them. The moonlight stripes the Mosque's high front of coloured enamel work in broad diagonal bands; and each separate dreaming pigeon in the niches and corners of the masonry throws a squab little shadow. Sheeted ghosts rise up wearily from their pallets, and flit into the dark depths of the building. Is it possible to climb to the top of the great Minars, and thence to look down on the city? At all events the attempt is worth making, and the chances are that the door of the staircase will be unlocked. Unlocked it is; but a deeply sleeping janitor lies across the threshold, face turned to the Moon. A rat dashes out of his turban at the sound of approaching footsteps. The man grunts, opens his eyes for a minute, turns round, and goes to sleep again. All the heat of a decade of fierce Indian summers is stored in the pitch-black, polished walls of the corkscrew staircase. Half-way up there is something alive, warm, and feathery; and it snores. Driven from step to step as it catches the sound of my advance, it flutters to the top and reveals itself as a yellow-eyed, angry kite. Dozens of kites are asleep on this and the other Minars, and on the domes below. There is the shadow of a cool, or at least a less sultry breeze at this height; and, refreshed thereby, turn to look on the City of Dreadful Night.

Doré might have drawn it! Zola could describe it – this spectacle of sleeping thousands in the moonlight and in the shadow of the Moon. The roof-tops are crammed with men, women, and children; and the air is full of undistinguishable noises. They are restless in the City of Dreadful Night; and small wonder. The marvel is that they can even breathe. If you gaze intently at the multitude you can see that they are almost as uneasy as a daylight crowd; but the tumult is subdued. Everywhere, in the strong light, you can watch the sleepers turning to and fro; shifting their beds and again resettling them. In the pit-like courtyards of the houses there is the same movement.

The pitiless Moon shows it all. Shows, too, the plains outside the city, and here and there a hand's-breadth of the Ravee without the walls. Shows lastly, a splash of glittering silver on a house-top almost directly below the mosque Minar. Some poor soul has risen to throw a jar of water over his fevered body; the tinkle of the falling water strikes faintly on the ear. Two or three other men, in far-off corners of the City of Dreadful Night, follow his example, and the water flashes like heliographic signals. A small cloud passes over the face of the Moon, and the city and its inhabitants – clear drawn in black and white before – fade into masses of black and deeper black. Still the unrestful noise continues, the sigh of a great city overwhelmed with the heat, and of a people seeking in vain for rest. It is only the lower-class women who sleep on the house-tops. What must the torment be in the latticed zenanas, where a few lamps are still twinkling? There are footfalls in the court below. It is the *Muezzin* – faithful minister; but he ought to have been here an hour ago to tell the Faithful that prayer is better than sleep – the sleep that will not come to the city.

The *Muezzin* fumbles for a moment with the door of one of the Minars, disappears awhile, and a bull-like roar – a magnificent bass thunder – tells that he has reached the top of the Minar. They must hear the cry to the banks of the shrunken Ravee itself! Even across the courtyard it is almost overpowering. The cloud drifts by and shows him outlined in black against the sky, hands laid upon his ears, and broad chest heaving with the play of his lungs – 'Allah ho Akbar'; then a pause while another *Muezzin* somewhere in the direction of the Golden Temple takes up the call – 'Allah ho Akbar.' Again and again; four times in all; and from the bedsteads a dozen men have risen up already. – 'I bear witness that there is no God but God.' What a splendid cry it is, the proclamation of the creed that brings men out of their beds by scores at midnight! Once again he thunders through the same phrase, shaking with the vehemence of his own voice; and then, far and near, the night air rings with 'Mahomed is the Prophet of God.' It is as though he were flinging his defiance to the far-off horizon, where the summer lightning plays and leaps like a bared sword. Every *Muezzin* in the city is in full cry, and some men on the roof-tops are beginning to kneel. A long pause precedes the last cry, '*La ilaha Illallah*,' and the silence closes up on it, as the ram on the head of a cotton-bale.

The *Muezzin* stumbles down the dark stairway grumbling in his beard. He passes the arch of the entrance and disappears. Then the stifling silence settles down over the City of Dreadful Night. The kites on the Minar sleep again, snoring more loudly, the hot breeze comes up in puffs and lazy eddies, and the Moon slides down towards the horizon. Seated with both elbows on the parapet of the tower, one can watch and wonder over that heat-tortured hive till the dawn. 'How do they live down there? What do they think of? When will they awake?' More tinkling of sluiced water-pots; faint jarring of wooden bedsteads moved into or out of the shadows; uncouth music of stringed instruments softened by distance into a plaintive wail, and one low grumble of far-off thunder. In the courtyard of the mosque the janitor, who lay across the threshold of the Minar when I came up, starts wildly in his sleep, throws his hands above his head, mutters something, and falls back again. Lulled by the snoring of the kites – they snore like over-gorged humans – I drop off into an uneasy doze, conscious that three o'clock has struck, and that there is a slight – a very slight – coolness in the atmosphere. The city is absolutely quiet now, but for some vagrant dog's love-song. Nothing save dead heavy sleep.

Several weeks of darkness pass after this. For the Moon has gone out. The very dogs are still, and I watch for the first light of the dawn before making my way homeward. Again the noise of shuffling feet. The morning call is about to begin, and my night watch is over. '*Allah ho Akbar! Allah ho Akbar!*' The east grows gray, and presently saffron; the dawn wind comes up as though the *Muezzin* had summoned it; and, as one man, the City of Dreadful Night rises from its bed and turns its face towards the dawning day. With return of life comes return of sound. First a low whisper, then a deep bass hum; for it must be remembered that the entire city is on the house-tops. My eyelids weighed down with the arrears of long deferred sleep, I escape from the Minar through the courtyard and out into the square beyond, where the sleepers have risen, stowed away the bedsteads, and are discussing the morning hookah. The minute's freshness of the air has gone, and it is as hot as at first.

'Will the Sahib, out of his kindness, make room?' What is it? Something borne on men's shoulders comes by in the half-light, and I stand back. A woman's corpse going down to the burning-ghat, and a bystander says, 'She died at midnight from the heat.' So the city was of Death as well as Night after all.

[*CMG*, 10 September 1885; *Life's Handicap*]

✠ ✠ ✠

IT LIES BETWEEN THE Coppersmith's Gully and the pipe-stem sellers' quarter, within a hundred yards, too, as the crow flies, of the Mosque of Wazir Khan. I don't mind telling anyone this much, but I defy him to find the Gate, however well he may think he knows the City. You might even go through the very gully it stands in a hundred times, and be none the wiser. We used to call the gully, 'The Gully of the Black Smoke,' but its native name is altogether different of course. A loaded donkey couldn't pass between the walls; and, at one point, just before you reach the Gate, a bulged house-front makes people go along all sideways.

It isn't really a gate, though. It's a house. Old Fung-Tching had it first five years ago. He was a boot-maker in Calcutta. They say that he murdered his wife there when he was drunk. That was why he dropped bazar-rum and took to the Black Smoke instead.

Later on, he came up north and opened the Gate as a house where you could get your smoke in peace and quiet. Mind you, it was a *pukka*, respectable opium-house, and not one of those stifling, sweltering *chandoo-khanas* that you can find all over the City. No; the old man knew his business thoroughly, and he was most clean for a Chinaman. He was a one-eyed little chap, not much more than five feet high, and both his middle fingers were gone. All the same, he was the handiest man at rolling black pills I have ever seen. Never seemed to be touched by the Smoke, either; and what he took day and night, night and day, was a caution. I've been at it five years, and I can do my fair share of the Smoke with any one; but I was a child to Fung-Tching that way. All the same, the old man was keen on his money: very keen; and that's what I can't understand. I heard he saved a good deal before he died, but his nephew has got all that now; and the old man's gone back to China to be buried.

['The Gate of the Hundred Sorrows', *CMG*, 26 September 1884;
Plain Tales from the Hills]

✷ ✷ ✷

Two years ago, Lahore at the end of the hot weather was enlivened by a small Mohurrum fight in the City, and the outcries of many bunniahs. A British regiment, to the extent of four companies, was dug out of its bed at Mian Mir, the 14th B[engal] L[ancers] smote with their lance-butts on the toes of the peace-breakers and Lahore Fort was crowded with riotous subalterns, while most of the high officials in the station mounted horses and ran hither and thither. In the dearth of other news, down-country papers called the scuffle 'Riots' and the 'Lahore Riots' it has remained in the memory of man ever since. Forty-one years ago, it may be mentioned incidentally, when an over-zealous sword-maker was hanged outside the Delhi gate in the early morning, the night's work in which he had taken a leading part was dignified with no loftier title than that of 'a disturbance'.

This year's Mohurrum has passed with a peace that was almost dullness. No one threw bricks into the tinselled *tazias*,

and none except the police excited their neighbours with *lathis*.
A 'processional' conflict in one of the narrow gullies, when
all are so tightly packed that they can do nothing save shout
abuse, is worth seeing, and still more impressive is the rush that
follows, on a rumour that the *gorah-log* are coming. But Lahore
has given up these dissipations under the benign influence of a
native municipality and the education of the University. Because
many hundreds of years ago Yezid, son of Mowwajib, first of the
Ommeiad Caliphs of Damascus, met, on the plains of Kerbela,
west of the Euphrates, and slew Hossain and Hussan, sons of
Ali, First or Fourth (as you are Shiah or Sunni) of the Caliphs,
and of Fatima, his wife, it is now necessary for every Deputy
Commissioner in the Province, once a year, to spend half the
night in a native city while the representations of the tombs
of the butchered and Blessed Imams stagger up and down the
ways. The consequences of any act, some moralists hold, are
infinite and eternal; and this instance backs the theory.

On Wednesday as soon as the darkness fell, the drums began
throbbing in the heart of the city though the three and twenty
tazias were not to begin moving till half-past eleven. This year as
in previous ones, there did not seem to be the slightest attempt
towards a massing of spectacular effect. As in the famous
Caucus race, witnessed by 'Alice in Wonderland', the *tazias*
began where they liked and left off as seemed good to them. A
little trouble on the part of the owners, a little fore-sight and a
careful disposition of torches would have done great things. The
City by night, and by moonlight more particularly, supplies one
of the most fascinating, if least savoury, walks in the station. The
yard-wide gullies into which the moonlight cannot struggle are
full of mystery, stories of life and death and intrigue of which
we, the Mall abiding, open-windowed, purdah-less English
know nothing and believe less. The open square, under the
great front of Wazir Khan's mosque where any man may find
a bed and remarkably good *kababs*, if he knows where to go, is
full of beauty even when the noonday heat silences the voices
of men and puts the pigeons of the mosque to sleep. Properly
exploited, our City, from the Taksali to the Delhi Gate, and from
the wrestling-ground to the Badami Bagh would yield a store

of novels to which the *City of Sunshine* would be as 'water unto wine'. However, until some one lifts its name into the light of a new fame, Lahore is only a fraction of a Deputy Commissioner's charge, to be watched, drained, coaxed and scolded as such. From the Delhi Gate to the Soneri Musjid – was it the founder or the architect of this mosque who, ignoble end, was slippered to death by a too powerful mistress? – runs the main artery of the city, the Road of Globe-Trotters and inferior folk of their kidney. At the Golden Musjid, a little beyond the cloth-seller's shops, the first *tazia*, a gorgeous arrangement in tin and tinselry was reeling and plunging like a ship in a heavy sea. It is the proud privilege of all the little boys who can, by any means, lay hands upon them to carry the torches of rolled rag dipped in oil. The boys were prancing and squealing with impatience, occasionally chasing each other across the road, and under the legs of the mounted policeman's horse who was a patient beast and went to sleep when the drums were beating under his venerable nose. As the hour of the general move forward to the Shalmi Gate drew nearer, the din increased; *tazia* answering *tazia* and the gullies holding the roll of the drums as the hills hold thunder.

The Mochi Darwaza *tazias* were some four or five in number and had packed themselves into an especially narrow street which they did their best to choke. Seen from the safe shelter of a well-curb the movement was picturesque; but after a few years the eye of the dweller in this country becomes scared and his heart hardens, so that the finest effects of red light and black shadow, seas of turbans, upturned faces and arms tossed aloft, fail to impress him as anything new or startling. The heat, and the heat in the City even on a September night was inconvenient, the smells and the noise touch him as keenly as ever; but it is impossible to wax enthusiastic over these things.

A *tazia* advanced, swayed, shook, retreated, was driven back, dived forward and passed with a yell, a shout, a patter of hundreds of feet, a blaze of torches and a rain of lighted tow, to be succeeded by another *tazia*, another mob and occasionally a brass band of terrible quality. In the pauses of the processions the *gutkas* leapt into the middle of the way and fought with lath swords carrying arm guards to the elbow. With the best will in the world, and all possible desire to recover 'the first fine careless rapture' of the griffin who gazes on the gaudier aspects of the East, the attention wandered from the crowd to the watch, and interest was swallowed up in a yawn. There had been no trouble, the City was quiet and another Mohurrum had been safely tided over. Beyond the city walls lay civilization in the shape of iced drinks and spacious roads.

[*CMG*, 1 October 1887]

✠ ✠ ✠

WHEN A BREEZE CAME you could see two *ekka* lengths ahead. When it dropped you could hear the driver yelling and the *ekkas* bumping into you like small boats round a big ship. No *ekka* held less than five persons – none at least of those I saw, and there was one long-necked cart with five and thirty people in it. Sixteen of them were children, but even then they had to pack close. When the dust allowed a clear view, you could see lanes of people closing in on Shalimar, through the green crops near Begumpora village and from the Mian Mir side too. Most of them were singing as they went along, and when they reached the main road, they chaffed the drivers of the *ekkas* and got in their way. One *ekka* lost a wheel and sat down like a hen in the middle of the traffic, while the fares rolled about in the dust and were nearly trodden on. This was considered a very superior joke. No one offered to help, but everyone laughed a good deal – except the pony and he kicked till the driver beat him over the head with a bamboo. Then he went off to graze; and the last I could see of the business was the driver trying to collect passage-money from the spilt fares and nursing the loose wheel under one arm.

The real crush began about five hundred yards before you came to the gates of the gardens. My friend the *chaprassi* said that there were fewer people at the *mela* than last year; but that a *lakh* at least must be present. He speaks the truth generally, but I don't think he understands figures. A Police Inspector Sahib, who has seen nearly as many *melas* as there are inches in his waist-belt, said that he reckoned the gathering at between thirteen and fourteen thousand. Putting the two estimates together, and deducting the proper percentages, we get between twenty and twenty five thousand. This is quite high enough, if you add a thousand or so for children too small to count, and only big enough to fall over.

It was the children's day out on Sunday. Perhaps there were twenty mothers of families. This is a very liberal estimate. The rest were children and men. I suppose it is not considered wholesome to let the womenfolk of the country enjoy themselves. It might over-excite them or lead to a revolution. A man mob isn't pretty to look at when you think of these things, and remember how for nearly every man enjoying himself over the *kabab* stalls or the sweetmeat booths there's a woman at home out of it, and getting the place in order against his return. My friend the *chaprassi* had put a thin book-muslin wrapper over his office kit, and was really very well turned out all over; but he was very much shocked at the notion that his wife might possibly care to join in the fun. He said that *tamashas* like the Chiragan Fair were not for women, and then went away to stuff himself with thin cakes fried in *ghi* and three *kababs* and a bottle of muddy lemonade. The whole picnic cost him one anna and a half, but he explained that I couldn't have got as much for four annas. I believed him implicitly, and I know that I wouldn't have eaten the messes for a thousand rupees. *Kababs* are made in a horrible way; so are the cakes fried in ghi, and so is the lemonade. To show there is no deception – nothing but good honest dirt – they are all three manufactured in public, and they command a ready sale. [. . .]

[*CMG*, 30 March 1886]

PESHAWAR

ROLLING THUNDER AMONG THE Khyber hills all day long; the day itself wasted in spiteful attempts to rain, varied by a shower of hail which clears the crowded streets as a mitrailleuse would do. Evening seems to have brought down the rain in earnest. A steady drizzling downpour blanketing the Fort, and the crops beyond, filling the roads with glutinous mire and the heart of man with despair.

[. . .]

Meantime, the City of Evil Countenances has become shrouded from sight by the incessant rain, and a journey to the Edwardes Gate means a mile-long struggle through soft oozy slime – to be undertaken only as a counter-irritant against the growing gloom of the evening. The road to the city is thronged with foot and horse passengers of all kinds; all utterly heedless of the downpour, and all, so it seems, shouting to a friend half a mile away. Strings of shaggy-haired camels, nearly as repulsive as their masters, jostle mule carts, ekkas and restive horses fretting under the punishment of their spiked bits. These ships of the desert can make but little headway through the ooze, blundering and swaying from side to side like rudderless galleons. Their long hair throws off the water as completely as a mackintosh, but the loads of bhoosa and green barley soak up as much as they can to the discomfort of the dripping driver atop. A camel's esprit de corps is an all-pervading essence which rain intensifies. His arrival is heralded on the wings of the wind, and his presence remembered long after he has passed away. Indeed, so powerful is the rank stench, that those who know least of him, maintain that it is the most offensive in the world. To this slander the unwashed camel driver gives the lie direct, and the Afghan no less. The healing rain that makes the onion to sprout and (six weeks later on) the white ant to suicide himself in the lamp flame, has no charms for these men, but rather acts on them as the sun on the rose. This evening the city road is witness to the fact.

Under the shadow of the Edwardes Gate, the crowd thickens, and the continuous tide of humanity is broken up into eddies, bays and cross-currents. The waning light is darkened here by the houses, and though it is barely six o'clock they have begun to light the shop *chirags*. Then you shall see a scene worthy almost of a place in the Inferno, for the city is unlovely even beneath bright sunshine, and when set off with heavy slime under foot, dark skies and rolling thunder overhead, and driving scotch mist, everywhere repulsive to every sense.

Under the shop lights in front of the sweet-meat and ghee seller's booths, the press and din of words is thickest. Faces of clogs, swine, weazles and goats, all the more hideous for being set on human bodies, and lighted with human intelligence, gather in front of the ring of lamp-light, where they may be studied for half an hour at a stretch. Pathans, Afreedees, Logas, Kohistanis, Turkomans, and a hundred other varieties of the turbulent Afghan race, are gathered in the vast human menagerie between the Gate and the Ghor Khutri. As an Englishman passes, they will turn to scowl upon him, and in many cases to spit fluently on the ground after he has passed. One burly big-paunched ruffian, with a shaven head and a neck creased and dimpled with rolls of fat, is specially zealous in this religious rite – contenting himself with no perfunctory performance, but with a whole-souled expectoration, that must be as refreshing to his comrades, as it is disgusting to the European, sir. As an unconscious compensation to the outraged Kafir, he poses himself magnificently on – degrading instance of civilization – a culvert, turning a very bull's head and throat to the light. Dirty *poshteen* melts into the back-ground of driving rain; neck, shoulders, and fiery red beard standing out in startling relief. But he is only one of twenty thousand. The main road teems with magnificent scoundrels and handsome ruffians; all giving the on-looker the impression of wild beasts held back from murder and violence, and chafing against the restraint. The impression may be wrong; and the Peshawari, the most innocent creature on earth, in spite of History's verdict against him; but not unless thin lips, scowling brows, deep set vulpine eyes and lineaments stamped with every brute passion known to man, go for nothing. Women of course are invisible in the streets, but here and there instead, some nameless and shame-

less boy in girl's clothes with long braided hair and jewellry
– the centre of a crowd of admirers.

[*CMG*, 1 April 1885]

🞕 🞕 🞕

NORTH-WEST FRONTIER

A GREAT AND GLORIOUS thing it is
  To learn, for seven years or so,
The Lord knows what of that and this,
  Ere reckoned fit to face the foe –
The flying bullet down the Pass,
That whistles clear: 'All flesh is grass.'

Three hundred pounds per annum spent
  On making brain and body meeter
For all the murderous intent
  Comprised in 'villanous saltpetre!'
And after – ask the Yusufzaies
What comes of all our 'ologies.

A scrimmage in a Border Station –
  A canter down some dark defile –
Two thousand pounds of education
  Drops to a ten-rupee *jezail* –
The Crammer's boast, the Squadron's pride,
Shot like a rabbit in a ride!

No proposition Euclid wrote,
  No formulae the text-books know,
Will turn the bullet from your coat,
  Or ward the tulwar's downward blow.
Strike hard who cares – shoot straight who can –
The odds are on the cheaper man.

> One sword-knot stolen from the camp
> Will pay for all the school expenses
> Of any Kurrum Valley scamp
> Who knows no word of moods and tenses,
> But, being blessed with perfect sight,
> Picks off our messmates left and right.
>
> With home-bred hordes the hillsides teem,
> The troop-ships bring us one by one,
> At vast expense of time and steam,
> To slay Afridis where they run.
> The 'captives of our bow and spear'
> Are cheap – alas! as we are dear.

['Arithmetic on the Frontier', *Departmental Ditties and Other Verses*]

⛑ ⛑ ⛑

UMBALLA

LATER ON, IN THIS journey, was another river with an Irish bridge through it; and the bridge was composed of large stones levelled atop and sunk in concrete. Here came fresh bullocks, and a jolting to which the [river] Gugga's performance was child's play. As the country cousin bounded like a parched pea on a grid-iron from side to side of his carriage, he imagined himself an invalid, weak and prostrated with fever; worn out with dysentery; broken down through overwork. Again he imagined himself a lady sent up to Simla for reasons which— but imagination failed him, as his head was thrown against the sliding-door hasp, and his toes rattled on the foot shelf. Revolving these things, he came to Kalka – and the rain stopped with the carriage; and the country cousin took heart about the roads 'up above'. All that he said about the *dak gharri* and fifty percent more, might with truth be said about the tonga.

In addition to the vices of the *dak gharri*, it has the violent sifting motion of the winnower of a threshing machine. Imagine a sick lady being violently shaken for eight hours with two minute breaks at half hour intervals. This is the treatment she must go through ere reaching Simla. We all know it, and we all put up with it, because we are a slack, limp, go-as-you-please, for-heaven's-sake-don't-make-a-fuss-about-it people; and it is good for us to be told this again and again. The sun shone at Kalka; there was dust at Dagshai; and glare and dust at Solon. According to our notions – we are contented with little – the journey had been a very successful one so far; and the country cousin, in the baby jumper back seat of the tonga, congratulated himself on his luck. The driver was a clever man and a bold, with no hesitation about sending his ponies spinning round corners at a hand gallop, and putting them along the level as fast as they could lay foot to the ground.

At the twentieth milestone a curious thing happened. The tonga driver spun merrily round a corner into a thick drizzle which ten minutes after turned to driving rain. Ten minutes later the tonga met a stream coming down the road in a hurry. This stream was broader than the tonga, and in depth halfway to the wheel axle. Said the driver: 'It has been raining much at Simla and Tara Devi. We will make haste.' From that time the rain began to fall in earnest, and the country cousin discovered the well known fact, that the only way in which you can keep yourself moderately dry in a tonga is by half sitting, half kneeling, half crouching on the back seat with your legs tucked under you, and the cape of your waterproof thrown over your right or windward cheek. You cannot open an umbrella to ward the rain off if it blows in behind, because you need both hands to hold on with. Hill rain has a trick of blowing all ways in five minutes, and is very, very chilly. A tonga is constructed to admit as much rain as possible. Again the country cousin imagined himself an invalid and a lady and his imaginings were not pleasant ones. Ladies cannot well sit cross-legged in tongas, and they suffer a good deal from chills nor does rain down the back of the neck improve their health or temper. About the sixteenth milestone the country cousin forgot about playing at imagination; and began to imagine in earnest. The streams down the road side, the little torrents from above that jumped half way out into the road, the chill and damp and discomfort, did not so much matter; the worst of it was that little rocks and handfuls of earth were beginning to trickle gently down from the base of the cliffs. Wherever one looked, a small handful of earth and a few stones were just moving or had just finished rolling. It was disquieting to watch this slither and slide all round – more disquieting in fact than if one big slip had taken place just in front and blocked up the road. At the twelfth milestone, the stones in the road were bigger and harder to get over. A tonga need not turn out of the way for a stone as big as a man's head; but the jolt and jar is not pleasant. There was another tonga just behind the country cousin's, and from time to time – four times in all – the leading driver instructed the country cousin to tell the rear tonga to hurry up, as a piece of cliff was going to fall. There are few things more unpleasant then galloping in blinding rain under an overhanging piece of rock or earth of doubtful reputation. So the ride went on – the ponies ploughing mud knee-deep through turbid yellow water, now running in-cliff where there was rock and the imperfectly protected road seemed rotten at the edge; now running outcliff where the hill was shaley and great stones had slid into the middle of the road; now pulling up invisible in clouds of steam to be succeeded by other ponies – wet but willing little brutes who did all that lay in their power; and were alternately abused and endeared by the driver. And the tonga jolted and bumped over submerged stones in the water, creaked and strained where there was mud instead of clear washed road or running stream, while the tonga-bar clinked and jingled merrily through it all and the bugle blared huskily and the stones 'skipped like rams'. Presently there was a soft crash – not a hard one – a wild lurch and a string of oaths from the driver. Convinced that the end of all things was at hand, the country cousin prepared to step forth into the ever-lasting hills and die, like a gentleman, of starvation instead of being pitched over-khud like rubbish. But the tonga righted itself, and he was aware that it had, at a particularly sharp and unpleasant turning, run over a dead camel – wet, shiny and puffy in the rain. Luckily only two hind legs lay in the direct route of traffic, or the consequences might have been almost as undignified as the country cousin feared. Then the ponies went on, and the rain fell, and the torrents spouted and once many big stones blocked the road completely, but a kindly hill coolie – who looked like a mountain gnome and made the ponies shy wildly – sprang from nowhere and removed the worst, and the tonga jolted forward and took no harm. Once, too, a string of camels, blundering down in the dusk on the wrong side of the road, gave trouble, and once again the Government Bullock train stopped the way; but the driver, like Thackeray's sailors, 'called upon the prophet and thought but little of it', and the tonga reached the last *chowki* but one, where a coolie announced that the road was bund. Without any exaggeration, it may be set down that the last six miles of road into Simla are, in the rains, nothing better than a stream bed; and the water channels them from six to eighteen inches deep. It seemed that the coolie's words might be only too true. 'Without doubt,' said the driver, however, 'that man is a liar. We will go on and see.' So the tonga went forward, and the country cousin (a little reassured by the nonchalance of the driver) perceived that the real difficulty of the journey began at this point. The roads were diabolical and very steep, and there were many stones and heaps of slided earth. The dusk shut down about this time, and a cart stood across the road while the driver slept inside and was picked out at the end of a deftly applied whiplash. 'The coolie said truth. The road is bund – I do not think – but we will try.' There lay a strip of stones across the road – a bank about six foot high on the cliff and three foot high on the khud side. He put the tonga back a few yards (luckily the ground was comparatively level) and went forward, but the ponies stayed in the middle of the trouble, and the sazk ran forward and smote them under their bellies with a wet rope's end, and they pulled horsefully and the tonga came down on the further side with a soul-shattering bump, and in due course arrived in the thick dark at Simla; everyone except one small dog being drenched to the skin.

[CMG, 13 July 1886]

✠   ✠   ✠

SIMLA

AT THIS POINT OF the weekly narrative, a green monkey, with pinky blue face, swings himself into the verandah, and suggests plantains and bread. He is the advance guard of a family nearly twenty strong – hirsute fathers with short tempers and base voices; unlovely mothers with babies not bigger than three penny dutch dolls at their breasts; and irreverent hobbledehoys who are always getting in some one's way and being bitten. The hill side is alive with their clamour, and presently they assemble in force on the lawn tennis court; despatching a deputation to warn me that the babies are tired and want fruit. It is impossible to explain to the deputation, that the sayings and doings of their descendants are of much greater importance than theirs. The leader of the gang has established himself on my dressing table, and investigates the brushes there. The flatsides would do splendidly to keep the babies in order. He tucks a brush under each arm, and strikes out for the open country, with a set of mother o' pearl shirt studs in his capacious pouch. Under these circumstances, I would ask all who know the ways of the monkey world, whether it is possible to continue writing? The deputation have fled down to the tennis court, leaving brushes and studs in the verandah. Virtue must be rewarded with bread crusts and over-ripe fruit. A tiny wizened dutch doll is one of the first to profit by my bounty; securing a large plantain skin, and essaying to nibble like its elders. The bonne bouche is unwieldy, and the dutch doll overbalances its little self. With a dolorous cry, materfamilias appropriates the dainty; catches the wailing monkeylet to her bosom, and feeds it by hand as she climbs along the top of the court fencing. The brush stealer, a 'strong masterless rogue' as the old statutes used to say, is deep in a packet of sugar. He scoops it up with human dexterity, and flings the paper away. A few crystals have dropped on the ground, and in the face of his sorrowing descendant, the brush stealer drops on his hands and knees, and licks them up like a dog. Darwin's theory must be faulty somewhere; for, behold, the manlike brush stealer has reverted to the beast, and a greedy beast at that. Yet a few more crystals are stuck in the fur of one sinewy leg. Clasping the knee with both hands, he swings a straight limb up to the level of his mouth, and mumbles it rapturously. Then he sits down to scratch and cuff an intrusive hobbledehoy across the back. Darwin's theory is correct after all. This is no monkey, but an irascible old gentleman with a short temper. He coughs consumptively and lies down for a nap, with his arm under his head.

[*CMG*, 24 June 1885]

✠ ✠ ✠

AT THE BEGINNING OF April of this year, 1885, I was at Simla – semi-deserted Simla – once more, and was deep in lover's talks and walks with Kitty. It was decided that we should be married at the end of June. You will understand, therefore, that, loving Kitty as I did, I am not saying too much when I pronounce myself to have been, at that time, the happiest man in India.

Fourteen delightful days passed almost before I noticed their flight. Then, aroused to the sense of what was proper among mortals circumstanced as we were, I pointed out to Kitty that an engagement ring was the outward and visible sign of her dignity as an engaged girl; and that she must forthwith come to Hamilton's to be measured for one. Up to that moment, I give you my word, we had completely forgotten so trivial a matter. To Hamilton's we accordingly went on the 15th of April, 1885. Remember that – whatever my doctor may say to the contrary – I was then in perfect health, enjoying a well-balanced mind and an *absolutely* tranquil spirit. Kitty and I entered Hamilton's shop together, and there, regardless of the order of affairs, I measured Kitty for the ring in the presence of the amused assistant. The ring was a sapphire with two diamonds. We then rode out down the slope that leads to the Combermere Bridge and Peliti's shop.

While my Waler was cautiously feeling his way over the loose shale, and Kitty was laughing and chattering at my side – while all Simla, that is to say as much of it as had then come from the Plains, was grouped round the Reading-room and Peliti's veranda, – I was aware that someone, apparently at a vast distance, was calling me by my Christian name. It struck me that I had heard the voice before, but when and where I could not at once determine. In the short space it took to cover the road between the path from Hamilton's shop and the first plank of the Combermere Bridge I had thought over half a dozen people who might have committed such a solecism, and had eventually decided that it must have been singing in my ears. Immediately opposite Peliti's shop my eye was arrested by the sight of four *jhampanies* in 'magpie' livery, pulling a yellow-paneled, cheap, bazar 'rickshaw. In a moment my mind flew back to the previous season and Mrs. Wessington with a sense of irritation and disgust. Was it not enough that the woman was dead and done with, without her black and white servitors reappearing to spoil the day's happiness?

['The Phantom Rickshaw', *The Phantom Rickshaw and Other Stories*]

✠ ✠ ✠

TAJ MAHAL AND 'THE GLOBE-TROTTER'

THERE IS A STORY of a Frenchman who feared not God, nor regarded man, sailing to Egypt for the express purpose of scoffing at the Pyramids and – though this is hard to believe – at the great Napoleon who had warred under their shadow. It is on record that that blasphemous Gaul came to the Great Pyramid and wept through mingled reverence and contrition; for he sprang from an emotional race. To understand his feelings it is necessary to have read a great deal too much about the Taj, its design and proportions, to have seen execrable pictures of it at the Simla Fine Arts Exhibition, to have had its praises sung by superior and travelled friends till the brain loathed the repetition of the word, and then, sulky with want of sleep, heavy-eyed, unwashed, and chilled, to come upon it suddenly. Under these circumstances everything, you will concede, is in favour of a cold critical, and not too partial verdict. As the Englishman leaned out of the carriage he saw first an opal-tinted cloud on the horizon, and, later, certain towers. The mists lay on the ground, so that the splendour seemed to be floating free of the earth; and the mists rose in the background, so that at no time could everything be seen clearly. Then as the train sped forward, and the mists shifted, and the sun shone upon the mists, the Taj took a hundred new shapes, each perfect and each beyond description. It was the Ivory Gate through which all good dreams come; it was the realisation of the gleaming halls of dawn that Tennyson sings of; it was veritably the 'aspiration fixed,' the 'sigh made stone' of a lesser poet; and over and above concrete comparisons, it seemed the embodiment of all things pure, all things holy, and all things unhappy. That was the mystery of the building. It may be that the mists wrought the witchery, and that the Taj seen in the dry sunlight is only, as guidebooks say, a noble structure. The Englishman could not tell, and has made a vow that he will never go nearer the spot, for fear of breaking the charm of the unearthly pavilions.

It may be, too, that each must view the Taj for himself with his own eyes, working out his own interpretation of the sight. It is certain that no man can in cold blood and colder ink set down his impressions if he has been in the least moved.

To the one who watched and wondered that November morning the thing seemed full of sorrow – the sorrow of the man who built it for the woman he loved, and the sorrow of the workmen who died in the building – used up like cattle. And in the face of this sorrow the Taj flushed in the sunlight and was beautiful, after the beauty of a woman who has done no wrong.

Here the train ran in under the walls of Agra Fort, and another train – of thought incoherent as that written above – came to an end. Let those who scoff at overmuch enthusiasm look at the Taj and thenceforward be dumb. It is well on the threshold of a journey to be taught reverence and awe.

But there is no reverence in the Globe-trotter: he is brazen. A Young Man from Manchester was travelling to Bombay in order – how the words hurt! – to be home by Christmas. He had come through America, New Zealand, and Australia, and finding that he had ten days to spare at Bombay, conceived the modest idea of 'doing India.' 'I don't say that I've done it all; but you may say that I've seen a good deal.' Then he explained that he had been 'much pleased' at Agra, 'much pleased' at Delhi, and, last profanation, 'very much pleased' at the Taj. Indeed, he seemed to be going through life just then 'much pleased' at everything. With rare and sparkling originality he remarked that India was a 'big place,' and that there were many things to buy. Verily, this Young Man must have been a delight to the Delhi boxwallahs. He had purchased shawls and embroidery 'to the tune of' a certain number of rupees duly set forth, and he had purchased jewellery to another tune. These were gifts for friends at home, and he considered them 'very Eastern.' If silver filigree work modelled on Palais Royal patterns, or aniline blue scarves be Eastern, he had succeeded in his heart's desire. For some inscrutable end it has been decreed that man shall take a delight in making his fellow-man miserable. The Englishman began to point out gravely the probable extent to which the Young Man from Manchester had been swindled, and the Young Man said: 'By Jove. You don't say so. I hate being done. If there's anything I hate, it's being done!'

He had been so happy in the 'thought of getting home by Christmas,' and so charmingly communicative as to the members of his family for whom such and such gifts were intended, that the Englishman cut short the record of fraud and soothed him by saying that he had not been so very badly 'done,' after all. This consideration was misplaced, for, his peace of mind restored, the Young Man from Manchester looked out of the window and, waving his hand over the Empire generally, said: 'I say. Look here. All those wells are wrong, you know!' The wells were on the wheel and inclined plane system; but he objected to the incline, and said that it would be much better for the bullocks if they walked on level ground. Then light dawned upon him, and he said: 'I suppose it's to exercise all their muscles. Y' know a canal-horse is no use after he has been on the tow-path for some time. He can't walk anywhere but on the flat, y' know, and I suppose it's just the same with bullocks.' The spurs of the Aravalis, under which the train was running, had evidently suggested this brilliant idea which passed uncontradicted, for the Englishman was looking out of the window.

[*Letters of Marque*]

✠ ✠ ✠

JAIPUR

IF ANY PART OF a land strewn with dead men's bones have a special claim to distinction, Rajputana, as the cock-pit of India, stands first. East of Suez men do not build towers on the tops of hills for the sake of the view, nor do they stripe the mountain sides with bastioned stone walls to keep in cattle. Since the beginning of time, if we are to credit the legends, there was fighting – heroic fighting – at the foot of the Aravalis and beyond, in the great deserts of sand penned by those kindly mountains from spreading over the heart of India. The 'Thirty-six Royal Races' fought as royal races know how to do, Chohan with Rahtor, brother against brother, son against father. Later – but excerpts from the tangled tale of force, fraud, cunning, desperate love and more desperate revenge, crime worthy of demons and virtues fit for gods, may be found, by all who care to look, in the book of the man who loved the Rajputs and gave a life's labours in their behalf.

From Delhi to Abu, and from the Indus to the Chambul, each yard of ground has witnessed slaughter, pillage, and rapine. But, to-day, the capital of the State, that Dhola Rae, son of Soora Singh, hacked out more than nine hundred years ago with the sword from some weaker ruler's realm, is lighted with gas, and possesses many striking and English peculiarities.

Dhola Rae was killed in due time, and for nine hundred years Jeypore, torn by the intrigues of unruly princes and princelings, fought Asiatically.

When and how Jeypore became a feudatory of British power and in what manner we put a slur upon Rajput honour – punctilious as the honour of the Pathan – are matters of which the Globe-trotter knows more than we do. He 'reads up' – to quote his own words – a city before he comes to us, and, straightway going to another city, forgets, or, worse still, mixes what he has learnt – so that in the end he writes down the Rajput a Mahratta, says that Lahore is in the North-West Provinces, and was once the capital of Sivaji, and piteously demands a 'guide-book on all India, a thing that you can carry in your trunk y' know – that gives you plain descriptions of things without mixing you up.' Here is a chance for a writer of discrimination and void of conscience!

But to return to Jeypore – a pink city set on the border of a blue lake, and surrounded by the low, red spurs of the Aravalis – a city to see and to puzzle over. There was once a ruler of the State, called Jey Singh, who lived in the days of Aurungzeb, and did him service with foot and horse. He must have been the Solomon of Rajputana, for through the forty-four years of his reign his 'wisdom remained with him.' He led armies, and when fighting was over, turned to literature; he intrigued desperately and successfully, but found time to gain a deep insight into astronomy, and, by what remains above ground now, we can tell that whatsoever his eyes desired, he kept not from him. Knowing his own worth, he deserted the city of Amber founded by Dhola Rae among the hills, and, six miles further, in the open plain, bade one Vedyadhar, his architect, build a new city, as seldom Indian city was built before – with huge streets straight as an arrow, sixty yards broad, and cross-streets broad and straight. Many years afterward the good people of America builded their towns after this pattern, but knowing nothing of Jey Singh, they took all the credit to themselves.

He built himself everything that pleased him, palaces and gardens and temples, and then died, and was buried under a white marble tomb on a hill overlooking the city. He was a traitor, if history speaks truth, to his own kin, and he was an accomplished murderer, but he did his best to check infanticide; he reformed the Mahometan calendar; he piled up a superb library and he made Jeypore a marvel.

Later on came a successor, educated and enlightened by all the lamps of British Progress, and converted the city of Jey Singh into a surprise – a big, bewildering, practical joke. He laid down sumptuous *trottoirs* of hewn stone, and central carriage drives, also of hewn stone, in the main street; he, that is to say, Colonel Jacob, the Superintending Engineer of the State, devised a water supply for the city and studded the ways with standpipes. He built gas works, set afoot a School of Art, a Museum – all the things in fact which are necessary to Western municipal welfare and comfort, and saw that they were the best of their kind. How much Colonel Jacob has done, not only for the good of Jeypore city but for the good of the State at large, will never be known, because the officer in question is one of the not small class who resolutely refuse to talk about their own work. The result of the good work is that the old and the new, the rampantly raw and the sullenly old, stand cheek-by-jowl in startling contrast. Thus the branded bull trips over the rails of a steel tramway which brings out the city rubbish; the lacquered and painted cart behind the two little stag-like trotting bullocks catches its primitive wheels in the cast-iron gas-lamp post with the brass nozzle a-top, and all Rajputana, gayly clad, small-turbaned, swaggering Rajputana, circulates along the magnificent pavements.

The fortress-crowned hills look down upon the strange medley. One of them bears on its flank in huge white letters the cheery inscript, 'Welcome!' This was made when the Prince of Wales visited Jeypore to shoot his first tiger; but the average traveller of to-day may appropriate the message to himself, for Jeypore takes great care of strangers and shows them all courtesy. This, by the way, demoralises the Globe-trotter, whose first cry is, 'Where can we get horses? Where can we get elephants? Who is the man to write to for all these things?'

[*Letters of Marque*]

✠ ✠ ✠

AMBER

AMBER LIES BETWEEN SIX and seven miles from Jeypore among the tumbled fragments of the hills, and is reachable by so prosaic a conveyance as a *ticca-gharri*, and so uncomfortable a one as an elephant. He is provided by the Maharaja, and the people who make India their prey are apt to accept his services as a matter of course.

Rise very early in the morning, before the stars have gone out, and drive through the sleeping city till the pavement gives place to cactus and sand, and educational and enlightened institutions to mile upon mile of semi-decayed Hindu temples – brown and weather-beaten – running down to the shores of the great Man Sagar Lake, wherein are more ruined temples, palaces, and fragments of causeways. The water-birds have their home in the half-submerged arcades and the crocodile nuzzles the shafts of the pillars. It is a fitting prelude to the desolation of Amber. Beyond the Man Sagar the road of to-day climbs uphill, and by its side runs the huge stone causeway of yesterday – blocks sunk in concrete. Down this path the swords of Amber went out to kill. A triple wall rings the city, and, at the third gate, the road drops into the valley of Amber. In the half light of dawn a great city sunk between hills and built round three sides of a lake is dimly visible, and one waits to catch the hum that should arise from it as the day breaks. The air in the valley is bitterly chill. With the growing light, Amber stands revealed, and the traveller sees that it is a city that will never wake. A few *meenas* live in huts at the end of the valley, but the temples, the shrines, the palaces, and the tiers on tiers of houses are desolate. Trees grow in and split upon the walls, the windows are filled with brushwood, and the cactus chokes the street. The Englishman made his way up the side of the hill to the great palace that overlooks everything except the red fort of Jeighur, guardian of Amber. As the elephant swung up the steep roads paved with stone and built out on the sides of the hill, the Englishman looked into empty houses where the little grey squirrel sat and scratched its ears. The peacock walked on the house-tops, and the blue pigeon roosted within. He passed under iron-studded gates whose hinges were eaten out with rust, and by walls plumed and crowned with grass, and under more gateways, till, at last, he reached the palace and came suddenly into a great quadrangle where two blinded, arrogant stallions, covered with red and gold trappings, screamed and neighed at each other from opposite ends of the vast space. For a little time these were the only visible living beings, and they were in perfect accord with the spirit of the spot. Afterwards certain workmen appeared, for it seems that the Maharaja keeps the old palace of his forefathers in good repair, but they were modern and mercenary, and with great difficulty were detached from the skirts of the traveller.

[*Letters of Marque*]

✠ ✠ ✠

CHITOR

THIS STANDS, LIKE ALL things in Chitor, among ruins, but Time and the other enemies have been good to it. It is a Jain edifice, nine stories high, crowned atop – was this designed insult or undesigned repair? – with a purely Mahometan dome, where the pigeons and the bats live. Excepting this blemish, the Tower of Victory is nearly as fair as when it left the hands of the builder whose name has not been handed down to us. It is to be observed here that the first, or more ruined, Tower of Victory, built in Alluji's days, when Chitor was comparatively young, was raised by some pious Jain as proof of conquest over things spiritual. The second tower is more worldly in intent.

Those who care to look, may find elsewhere a definition of its architecture and its more striking peculiarities. It was in kind, but not in degree, like the Jugdesh Temple at Udaipur, and, as it exceeded it in magnificence, so its effect upon the mind was more intense. The confusing intricacy of the figures with which it was wreathed from top to bottom, the recurrence of the one calm face, the God enthroned, holding the Wheel of the Law, and the appalling lavishness of decoration, all worked toward the instilment of fear and aversion.

Surely this must have been one of the objects of the architect. The tower, in the arrangement of its stairways, is like the interior of a Chinese carved ivory puzzle-ball. The idea given is that, even while you are ascending, you are wrapping yourself deeper and deeper in the tangle of a mighty maze. Add to this the half-light, the thronging armies of sculptured figures, the mad profusion of design splashed as impartially upon the undersides of the stone window-slabs as upon the door-beam of the threshold – add, most abhorrent of all, the slippery sliminess of the walls always worn smooth by naked men, and you will understand that the tower is not a soothing place to visit. The Englishman fancied presumptuously that he had, in a way, grasped the builder's idea; and when he came to the top storey and sat among the pigeons his theory was this: To attain power, wrote the builder of old, in sentences of fine stone, it is necessary to pass through all sorts of close-packed horrors, treacheries, battles, and insults, in darkness and without knowledge whether the road leads upward or into a hopeless *cul-de-sac*. Kumbha Rana must many times have climbed to the top storey, and looked out toward the uplands of Malwa on the one side and his own great Mewar on the other, in the days when all the rock hummed with life and the clatter of hooves upon the stony ways, and Mahmoud of Malwa was safe in hold. How he must have swelled with pride – fine insolent pride of life and rule and power – power not only to break things but to compel such builders as those who piled the tower to his royal will! There was no decoration in the top storey to bewilder or amaze – nothing but well-grooved stone slabs, and a boundless view fit for kings who traced their ancestry –

> From times when forth from the sunlight, the first of our
> Kings came down,
> And had the earth for his footstool, and wore the stars for his
> crown.

The builder had left no mark behind him – not even a mark on the threshold of the door, or a sign in the head of the topmost step. The Englishman looked in both places, believing that those were the places generally chosen for mark cutting. So he sat and meditated on the beauties of kingship and the unholiness of Hindu art, and what power a shadow land of lewd monstrosities had upon those who believed in it, and what Lord Dufferin, who is the nearest approach to a king in this India, must have thought when aide-de-camps clanked after him up the narrow steps. But the day was wearing, and he came down – in both senses – and, in his descent, the carven things on every side of the tower, and above and below, once more took hold of and perverted his fancy, so that he arrived at the bottom in a frame of mind eminently fitted for a descent into the Gau-Mukh, which is nothing more terrible than a little spring, falling into a reservoir, in the side of the hill.

He stumbled across more ruins and passed between tombs of dead Ranis, till he came to a flight of steps, built out and cut out from rock, going down as far as he could see into a growth of trees on a terrace below him. The stone of the steps had been worn and polished by the terrible naked feet till it showed its markings clearly as agate; and where the steps ended in a rock-slope, there was a visible glair, a great snail-track, upon the rocks. It was hard to keep safe footing upon the sliminess. The air was thick with the sick smell of stale incense, and grains of rice were scattered upon the steps. But there was no one to be seen. Now this in itself was not specially alarming; but the Genius of the Place must be responsible for making it so. The Englishman slipped and bumped on the rocks, and arrived, more suddenly than he desired, upon the edge of a dull blue tank, sunk between walls of timeless masonry. In a slabbed-in recess, water was pouring through a shapeless stone gargoyle, into a trough; which trough again dripped into the tank. Almost under the little trickle of water, was the loathsome Emblem of Creation, and there were flowers and rice around it. Water was trickling from a score of places in the cut face of the hill; oozing between the edges of the steps and welling up between the stone slabs of the terrace. Trees sprouted in the sides of the tank and hid its surroundings. It seemed as though the descent had led the Englishman, firstly, two thousand years away from his own century, and secondly, into a trap, and that he would fall off the polished stones into the stinking tank, or that the Gau-Mukh would continue to pour water until the tank rose up and swamped him, or that some of the stone slabs would fall forward and crush him flat.

Then he was conscious of remembering, with peculiar and unnecessary distinctness, that, from the Gau-Mukh, a passage led to the subterranean chambers in which the fair Pudmini and her handmaids had slain themselves. And, that Tod had written and the Stationmaster at Chitor had said, that some sort of devil, or ghoul, or Something, stood at the entrance of that approach.

All of which was a nightmare bred in full day and folly to boot; but it was the fault of the Genius of the Place, who made the Englishman feel that he had done a great wrong in trespassing into the very heart and soul of all Chitor. And, behind him, the Gau-Mukh gurgled and choked like a man in his death-throe. The Englishman endured as long as he could – about two minutes. Then it came upon him that he must go quickly out of this place of years and blood – must get back to the afternoon sunshine, and Gerowlia, and the dak-bungalow with the French bedstead. He desired no archæological information, he wished to take no notes, and, above all, he did not care to look behind him, where stood the reminder that he was no better than the beasts that perish. But he had to cross the smooth, worn rocks, and he felt their sliminess through his boot-soles. It was as though he were treading on the soft, oiled skin of a Hindu. As soon as the steps gave refuge, he floundered up them, and so came out of the Gau-Mukh, bedewed with that perspiration which follows alike on honest toil or – childish fear.

'This,' said he to himself, 'is absurd!' and sat down on the fallen top of a temple to review the situation. But the Gau-Mukh had disappeared. He could see the dip in the ground and the beginning of the steps, but nothing more.

Perhaps it was absurd. It undoubtedly appeared so, later. Yet there was something uncanny about it all. It was not exactly a feeling of danger or pain, but an apprehension of great evil.

In defence, it may be urged that there is moral, just as much as there is mine, choke-damp. If you get into a place laden with the latter you die, and if into the home of the former you . . . behave unwisely, as constitution and temperament prompt. If any man doubt this, let him sit for two hours in a hot sun on an elephant, stay half an hour in the Tower of Victory, and then go down into the Gau-Mukh, which, it must never be forgotten, is merely a set of springs 'three or four in number, issuing from the cliff face at cow-mouth carvings, now mutilated. The water, evidently percolating from the Hathi Kund above, falls first in an old pillared hall and thence into the masonry reservoir below, eventually, when abundant enough, supplying a little waterfall lower down.' That, Gentlemen and Ladies, on the honour of one who has been frightened of the dark in broad daylight, is the Gau-Mukh, as though photographed!

[*Letters of Marque*]

❈ ❈ ❈

JODHPUR

JODHPUR DIFFERS FROM THE other States of Rajputana in that its Royalty is peculiarly accessible to an inquiring public. There are wanderers, the desire of whose life it is 'to see Nabobs,' which is the Globe-trotter's title for any one in unusually clean clothes, or an Oudh Taluqdar in gala dress. Men asked in Jodhpur whether the Englishman would like to see His Highness. The Englishman had a great desire to do so, if His Highness would be in no way inconvenienced. Then they scoffed: 'Oh, he won't *durbar* you, you needn't flatter yourself. If he's in the humour he'll receive you like an English country-gentleman.' How in the world could the owner of such a place as Jodhpur Palace be in any way like an English country-gentleman? The Englishman had not long to wait in doubt. His Highness intimated his readiness to see the Englishman between eight and nine in the morning at the Raika-Bagh. The Raika-Bagh is not a Palace, for the lower storey and all the detached buildings round it are filled with horses. Nor can it in any way be called a stable, because the upper storey contains sumptuous apartments full of all manner of valuables both of the East and the West. Nor is it in any sense a pleasure-garden, for it stands on soft white sand, close to a multitude of litter and sand training tracks, and is devoid of trees for the most part. Therefore the Raika-Bagh is simply the Raika-Bagh and nothing else. It is now the chosen residence of the Maharaja, who loves to live among his four hundred or more horses. All Jodhpur is horse-mad by the way, and it behoves anyone who wishes to be anyone to keep his own race-course. The Englishman went to the Raika-Bagh, which stands half a mile or so from the city, and passing through a long room filled with saddles by the dozen, bridles by the score, and bits by the hundred, was aware of a very small and lively little cherub on the roof of a garden-house. He was carefully muffled, for the morning was chill. 'Good morning,' he cried cheerfully in English, waving a mittened hand. 'Are you going to see my faver and the horses?' It was the Maharaja Kanwar, the Crown Prince, the apple of the Maharaja's eye, and one of the quaintest little bodies that ever set an Englishman disrespectfully laughing. He studies English daily with one of the English officials of the State, and stands a very good chance of being thoroughly spoiled, for he is a general pet. As befits his dignity, he has his own carriage or carriages, his own twelve-hand stable, his own house and retinue.

A few steps further on, in a little enclosure in front of a small two-storeyed white bungalow, sat His Highness the Maharaja, deep in discussion with the State Engineer. He wore an English ulster, and within ten paces of him was the first of a long range of stalls. There was an informality of procedure about Jodhpur which, after the strained etiquette of other States, was very refreshing. The State Engineer, who has a growing line to attend to, cantered away, and His Highness, after a few introductory words, knowing what the Englishman would be after, said: 'Come along, and look at the horses.' Other formality there was absolutely none. Even the indispensable knot of hangers-on stood at a distance, and behind a paling, in this most rustic country residence. A well-bred fox-terrier took command of the proceedings, after the manner of dogs the world over, and the Maharaja led to the horse-boxes. But a man turned up, bending under the weight of much bacon. 'Oh! here's the pig I shot for Udaipur last night. You see that is the best piece. It's pickled, and that's what makes it yellow to look at.' He patted the great side that was held up. 'There will be a camel sowar to meet it half way to Udaipur; and I hope Udaipur will be pleased with it. It was a very big pig.' 'And where did you shoot it, Maharaja Sahib?' 'Here,' said His Highness, smiting himself high up under the armpit. 'Where else would you have it?' Certainly this descendant of Raja Maun was more like an English country-gentleman than the Englishman in his ignorance had deemed possible. He led on from horse-box to horse-box, the terrier at his heels, pointing out each horse of note; and Jodhpur has many. 'There's *Raja*, twice winner of the Civil Service Cup.' The Englishman looked reverently and *Raja* rewarded his curiosity with a vicious snap, for he was being dressed over, and his temper was out of joint. Close to him stood *Autocrat*, the grey with the nutmeg marks on the off-shoulder, a picture of a horse, also disturbed in his mind. Next to him was a chestnut Arab, a hopeless cripple, for one of his knees had been smashed and the leg was doubled up under him. It was *Turquoise*, who, six or eight years ago, rewarded good feeding by getting away from his groom, falling down and ruining himself, but who, none the less, has lived an honoured pensioner on the Maharaja's bounty ever since. No horses are shot in the Jodhpur stables, and when one dies – they have lost not more than twenty-five in six years – his funeral is an event. He is wrapped in a white sheet which is strewn with flowers, and, amid the weeping of the *saises*, is borne away to the burial ground.

[*Letters of Marque*]

❁ ❁ ❁

JAMALPUR

JAMALPUR IS THE HEADQUARTERS of the East India Railway. This in itself is not a startling statement. The wonder begins with the exploration of Jamalpur, which is a station entirely made by, and devoted to, the use of those untiring servants of the public, the railway folk. They have towns of their own at Toondla and Assensole; a sun-dried sanitarium at Bandikui; and Howrah, Ajmir, Allahabad, Lahore, and Pindi know their colonies. But Jamalpur is unadulteratedly 'Railway,' and he who has nothing to do with the E.I. Railway in some shape or another feels a stranger and an interloper. Running always east and southerly, the train carries him from the torments of the North-west into the wet, woolly warmth of Bengal, where may be found the hothouse heat that has ruined the temper of the good people of Calcutta. The land is fat and greasy with good living, and the wealth of the bodies of innumerable dead things; and here – just above Mokameh – may be seen fields stretching, without stick, stone, or bush to break the view, from the railway line to the horizon.

Up-country innocents must look at the map to learn that Jamalpur is near the top left-hand corner of the big loop that the E.I.R. throws out round Bhagalpur and part of the Bara-Banki districts. Northward of Jamalpur, as near as may be, lies the Ganges and Tirhoot, and eastward an offshoot of the volcanic Rajmehal range blocks the view.

[. . .]

The heart of Jamalpur is the 'shops,' and here a visitor will see more things in an hour than he can understand in a year. Steam Street very appropriately leads to the forty or fifty acres that the 'shops' cover, and to the busy silence of the loco. super-intendent's office, where a man must put down his name and his business on a slip of paper before he can penetrate into the Temple of Vulcan. About three thousand five hundred men are in the 'shops,' and, ten minutes after the day's work has begun, the assistant superintendent knows exactly how many are 'in.' The heads of departments – silent, heavy-handed men, captains of five hundred or more – have their names fairly printed on a board which is exactly like a pool-marker. They 'star a life' when they come in, and their few names alone represent sala-ries to the extent of six thousand a month. They are men worth hearing deferentially. They hail from Manchester and the Clyde, and the great ironworks of the North: pleasant as cold water in a thirsty land is it to hear again the full Northumbrian burr or the long-drawn Yorkshire 'aye.' Under their great gravity of demeanour – a man who is in charge of a few lakhs' worth of plant cannot afford to be riotously mirthful – lurks melody and humour. They can sing like north-countrymen, and in their hours of ease go back to the speech of the iron countries they have left behind, when 'Ab o' th' yate 'and all 'Ben Briarly's' shrewd wit shakes the warm air of Bengal with deep-chested laughter. Hear 'Ruglan' Toon,' with a chorus as true as the fall of trip-hammers, and fancy that you are back again in the smoky, rattling North!

But this is the 'unofficial' side. Go forward through the gates under the mango trees, and set foot at once in sheds which have as little to do with mangoes as a locomotive with Lakshmi, The 'buzzer' howls, for it is nearly tiffin time. There is a rush from every quarter of the shops, a cloud of flying natives, and a procession of more sedately pacing Englishmen, and in three short minutes you are left absolutely alone among arrested wheels and belts, pulleys, cranks, and cranes – in a silence only broken by the soft sigh of a far-away steam-valve or the cooing of pigeons. You are, by favour freely granted, at liberty to wander anywhere you please through the deserted works. Walk into a huge, brick-built, tin-roofed stable, capable of holding twenty-four locomotives under treatment, and see what must be done to the Iron Horse once in every three years if he is to do his work well. On reflection, Iron Horse is wrong. An engine is a she – as distinctly feminine as a ship or a mine. Here stands the *Echo*, her wheels off, resting on blocks, her underside machinery taken out, and her side scrawled with mysterious hieroglyphics in chalk. An enormous green-painted iron harness-rack bears her piston and eccentric rods, and a neatly painted board shows that such and such Englishmen are the fitter, assistant, and apprentice engaged in editing that *Echo*. An engine seen from the platform and an engine viewed from underneath are two very different things. The one is as unimpressive as a cart; the other as imposing as a man-of-war in the yard.

In this manner is an engine treated for navicular, laminitis, back-sinew, or whatever it is that engines most suffer from. No. 607, we will say, goes wrong at Dinapore, Assensole, Buxar, or wherever it may be, after three years' work. The place she came from is stencilled on the boiler, and the foreman examines her. Then he fills in a hospital sheet, which bears one hundred and eighty printed heads under which an engine can come into the shops. No. 607 needs repair in only one hundred and eighteen particulars, ranging from mud-hole-flanges and blower-cocks to lead-plugs, and platform brackets which have shaken loose. This certificate the foreman signs, and it is framed near the engine for the benefit of the three Europeans and the eight or nine natives who have to mend No. 607. To the ignorant the superhuman wisdom of the examiner seems only equalled by the audacity of the two men and the boy who are to undertake what is frivolously called the 'job.' No. 607 is in a sorely mangled condition, but 403 is much worse. She is reduced to a shell – is a very elle-woman of an engine, bearing only her funnel, the iron frame and the saddle that supports the boiler.

Four-and-twenty engines in every stage of decomposition stand in one huge shop. A travelling crane runs overhead, and the men have hauled up one end of a bright vermilion loco, The effect is the silence of a scornful stare – just such a look as a colonel's portly wife gives through her *pince-nez* at the audacious subaltern. Engines are the 'livest' things that man ever made. They glare through their spectacle-plates, they tilt their noses contemptuously, and when their insides are gone they adorn themselves with red lead, and leer like decayed beauties; and in the Jamalpur works there is no escape from them. The shops can hold fifty without pressure, and on occasion as many again. Everywhere there are engines, and everywhere brass domes lie about on the ground like huge helmets in a pantomime.

['Among the Railway Folk', *The City of Dreadful Night and Other Places*]

✠ ✠ ✠

GHAZIPUR

ON THE BANKS OF the Ganges, forty miles below Benares as the crow flies, stands the Ghazipur Factory, an opium mint as it were, whence issue the precious cakes that are to replenish the coffers of the Indian Government. The busy season is setting in, for with April the opium comes up from the districts after having run the gauntlet of the district officers of the Opium Department, who will pass it as fit for use. Then the really serious work opens, under a roasting sun. The opium arrives by *challans*, regiments of one hundred jars, each holding one maund, and each packed in a basket and sealed atop. The district officer submits forms – never was such a place for forms as the Ghazipur Factory – showing the quality and weight of each pot, and with the jars comes a person responsible for the safe carriage of the string, their delivery, and their virginity. If any pots are broken or tampered with, an unfortunate individual called the import-officer, and appointed to work like a horse from dawn till dewy eve, must examine the man in charge of the *challan* and reduce his statement to writing. Fancy getting any native to explain how a jar has been smashed! But the Perfect Flower is about as valuable as silver.

Then all the pots have to be weighed, and the weight of each pot is recorded on the pot, in a book, and goodness knows where else, and every one has to sign certificates that the weighing is correct. The pots have been weighed once in the district and once in the factory. None the less a certain number of them are taken at random and weighed afresh before they are opened. This is only the beginning of a long series of checks. Then the testing begins. Every single pot has to be tested for quality. A native, called the *purkhea*, drives his fist into the opium, rubs and smells it, and calls out the class for the benefit of the opium examiner. A sample picked between finger and thumb is thrown into a jar, and if the opium examiner thinks the *purkhea* has said sooth, the class of that jar is marked in chalk, and everything is entered in a book. Every ten samples are put in a locked box with duplicate keys, and sent over to the laboratory for assay. With the tenth boxful – and this marks the end of the *challan* of a hundred jars – the Englishman in charge of the testing signs the test-paper, and enters the name of the native tester and sends it over to the laboratory. For convenience' sake, it may be as well to say that, unless distinctly stated to the contrary, every single thing in Ghazipur is locked, and every operation is conducted under more than police supervision.

In the laboratory each set of ten samples is thoroughly mixed by hand: a quarter-ounce lump is then tested for starch adulteration by iodine, which turns the decoction blue, and, if necessary, for gum adulteration by alcohol, which makes the decoction filmy. If adulteration be shown, all the ten pots of that set are tested separately till the sinful pot is discovered. Over and above this test, three samples of one hundred grains each are taken from the mixed set of ten samples, dried on a steam-table, and then weighed for consistence. The result is written down in a ten-columned form in the assay register, and by the mean result are those ten pots paid for. This, after everything has been done in duplicate and countersigned, completes the test and assay. If a district officer has classed the opium in a glaringly wrong way, he is thus caught and reminded of his error. No one trusts anyone in Ghazipur. They are always weighing, testing, and assaying.

Before the opium can be used it must be 'alligated' in big vats. The pots are emptied into these, and special care is taken that none of the drug sticks to the hands of the coolies. Opium has a knack of doing this, and therefore coolies are searched at most inopportune moments. There are a good many Mahometans in Ghazipur, and they would all like a little opium. The pots after emptying are smashed up and scraped, and heaved down the steep river-bank of the factory, where they help to keep the Ganges in its place, so many are they and the little earthen bowls in which the opium cakes are made. People are forbidden to wander about the river-front of the factory in search of remnants of opium on the shards. There are no remnants, but people will not credit this. After vatting, the big vats, holding from one to three thousand maunds, are probed with test-rods, and the samples are treated just like the samples of the *challans*, everybody writing everything in duplicate and signing it. Having secured the mean consistence of each vat, the requisite quantity of each blend is weighed out, thrown into an alligating vat, of 250 maunds, and worked up by the feet of coolies.

This completes the working of the opium. It is now ready to be made into cakes after a final assay. Man has done nothing to improve it since it streaked the capsule of the poppy – this mysterious drug. April, May, and June are the months for receiving and manufacturing opium, and in the winter months come the packing and the despatch.

At the beginning of the cold weather Ghazipur holds, locked up, a trifle, say, of three and a half millions sterling in opium. Now, there may be only a paltry three-quarters of a million on hand, and that is going out at the rate per diem of one Viceroy's salary for two and a half years.

['In an Opium Factory', *The City of Dreadful Night and Other Places*]

❈ ❈ ❈

CALCUTTA (KOLKATA)

A FIRST INTRODUCTION TO the Calcutta *durwân* or door-keeper is not nice. If he is chewing *pân*, he does not take the trouble to get rid of his quid. If he is sitting on his cot chewing sugar-cane, he does not think it worth his while to rise. He has to be taught those things, and he cannot understand why he should be reproved. Clearly he is a survival of a played-out system. Providence never intended that any native should be made a *concierge* more insolent than any of the French variety. The people of Calcutta put a man in a little lodge close to the gate of their house, in order that loafers may be turned away, and the houses protected from theft. The natural result is that the *durwân* treats everybody whom he does not know as a loafer, has an intimate and vendible knowledge of all the outgoings and incomings in that house, and controls, to a large extent, the nomination of the servants. They say that one of the estimable class is now suing a bank for about three lakhs of rupees. Up-country, a Lieutenant-Governor's servant has to work for thirty years before he can retire on seventy thousand rupees of savings. The Calcutta *durwân* is a great institution. The head and front of his offence is that he will insist upon trying to talk English. How he protects the houses Calcutta only knows. He can be frightened out of his wits by severe speech, and is generally asleep in calling hours. If a rough round of visits be any guide, three times out of seven he is fragrant of drink. So much for the *durwân*. Now for the houses he guards. . . . . .

The thick, greasy night shuts in everything. We have gone beyond the ancestral houses of the Ghoses and the Boses, beyond the lamps, the smells, and the crowd of Chitpore Road, and have come to a great wilderness of packed houses – just such mysterious, conspiring tenements as Dickens would have loved. There is no breeze here, and the air is perceptibly warmer. If Calcutta keeps such luxuries as Commissioners of Sewers and Paving, they die before they reach this place. The air is heavy with a faint, sour stench – the essence of long-neglected abominations – and it cannot escape from among the tall, three-storeyed houses. 'This, my dear Sir, is a *perfectly* respectable quarter as quarters go. That house at the head of the alley, with the elaborate stucco-work round the top of the door, was built long ago by a celebrated midwife. Great people used to live here once. Now it's the—, Aha! Look out for that carriage.' A big mail-phaeton crashes out of the darkness and, recklessly driven, disappears. The wonder is how it ever got into this maze of narrow streets, where nobody seems to be moving, and where the dull throbbing of the city's life only comes faintly and by snatches. 'Now it's the what?' 'The St. John's Wood of Calcutta – for the rich Babus. That "fitton" belonged to one of them.' 'Well, it's not much of a place to look at!' 'Don't judge by appearances. About here live the women who have beggared kings. We aren't going to let you down into unadulterated vice all at once. You must see it first with the gilding on – and mind that rotten board.'

Stand at the bottom of a lift-shaft and look upwards. Then you will get both the size and the design of the tiny courtyard round which one of these big dark houses is built. The central square may be perhaps ten feet every way, but the balconies that run inside it overhang, and seem to cut away half the available space. To reach the square a man must go round many corners, down a covered-in way, and up and down two or three baffling and confused steps. 'Now you will understand,' say the Police kindly, as their charge blunders, shin-first, into a well-dark winding staircase, 'that these are not the sort of places to visit alone.' 'Who wants to? Of all the disgusting, inaccessible dens – Holy Cupid, what's this?'

A glare of light on the stair-head, a clink of innumerable bangles, a rustle of much fine gauze, and the Dainty Iniquity stands revealed, blazing – literally blazing – with jewellery from head to foot. Take one of the fairest miniatures that the Delhi painters draw, and multiply it by ten; throw in one of Angelica Kaufmann's best portraits, and add anything that you can think of from Beckford to *Lalla Rookh*, and you will still fall short of the merits of that perfect face! For an instant, even the grim, professional gravity of the Police is relaxed in the presence of the Dainty Iniquity with the gems, who so prettily invites every one to be seated, and proffers such refreshments as she conceives the palates of the barbarians would prefer. Her maids are only one degree less gorgeous than she. Half a lakh, or fifty thousand pounds' worth – it is easier to credit the latter statement than the former – are disposed upon her little body. Each hand carries five jewelled rings which are connected by golden chains to a great jewelled boss of gold in the centre of the back of the hand. Ear-rings weighted with emeralds and pearls, diamond nose-rings, and how many other hundred articles make up the list of adornments. English furniture of a gorgeous and gimcrack kind, unlimited chandeliers, and a collection of atrocious Continental prints are scattered about the house, and on every landing squats or loafs a Bengali who can talk English with unholy fluency. The recurrence suggests – only suggests, mind – a grim possibility of the affectation of excessive virtue by day, tempered with the sort of unwholesome enjoyment after dusk – this loafing and lobbying and chattering and smoking, and unless the bottles lie, tippling, among the foul-tongued handmaidens of the Dainty Iniquity. How many men follow this double, deleterious sort of life? The Police are discreetly dumb.

'Now don't go talking about "domiciliary visits" just because this one happens to be a pretty woman. We've *got* to know these creatures. They make the rich man and the poor spend their money; and when a man can't get money for 'em honestly, he comes under *our* notice. Now do you see? If there was any "domiciliary visit" about it, the whole houseful would be hidden past our finding as soon as we turned up in the courtyard. We're friends – to a certain extent.' And, indeed, it seemed no difficult thing to be friends to any extent with the Dainty Iniquity who was so surpassingly different from all that experience taught of the beauty of the East. Here was the face from which a man could write *Lalla Rookhs* by the dozen, and believe every word that he wrote. Hers was the beauty that Byron sang of when he wrote . . .

'Remember, if you come here alone, the chances are that you'll be clubbed, or stuck, or, anyhow, mobbed. You'll understand that this part of the world is shut to Europeans – absolutely. Mind the steps, and follow on.' The vision dies out in the smells and gross darkness of the night, in evil, time-rotten brickwork, and another wilderness of shut-up houses.

Follows, after another plunge into a passage of a courtyard, and up a staircase, the apparition of a Fat Vice, in whom is no sort of romance, nor beauty, but unlimited coarse humour. She too is studded with jewels, and her house is even finer than the house of the other, and more infested with the extraordinary men who speak such good English and are so deferential to the Police. The Fat Vice has been a great leader of fashion in her day, and stripped a zemindar Raja to his last acre – insomuch that he ended in the House of Correction for a theft committed for her sake. Native opinion has it that she is a 'monstrous well-preserved woman.' On this point, as on some others, the races will agree to differ.

The scene changes suddenly as a slide in a magic-lantern. Dainty Iniquity and Fat Vice slide away on a roll of streets and alleys, each more squalid than its predecessor. We are 'somewhere at the back of the Machua Bazar,' well in the heart of the city. There are no houses here – nothing but acres and acres, it seems, of foul wattle-and-daub huts, any one of which would be a disgrace to a frontier village. The whole arrangement is a neatly contrived germ and fire trap, reflecting great credit upon the Calcutta Municipality.

[from *The City of Dreadful Night and Other Places*]

✠   ✠   ✠

WHEN I HAD DISGUSTED all who knew me, I fled to Calcutta, which, I was pained to see, still persisted in being a city and transacting commerce after I had formally cursed it one year ago. That curse I now repeat, in the hope that the unsavoury capital will collapse. One must begin to smoke at five in the morning – which is neither night nor day – on coming across the Howrah Bridge, for it is better to get a headache from honest nicotine than to be poisoned by evil smells. And a man, who otherwise was a nice man, though he worked with his hands and his head, asked me why the scandal of the Simla Exodus was allowed to continue. To him I made answer: 'It is because this sewer is unfit for human habitation. It is because you are all one gigantic mistake, – you and your monuments and your merchants and everything about you. I rejoice to think that scores of lakhs of rupees have been spent on public offices at a place called Simla, that scores and scores will be spent on the Delhi–Kalka line, in order that civilised people may go there in comfort. When that line is opened, your big city will be dead and buried and done with, and I hope it will teach you a lesson. Your city will rot, Sir.' And he said: 'When people are buried here, they turn into adipocere in five days if the weather is rainy. They saponify, you know.' I said: 'Go and saponify, for I hate Calcutta.' But he took me to the Eden Gardens instead, and begged me for my own sake not to go round the world in this prejudiced spirit. I was unhappy and ill, but he vowed that my spleen was due to my 'Simla way of looking at things.'

All this world of ours knows something about the Eden Gardens, which are supposed by the uninitiated of the mofussil to represent the gilded luxury of the metropolis. As a matter of fact they are hideously dull. The inhabitants appear in top-hats and frock-coats, and walk dolorously to and fro under the glare of jerking electric lamps, when they ought to be sitting in their shirt-sleeves round little tables and treating their wives to iced lager beer. My friend – it was a muggy March night – wrapped himself in the prescribed garments and said graciously: 'You can wear a round hat, but you mustn't wear deck-shoes; and for goodness' sake, my dear fellow, don't smoke on the Red Road – all the people one knows go there.' Most of the people who were people sat in their carriages, in an atmosphere of hot horse, harness, and panel-lacquer, outside the gardens, and the remnant tramped up and down, by twos and threes, upon squashy green grass, until they were wearied, while a band played at them. 'And is this all you do?' I asked. 'It is,' said my friend. 'Isn't it good enough? We meet every one we know here, and walk with him or her, unless he or she is among the carriages.'

Overhead was a woolly warm sky; underfoot feverish soft grass; and from all quarters the languorous breeze bore faint reminiscences of stale sewage upon its wings. Round the horizon were stacked lines of carriages, and the electric flare bred aches in the strained eyebrow. It was a strange sight and fascinating. The doomed creatures walked up and down without cessation, for when one fled away into the lamp-spangled gloom twenty came to take his place. Slop-hatted members of the mercantile marine, Armenian merchants, Bengal civilians, shop-girls and shop-men, Jews, Parthians, and Mesopotamians, were all there in the tepid heat and the fetid smell.

[*From Sea to Sea*]

❊ ❊ ❊

INDIAN RAILWAYS

The beginning of everything was in a railway train upon the road to Mhow from Ajmir. There had been a Deficit in the Budget, which necessitated travelling, not Second-class, which is only half as dear as First-class, but by Intermediate, which is very awful indeed. There are no cushions in the Intermediate class, and the population are either Intermediate, which is Eurasian, or native, which for a long night journey is nasty, or Loafer, which is amusing though intoxicated. Intermediates do not buy from refreshment-rooms. They carry their food in bundles and pots, and buy sweets from the native sweetmeat-sellers, and drink the road-side water. That is why in the hot weather Intermediates are taken out of the carriages dead, and in all weathers are most properly looked down upon.

['The Man Who Would Be King', *The Phantom Rickshaw and Other Tales*]

TO LAHORE BY TRAIN

THE LONGING BEGAN AT least a league off shore from Colombo, when the *Chusan*, Calcutta bound, swung out around the breakwater under the *Valetta's* nose, and we who were Anglo-Indians separated ourselves a little from the crowd. A smell came up over the sea – a smell of damp earth, coconut oil, ginger, onions and mankind.

It spoke with a strong voice, recalling many things; but the most curious revelation to one man was the sudden knowledge that under these skies lay home and the dearest places in all the world. Even the first sniff of London had not caused so big a choke in the throat, or so strict a tightening over the heart.

There was a most urgent necessity to get away to Lahore swiftly. The *Valetta* ploughed on to Aden; a big B.I. boat took charge of me to Tuticorin, and at the first turn of her screw, the first glimpse of the *khit-magars* on deck, Australia, the Cape, New Zealand, and the British Isles dropped under the sea. I was going home for Christmas, largely and expansively – as an Anglo-Indian should go – by train for the better part of a week, as soon as the *Nerbudda* should make Tuticorin.

With me, sole survivor of a scattered card-party, was the Post Officer of Vizagatapam, and he promised me breakfast on shore in the old casual Anglo-Indian fashion. 'I know the Post Officer here', he said, 'met him once. No, I didn't, by Jove – he was out when I came – but I can put up at his house. He'll give us breakfast.' By this I knew where I was, and rejoiced.

Then we stepped on to Indian soil under the green fig trees that face the beach, where the cotton trains go to and fro, and the Tamil women weave onion baskets of green reeds while their babies hang like cocoons in the blight of a loin-cloth flung over a branch. Allah be praised, we stepped straight into India again. It was not quite the real India, but the India that the English know – the *Little Henry and his Bearer* country, all paddy, palmyra, and coconut palms, as the books draw it. Hindu temples jostled old Dutch-built Roman Catholic Churches where the Virgin, I believe, has twelve arms and the saints are rather like Krishnas. The people, too, were hereditary Christians, and spoke English, many of them. Small wonder that the South Indian papers point out that one writer at least does not describe India – their India. Could a Swede from the Baltic write of Algiers?

But the beautiful smell was there, the brown, slow-moving crowds were there (white is rather a leprous tint when you come to think of it, and it doesn't match backgrounds), the crumbling *kutcha* walls and the deep; bowed bungalows were all waiting there. Best of all there was the Post Officer, first met of our breed, a khaki-clad Anglo-Indian, not one whit disturbed because two utter strangers from the sea demanded breakfast.

Oh! that breakfast, eaten under the slow-swinging *punkahs* with white-robed butlers behind our chairs – the fish fresh from the sea that was lapping twenty yards away outside in the glare, the teal bagged yesterday, the Madras curry with its rich allowance of spices, and the first long pull of Pilsener, the ice clinking in the tall glass. Afterwards – this was even more perfect – there came the self-assured and confident flop into the long chair – our long chair – where you put up your feet by right and not by permission, and jamming a black rank Dawson No. 1 between your teeth puff the well remembered incense and thank Heaven you are back among your fellows once more. There were no 'Misters' in that bungalow after first introductions; we keep 'Mister' for the Globe-Trotter.

Even then, with two thousand four hundred miles to cover before I got home, it was manifestly absurd to pretend that I had been away for a day.

The *Nerbudda*, just visible on the horizon, was an accident I could not explain. She probably came from Colombo. I was from the North, the men on the long chairs were talking shop – cotton and harbour improvements, with allusions to sick friends and a fever-stricken householder in the station. They talked in their own way, but as I listened a memory came up through the tobacco smoke 'touching the life I led before this life' – a worritsome gabbling life somewhere overseas. In that life surely there was a man – a reviewer – who whiningly wanted to know y'know, whether anywhere in the world men talk as they are represented in certain books – that is to say, like telegraph forms. I think his words were 'cynically, brusquely and like telegraph forms'. Oh, reviewer they do, indeed they do. That is why I made it so. Probably they would not talk to you in that fashion, because you are not of their household, but among themselves they speak – they are speaking now of a man down with small-pox – word for word, as these hands have written before. It is all one big family and if you do not know the catchwords of the family, you must stand outside.

We loafed through the bazaar to the train, paralysed booking and telegraph clerk by trying to get a ticket and send a telegram in under half-an-hour, and at noon in the brilliant moist sunshine slouched off by the S.I.R. on a four hundred mile run to Madras. The warm rain began to fall steadily, and in an hour or two the flat red soil was under water as far as the eye could reach. Then came the perfect tropical moon, turning the embankment aloes to frosted silver, and the frogs sang songs at the stations where we halted, and the palms dripped heavily and gave out all their smell.

Moreover Asia, taking me back without reserve, threw her mantle over me from head to foot. To think that a man should be thankful for prickly heat!

After interminable hours – twenty-eight of them – and flood all the way, there was Arconum and a parting. The Post Officer of Vizag went his way to his harbour and I to mine, hopping from train to train and wrestling with booking clerks who denied the existence of Lahore. One fat Madrassi pinned me in a corner – indeed I wanted no more than a ticket to Khundwa – and waving a triplicate form-book over my head, shouted: 'Do you know what work is?'

In free America or enlightened England he would have been badly injured, but the brutal and overbearing Anglo-Indian – who talks, as you will know, of the 'damned nigger' all day and kicks his servant all night – takes this sort of thing as part of the day's work. I would have given a month's pay to have turned one or two howling philanthropists of my England acquaint-ance loose among the booking offices. Nay, more, I would have paid their fines for assault with intent to kill.

Then north to Raichur and Wadi where the look of the land changed and there was a prophecy of drought in the air. Two men entered, one a Major of seventeen years' service and the other a Subaltern of two. He was on transfer to the Staff Corps, had bagged his live tigers, desired more *shikar* and more than *shikar* lusted for active service. The elder man got out at some unholy hour of the night for a twenty-mile tonga drive and a fifty-mile ride; and the last we saw of him was a figure in the moonlight suavely assuring the tonga driver that never since the British Raj was founded had an officer travelled with less kit. 'And it will all go into the tonga – because it must all go into the tonga,' he said. It was sound logic and the principle upon which the Government servant is administered.

Then did the Subaltern and myself, climbing into our bunks on the Dhond–Manmar line seriously discuss the ordering of a young man's future. Was it better for a man who had just entered the Staff Corps – 'and that means India all my life' – to try for the Guides, the Goorkhas or Bengal cavalry. After much argument, we agreed to refer the matter unofficially to any man over ten years' service whom we might catch. At Manmar junction we found that man by the simple process of falling over his feet in the dawn.

He was guarded by a rampart of kit and two superb bull-terriers. Over the dogs and the tea we fraternised in the blessed Anglo-Indian custom. Fancy waking up an Englishman in his pyjamas on the Edinburgh Express, let us say, and expecting him to be amiable. Presently we laid the Subaltern's difficulty before him, and he said 'Cavalry of course – Go for the horses by all means.' He was in the Cavalry himself and prejudiced. He, well knowing me to be a Punjabi, told me how some Hyderabadi troopers came up to Muridki camp last year for *dugabashi*, and 'knocked spots out of your Pathans, by Jove!' Now everybody knows that one Punjabi is worth five down-country *sowars*. I hate a prejudiced man.

We talked together and apart while the red-eyed bull-terriers fawned upon us, and the Subaltern, whose arms were splashed with the red sun tar, far up the elbows, showed us his guns and told me how there was no one in the world so wise, so full of resource and such a 'ripping good man all round' as his Skipper. He, the Subaltern, had been learning the mystery of managing men, and getting to know his half-company as an officer should.

The subject was a fascinating one – 'it's an awful grind, though' – and it ended all too soon when he packed up his things and went eastward to his first Staff Corps Regiment. God be very good to him, for those square shoulders may have to uphold the weight of an Empire's honour alone in some lone outpost before a year is done.

One vision of the night-time stays with me. There was a Globe-Trotter with his neatly locked bag of washing fresh from the steamer. He came and slept and went but [I was] awake when he climbed into the upper bunk, and behold he wore a night-gown, a beautiful ample-tailed slashed and lily white English night-gown! See a man manoeuvre into an upper bunk with a night-gown, and die, as I nearly did.

All this time India was rolling back behind the wheels – level, burned and dusty. We ploughed through the Asseerghur jungle, in company with a Forest Officer and a young 'Stunt two months out from home, a little bewildered at the new life, but very resolute to make the best of it. The Forest Officer melted nearly to tears at the sight of an English half crown, handled it lovingly and offered three rupees in exchange.

Now was it yesterday, or ten years ago, that in a railway carriage by Neemuch I found a Globe-Trotter and sighed when he showed me an English penny? It must have been the better part of ten years; and to-day it is our poor one and four-penny rupee that makes me home-sick.

The first suggestion of the cold weather – our own real cold weather – began at Bhopal, where the train ran through the dank white layers of evening wood smoke and there came a smell of dried earth and burned cowdung. Morning – a clear dry morning – brought 'the hottest town, in all this land of Ind' – Agra, with her red Fort and disreputable monkeys. There was a 'homey' look about the fields; the village boundary pillars were familiar, and the cattle such as one knows.

But the people on the platform were only North-West men – down-country folk and they did not carry the proper kind of huqqa. By noon we should be in our proper territories, and it was more than likely that some old faces . . . . Now observe the kindness of Providence! Three years ago it was the Lord of the Iron Horses of the North-Western Railway who saw me off the premises in his inspection carriage. Therefore it was right and proper that the first train into Ghaziabad – Ghaziabad with its awful tiffins and vault-like refreshment rooms – should bring up from Ajmir on his way to Lahore, that same Lord of the Iron Horses.

'Back again?' said he. 'Back again', said I. 'Well, you're a nice sort of a Globe-Trotter!' said he. I pocketed the insult, for there were three years arrears of news to make good of what had happened up at home? Who was dead, married, transferred, promoted or gone under? In the evening light, flying up to Meerut, my questions were answered simply and monosyllabically as is our custom. Thus: – 'A?' 'He's dead. Didn't you hear?' 'B?' 'Transferred – Poona.' C? 'Still at Gurdaspore.' D? 'He married Miss Such-An-one. They've both gone home on six months.' 'Mrs E.?' 'Dead – died of typhoid last July. It was a bad hot weather.'

'And you yourself?' I said, knowing he had had no leave for eleven years. 'Oh, I don't care. I know that the weather can't be worse than I've known it, so I stick it out. I say, though, what a fuss you kicked up at Home about that Manipur business; might have thought all India was being sacked.'

'You at Home' sticks unpleasantly in the throat; confound the Lord of the Iron Horses. What have I to do with the people at 'Home'. I am here, and the North-Western Railway is running disgracefully late as usual.

'Don't you fret,' he answers calmly. 'She'll leg it in the night. Look at Meerut. There's a Cavalry camp on.'

A line of white tents and a cloud of dust fringes the station of the Race Course. Another young Subaltern – keen as mustard on his profession, who has stolen a few days and travelled a few hundred miles to see the show – leans forward intently. He is going to the camp. Everybody will be there, and General Luck, or whoever it is, will bucket them about royally.

Only . . . Only I am out of it, no camp for me. Officers in wonderful *khaki* undress are walking about the platform. Their *putties* are white with the beautiful dust and their noses are skinned by the sun. The Subaltern goes away, and the last stretch of rail begins.

'S – if you love me, make her go. We shall be late at Lahore to-morrow.'

'She'll leg it in the night,' is the answer. 'What's the good of getting into Lahore in the dawn?'

She legs it. After Saharanpur she lies down to her work in earnest with an hour and a half to make up. The Jhelum bridge rings and rattles under her heels. There is a glimpse of lean, dry sand under the moon, and with a whistle she sails into the Punjab. The rest is easy. How do the Stations run?

Umballa, Phillour, Beas East, Jullundur, Amritsar and Ataree, and then Lahore. Colder and colder grows the Northern night. Somebody shouts Umballa through my dreams – Umballa of a hundred Simla memories in the days before you went to Kalka by rail. Now that I know every tie and fish plate from here to home I will sleep . . .

* * *

'Hi! Ho! We're past Amritsar. Here's Ataree. There's *chota hazri* in K's carriage!' It is the diamond-clear cold-weather dawn – dawn among the ferashes, the creaking well-wheels and the *Jats* – the huge-thighed *Jats* – each man head-blanketted from the cold and each trailing his lumbering *huqqa*. The land looks sick and drouthy. But it is home – every dusty inch of it. We invade K's carriage, and finding him defenceless in his pyjamas make a mock of him. The elephant lines and a couple of rocking tethered *hathis* show grey through the last patches of the morning mist, and rattling over the facing points, past the back of the railway theatre – who remembers *Plot and Passion* there eight years ago, when the locomotives whistled down all the love-scenes? – pull up at Lahore platform. Four and a half days from Tuticorin. One can move in the Empire.

Now, certainly, I have never been one day absent. There was an agricultural exhibition at Jullundur yesterday, which I was sent to describe, and after breakfast there will be just time to get back to office, send in the report and take the day's mail. The old life will begin again . . . after breakfast. Up start the brown faces in the familiar verandah that takes the dust of Mozung. 'Yes, by the Sahib's favour we be all well. Other of the Sahib's household be coming to make salutations after breakfast. Yes. He that was the scullion is now promoted to be the butler by the Honoured one's favour and' – Kadir Buksh, pearl among *khitmatgars*, the voice was thine! – 'There is *Hussaini Kabab* for *hazri*.'

A pious Musalman would be shocked if he were violently hugged by a Kafir. None the less, I should like to dance sarabands with Kadir as he grins and hands the curry. There is only one curry in the world, and Kadir Buksh makes it, and – oh the forgotten decency, that the English cannot understand! – sets out the finger-bowls after meat. For the rest, looking round the old home there is not much of the luxury we read about in the books. How would an English *memsahib* approve whitewashed walls, raw-timbered roofs split and cracked with old summers, the whitewash splashed impartially over the timbers, doors that never shut, and glass puttied as for an outhouse. But these things, with the old jail *dhurries*, the ruggled *chitai* in the verandah, the cock-eyed *almirahs*, the *choukuts* that catch a forgetful foot on the threshold, and the rude printed cloth dadoes make homes. To clinch everything, the Very Dearest Dog in All the World recognises a long-lost master, and behaves accordingly. Vixen, do you remember the hot weathers we shared together when you lay in the thermantidote and penked? Do you remember the wet tonga drives to Simla, and rat-catching in the office? Vixen, it's nearly seven years since I bought you at the sale of a dead man's kit, and you are getting old. 'Take me out', says Vixen, 'show me a squirrel and see.'

No *chaprassi* comes with an office box; there is no dogcart for Vixen to direct and – all the world is going off to its work except myself. Vixen, we will to the old *duftar* and pretend that we belong there? Therefore, in the morning sunshine, sifted through the dusty *ferashes*, we take stock of the land. As usual they have been excavating old graveyards, and then they wonder Lahore is unhealthy. You and I used to dig out skulls, Vixen, scrape them up with a fire shovel all round the foundations of the new Law Courts.

Now who in the exercise of his discretion has been splitting the Mall length ways with brick paths? What is the use of *surki* on the side walks? That was the only soft place to ride on. Central lamp posts invite a man to drive his dogcart into them, and Lahore Mall will never be a boulevard. It's just the Mall – the old *thunda suruk* – and even in the morning sunshine it is packed with ghosts. We've seen it in every light, Vixen – muddy and frosted and bare, drenched with the warmth of the rains, and hot as a station rail in June when the dust clouds danced down it like devils, and you wallowed, poor little beastie, in the spillage of the wells. It looks pretty enough now to a Globe-Trotter's eye. He couldn't guess that we have had no rain to speak of for twelve months. The frost has touched the roses a little too, and there are crowds of dead people driving up and down.

'Sahib, this is indeed the office of the *chappar kargaz* and I was your old *chaprassi*, but the paper itself is printed at another office and elsewhere.' This is really pleasant. It reminds you who you are, to go to your own office and find that it isn't there any longer, and that you don't know where it is. Once before, the mother-paper changed her place, but then one knew all about it. Now, one is only a rank outsider – a Globe-Trotter who must be piloted about Lahore. Yet it is good to think that the paper has prospered. To the new office, therefore, with a big, big lump in one's throat. No man can put in his seven years on an Indian journal when he is half the staff, and the sheet is part of his being without loving her dearly. The smell of the office comes out through the orange trees, and there is the thump of an old columbiad (I think I know which one it is) running off the galley proofs for the editor. Then, through a cautiously lifted *chick*, the old scene stands revealed, and there rush back on the memory the names of a score of natives buried for a time under the drift of the months. The brown comps. are bending over the cases, the little distributing boys are sitting cross-legged on the floor and – Yes ! *He* has not changed in the least – the man who broke my heart daily for years is getting together the standing matter. What would happen if one called out: '*Kitna* in hand *hai, kul se*?' The lemon and green turbans shake like a bed of tulips in a high wind, and they come up by the dozen, from the foreman, whom nothing could flurry, to the man who locks up the formes and has a detestable trick of doing it at least ten minutes too soon.

One cannot say much, but one thinks a good deal. Of the old Staff of '82, the foreman, perhaps three other hands and myself are the sole survivors. And now I am on the Staff no longer. No word of mine can make the old wheels spin, and Mahmud would only grin if I rated him for his sins. It isn't a nice feeling, but I know it will be worse this evening among the men at the Hall and the Club.

Into the office and the piles of the dusty exchanges, to fall over the eternal *duftri* and to watch with envy the loaded and littered tables. There is a long talk here – talk of the old days, reminiscence of catchwords, bygone practical jokes, and all the intimacies, squabbles and crises between two yoke-mates for years and then – it had to come, but it hurt – 'Well, I must get through the *dak*, old man. Can you give us something while you're here?'

'*You* give *us.*' Yes, I think so. An epic if I had it in hand. 'There is no demand for epics in the Punjab; men live them: but anything else will do.' So, back again with the 'You give us' rankling in my breast. Yet, it was absurd to think that a man would sit down and get back to work for a day or two, feel the snap of the shears again, stir up the 'Kingdom of Bombay' with irreverent jests, battle with the *Englishman* over Capua and the Exodus, and ask Madras whether it had an army, and if so, how many. That time is over, rightly and properly so; but one can still do a little work for one's own country otherwhere than on the old Staff. I comforted myself with that thought, and went off to the happy hunting grounds in the city.

The Lahore Municipality have sold the Taksali Gate for brick-work, leaving an ugly scar in the city wall. Gentlemen, whose souls would be dear at one brick a piece, you have done a sin; for that gate was built like the Pyramids. It had little beauty save of age and time, but while it stood it was full of beautiful light and shade, corners where an idle man could plant his charpoy and dream, niches where the burnished doves sat in the hot hours and the kine of the city used to troop under its arch twice a day, making a golden haze of dust without before they plunged into the cool darkness within. You could have bought bricks from the potter, but you will never build another Taksali Gate.

As second wind to a runner, or wine to a wearied man, was this second view of the city of Lahore – the oldest and surely the most picturesque city in the world. Thomas – of the K.O.S.B.'s – was on guard at the main gate of the Fort (I wonder which of us two best knew the guardroom on the wall) and the sunlight was splashing the mouldering tile work of the main face – the gay tile-wrought angels and elephants of Akbar. The minars of Shadera where Jahangir lies dead, and with him the memories of many moonlight picnics and wild words under the roses, showed above the belt of green by the Ravi. Thomas – a spot of vermillion – was loafing down the sunk way to the gate, his dog at his heels. Thomas with a *chilumchee* and bare headed – will nothing teach Thomas that he must not play even with the cold-weather sun? – was scuffling from barrack to barrack, and Thomas (fever-stricken Thomas) in his greatcoat was hanging over the balcony of the hospital, half a dozen superb Pathan soldiers in undress were swinging across the path by the glaring native guardroom where Sikh sepoys rested near their speckless rifles, rising to salute and standing one bar of blood red against the whitewashed wall. It is awful to think that in England they have never seen any of the primary colours, and that they know nothing of drapery, the folds of well-worn unsewn clothing that falls in great laps and curves, and gathered round the neck and under the armpit in robes of richest deep-shadowed wrinkles. The square of the Naulakha pavilion ached in the sunshine, and there tramping across the white marble, his belt well down over his hips, his coat open and his helmet at the back of his head, was Thomas – affable and a citizen of the world – Thomas with four years' service and very pronounced views on men and things. We talked together sitting under the painted, mirror-inlaid ceilings till he said with cheerful irrelevance that it was near canteen opening time. O Thomas, Thomas! to think that I should have been taken in by that stale old trick. But it was Simla beer, and no muddy English porter.

There was a glimpse of the fort barrack room with its monstrous under-strutting of masonry – and the spider-legged cots disposed in the hall of dead kings, the pillars of black and white marble defiled with whitewash, and the marvellous painted relief work daubed out of all knowledge. In the vast cool silence of this echoing hall, Thomas in every stage of undress came and went; and Thomas's dog lay on the cot and barked. The verandah arches showed pure raw sunlight and blue, and Thomas stood there in red, the points of light twinkling off his accoutrements as he went to relieve guard. It was home indeed!

Out of the Fort into the city, across the ground, where the cavalry camped on the night of the Mohurrum riots – how long ago? Is there 'Captain, Colonel or knight at arms' who remembers a scandalous night on an open gallery when the swords of fifteen skylarking subalterns came near to being thrown into the Fort ditch? Here, by the dusty outskirts was the spot where the troopers cut across the track of an infuriated procession of Moslems. Here at the corner of the Roshnai Gate they headed off a *tazia*, and it was at the Soneri Musjid that horse and foot stuck fast in the roaring press – that was a night among many nights and of those who were there, none remain except – a Globe-Trotter.

If the Civil station hinted at the memories of years, the city shouted them aloud. House upon piled house, the time-worn wood tracery standing askew on the rotten brickwork, well gulley mouth, ruinous dead wall and crumbling heap of sheer stark red rotten rubbish overrun by the crowd, the cattle and the asses – all spoke with the voice of the years. Here lived the Jews of Shushan, there, arrogant and unashamed, was Lalun's naughty little house, Azizan of the Douri Bagh was a little beyond, and the house of Suddhoo was not far off the ringing roaring gulley of the coppersmiths, where the lean traders sat by piles of beaten gold vessels selling the splendour of the East for a few annas. Here were the Pathan horse-dealers chattering with the seal cutters for a new signet ring. Not till one understands in some small measure the heart of the city, does one realise how much the poorest country in the world has to spend on fripperies – four-anna embroidered caps for the babies, cheap jewellry, bats and stumps (a new industry since my time – cricket is more than ever naturalised with us), kites, cheap lithographs of the gods, tinsel-stuck shoes and slippers, necklaces, beads, mirror-rings and a hundred other toys. Here and there through the jostling crowd where buffalo calves and led ponies share all the rights of way with men, a face passes that I know, and once or twice an old friend stops me to give greeting. The Dubbi Bazaar is full of old friends, from the fat *bunnia* among the turmeric heaps to the policeman with the *kullam* and the green-glazed inkpot in his hand. They don't know me, but I know them.

How shall one describe the sun-lit river bed of people whose daily passage has oil polished the wooden posts of the shop boards, smoothed the angles of the brickwork and faced the very ground with glair as a glacier polishes a rock. As if its own beauty were not enough, the dyers have spread filmy muslins of palest blue and pink across the street, and you look upon the old witchery of the old life through the pearl-tinted mists of dawn. It is noon and past, and high overhead a boy's yellow paper kite is sawing and jigging into the restful blue like a big sulphur butterfly. Below there is the hurry and the shouting, the broken waves of colour, the deep shadows that heighten colour as velvet displays the diamond, and above all, and apart from all, as a prayer from a tortured heart, the mosque of Wazir Khan flings up its four minars to heaven? What need to cry five times a day that God is great?

At the shadow of the Delhi Gate the picture of the city ends for the sight – to be graven deeper on the mind. Again comes the memory of the murmurs of a little city called London – a city where there is neither colour nor light nor air. Who was the particular *pagal* over there who wrote of extravagance of description and the Lord knows what else? If he were here between that broken-hatted, unbuttoned English loafer slinking red nosed in the sunshine and the dusty swaying plantain leaves of the Badami Bagh – here when I stand looking at the heaped-up roofs of the city, the proud arch of the gateway and the torrent of turbulent colour that rolls beneath it, what would he write? And if he had seen that Jubilee night in '87, when the city of Lahore flamed out of the dusk as a jewelled queen from the door of the palace of night – dome, minaret, bastion, wall and house-front drawn in dotted fire, what would he have said of extravagance then? But who can show a blind man colour?

['Home', *CMG*, 25 December 1891]

2

ASIA

Eastern Promise

Rangoon – Moulmein – Mandalay – Penang – Singapore – Hong Kong – China – Canton – Japan – Nagasaki – Tokyo – Kamakura.

Before Kipling embarked from Calcutta on his eastward voyage to America and England in March 1899, he had had little reason to think much about the Far East. The Muslim culture he revered in India looked west to Iran and Central Asia for its traditions and contacts.

As soon as he reached Burma, he realised he was somewhere different. As he wrote in his articles for the *Pioneer*, later collected under the title *From Sea to Sea*, Kipling was quickly attracted to the easy manners and iridescence of the inhabitants (particularly the women) in both Rangoon, his first port of call, and Moulmein (nowadays known as Mawlamyine or Mawlamyaing).

Kipling's best-known commentary on Burma came in his poem 'Mandalay', published later, after he reached Britain, as one of his 'Barrack-Room Ballads' in the *Scots Observer* on 21 June 1890. As he did not actually visit Mandalay (and the topography of these verses has been called into question), the poem should be read as a soldier's romanticised idyll for the strange, enticing existence he once (by accident of imperial reach) happened to experience 'somewheres east of Suez, where the best is like the worst,/ Where there aren't no Ten Commandments an' a man can raise a thirst'. Such reminiscences are an essential element in the psychic legacy of empire that Kipling understood so well.

After first encountering the Chinese in Penang, Kipling was taken aback and rather frightened by their unworldly capacity for work – a view that only intensified as he made his way on

the SS *Madura* through the Malacca Straits and the South China Sea to Hong Kong and Canton, where his chancing upon a site for executions only confirmed his growing prejudices against this particular race.

He much preferred Japan, finding it so much more civilised that he returned there on honeymoon with his new wife Caroline (née Balestier) in 1892. She had links to the country since her grandfather Erasmus Peshine Smith had been legal adviser to the Mikado.

On this second trip Kipling visited Kamakura, a city of many temples, one of which provided the site for the giant outdoor Buddha, whose calm magnificence Kipling evoked in 'Buddha at Kamakura', a poem that reflected his ecumenical views on religion.

RANGOON

THEN, A GOLDEN MYSTERY upheaved itself on the horizon, a beautiful winking wonder that blazed in the sun, of a shape that was neither Moslem dome nor Hindu temple-spire. It stood upon a green knoll, and below it were lines of warehouses, sheds, and mills. Under what new god, thought I, are we irrepressible English sitting now?

'There's the old Shway Dagon' (pronounced Dagone, *not* like the god in the Scriptures), said my companion. 'Confound it!' But it was not a thing to be sworn at. It explained in the first place why we took Rangoon, and in the second why we pushed on to see what more of rich or rare the land held. Up till that sight my uninstructed eyes could not see that the land differed much in appearance from the Sunderbuns, but the golden dome said: 'This is Burma, and it will be quite unlike any land you know about.' 'It's a famous old shrine o' sorts,' said my companion, 'and now the Tounghoo–Mandalay line is open, pilgrims are flocking down by the thousand to see it. It lost its big gold top – 'thing that they call a *'htee* – in an earthquake: that's why it's all hidden by bamboo-work for a third of its height. You should see it when it's all uncovered. They're regilding it now.'

Why is it that when one views for the first time any of the wonders of the earth a bystander always strikes in with, 'You should see it, etc.'? Such men given twenty minutes from the tomb at the Day of Judgment, would patronise the naked souls as they hurried up with the glare of Tophet on their faces, and say: 'You should have seen this when Gabriel first began to blow.' What the Shway Dagon really is and how many books may have been written upon its history and archaeology is no part of my business. As it stood overlooking everything it seemed to explain all about Burma – why the boys had gone north and died, why the troopers bustled to and fro, and why the steamers of the Irrawaddy Flotilla lay like black-backed gulls upon the water.

Then we came to a new land, and the first thing that one of the regular residents said was 'This place isn't India at all. They ought to have made it a Crown colony.' Judging the Empire as it ought to be judged, by its most prominent points – *videlicet*, its smells – he was right; for though there is one stink in Calcutta, another in Bombay, and a third and most pungent one in the Punjab, yet they have a kinship of stinks, whereas Burma smells quite otherwise. It is not exactly what China ought to smell like, but it is not India. 'What is it?' I asked; and the man said '*Napi*,' which is fish pickled when it ought to have been buried long ago. This food, in guide-book language, is inordinately consumed by . . . . but everybody who has been within downwind range of Rangoon knows what *napi* means, and those who do not will not understand.

Yes, it was a very new land – a land where the people understood colour – a delightfully lazy land full of pretty girls and very bad cheroots.

The worst of it was that the Anglo-Indian was a foreigner, a creature of no account. He did not know Burman, – which was no great loss, – and the Madrassi insisted upon addressing him in English. The Madrassi, by the way, is a great institution. He takes the place of the Burman, who will not work, and in a few years returns to his native coast with rings on his fingers and bells on his toes. The consequences are obvious. The Madrassi demands, and receives, enormous wages, and gets to know that he is indispensable. The Burman exists beautifully, while his women-folk marry the Madrassi and the Chinaman, because these support them in affluence. When the Burman wishes to work he gets a Madrassi to do it for him. How he finds the money to pay the Madrassi I was not informed, but all men were agreed in saying that under no circumstances will the Burman exert himself in the paths of honest industry. Now, if a bountiful Providence had clothed you in a purple, green, amber or puce petticoat, had thrown a rose-pink scarf-turban over your head, and had put you in a pleasant damp country where rice grew of itself and fish came up to be caught, putrefied and pickled, would *you* work? Would you not rather take a cheroot and loaf about the streets seeing what was to be seen? If two-thirds of your girls were grinning, good-humoured little maidens and the remainder positively pretty, would you not spend your time in making love?

The Burman does both these things, and the Englishman, who after all worked himself to Burma, says hard things about him. Personally I love the Burman with the blind favouritism born of first impression. When I die I will be a Burman, with twenty yards of real King's silk, that has been made in Mandalay, about my body, and a succession of cigarettes between my lips. I will wave the cigarette to emphasise my conversation, which shall be full of jest and repartee, and I will always walk about with a pretty almond-coloured girl who shall laugh and jest too, as a young maiden ought. She shall not pull a sari over her head when a man looks at her and glare suggestively from behind it, nor shall she tramp behind me when I walk: for these are the customs of India. She shall look all the world between the eyes, in honesty and good fellowship, and I will teach her not to defile her pretty mouth with chopped tobacco in a cabbage leaf, but to inhale good cigarettes of Egypt's best brand.

Seriously, the Burmese girls are very pretty, and when I saw them I understood much that I had heard about — about our army in Flanders let us say.

[*From Sea to Sea*]

❂ ❂ ❂

MOULMEIN

MOULMEIN IS SITUATED UP the mouth of a river which ought to flow through South America, and all manner of dissolute native craft appear to make the place their home. Ugly cargo-steamers that the initiated call 'Geordie tramps' grunt and bellow at the beautiful hills all round, and the pot-bellied British India liners wallow down the reaches. Visitors are rare in Moulmein – so rare that few but cargo-boats think it worth their while to come off from the shore.

Strictly in confidence I will tell you that Moulmein is not a city of this earth at all. Sindbad the Sailor visited it, if you recollect, on that memorable voyage when he discovered the burial-ground of the elephants.

As the steamer came up the river we were aware of first one elephant and then another hard at work in timber-yards that faced the shore. A few narrow-minded folk with binoculars said that there were *mahouts* upon their backs, but this was never clearly proven. I prefer to believe in what I saw – a sleepy town, just one house thick, scattered along a lovely stream and inhabited by slow, solemn elephants, building stockades for their own diversion. There was a strong scent of freshly sawn teak in the air – we could not see any elephants sawing – and occasionally the warm stillness was broken by the crash of the log. When the elephants had got an appetite for luncheon they loafed off in couples to their club, and did not take the trouble to give us greeting and the latest mail papers; at which we were much disappointed, but took heart when we saw upon a hill a large white pagoda surrounded by scores of little pagodas. 'This,' we said with one voice, 'is the place to make an excursion to,' and then shuddered at our own profanity, for above all things we did not wish to behave like mere vulgar tourists.

The *ticca-gharries* at Moulmein are three sizes smaller than those of Rangoon, for the ponies are no bigger than decent sheep. Their drovers trot them uphill and down, and as the *gharri* is extremely narrow and the roads are anything but good, the exercise is refreshing. Here again all the drivers are Madrassis.

I should better remember what that pagoda was like had I not fallen deeply and irrevocably in love with a Burmese girl at the foot of the first flight of steps. Only the fact of the steamer starting next noon prevented me from staying at Moulmein forever and owning a pair of elephants. These are so common that they wander about the streets, and, I make no doubt, could be obtained for a piece of sugar-cane.

Leaving this far too lovely maiden, I went up the steps only a few yards, and, turning me round, looked upon a view of water, island, broad river, fair grazing ground, and belted wood that made me rejoice that I was alive. The hillside below me and above me was ablaze with pagodas – from a gorgeous golden and vermilion beauty to a delicate grey stone one just completed in honour of an eminent priest lately deceased at Mandalay. Far above my head there was a faint tinkle, as of golden bells, and a talking of the breezes in the tops of the toddy-palms. Wherefore I climbed higher and higher up the steps till I reached a place of great peace, dotted with Burmese images, spotlessly clean. Here women now and again paid reverence. They bowed their heads and their lips moved, because they were praying. I had an umbrella – a black one – in my hand, deck-shoes upon my feet, and a helmet upon my head. I did not pray – I swore at myself for being a Globetrotter, and wished that I had enough Burmese to explain to these ladies that I was sorry and would have taken off my hat but for the sun. A Globetrotter is a brute. I had the grace to blush as I tramped round the pagoda. That will be remembered to me for righteousness. But I stared horribly – at a gold and red side-temple with a beautifully gilt image of Buddha in it – at the grim figures in the niches at the base of the main pagoda – at the little palms that grew out of the cracks in the tiled paving of the court – at the big palms above, and at the low-hung bronze bells that stood at each corner for the women to smite with staghorns. Upon one bell rang this amazing triplet in English – evidently the composition of the caster, who completed his work – and now, let us hope, has reached Nibban – thirty-five years ago:–

> He who destroyed this Bell
> They must be in the great Hel
> And unable to coming out.

I respect a man who is not able to spell Hell properly. It shows that he has been brought up in an amiable creed. You who come to Moulmein treat this bell with respect, and refrain from playing with it, for that hurts the feelings of the worshippers.

[*From Sea to Sea*]

✠ ✠ ✠

MANDALAY

By THE OLD MOULMEIN Pagoda, lookin' eastward to the sea,
There's a Burma girl a-settin', and I know she thinks o' me;
For the wind is in the palm-trees, and the temple-bells they say:
'Come you back, you British soldier; come you back to
        Mandalay!'
        Come you back to Mandalay,
        Where the old Flotilla lay:
        Can't you 'ear their paddles chunkin' from Rangoon to
            Mandalay?
        On the road to Mandalay,
        Where the flyin'-fishes play,
        An' the dawn comes up like thunder outer China 'crost
            the Bay!

'Er petticoat was yaller an' 'er little cap was green,
An' 'er name was Supi-yaw-lat – jes' the same as Theebaw's
        Queen,
An' I seed her first a-smokin' of a whackin' white cheroot,
An' a-wastin' Christian kisses on an 'eathen idol's foot:
        Bloomin' idol made o'mud –
        Wot they called the Great Gawd Budd –
        Plucky lot she cared for idols when I kissed 'er where she
            stud!
        On the road to Mandalay . . .

When the mist was on the rice-fields an' the sun was droppin'
        slow,
She'd git 'er little banjo an' she'd sing 'Kulla-lo-lo!'
With 'er arm upon my shoulder an' 'er cheek agin' my cheek
We useter watch the steamers an' the hathis pilin' teak.
        Elephints a-pilin' teak
        In the sludgy, squdgy creek,
        Where the silence 'ung that 'eavy you was 'arf afraid to
            speak!
        On the road to Mandalay . . .

But that's all shove be'ind me – long ago an' fur away,
An' there ain't no 'busses runnin' from the Bank to Mandalay;
An' I'm learnin' 'ere in London what the ten-year soldier tells:
'If you've 'eard the East a-callin', you won't never 'eed naught
      else.'
    No! you won't 'eed nothin' else
    But them spicy garlic smells,
    An' the sunshine an' the palm-trees an' the tinkly temple-
      bells;
    On the road to Mandalay . . .

I am sick o' wastin' leather on these gritty pavin'-stones,
An' the blasted Henglish drizzle wakes the fever in my bones;
Tho' I walks with fifty 'ousemaids outer Chelsea to the Strand,
An' they talks a lot o' lovin', but wot do they understand?
    Beefy face an' grubby 'and –
    Law! wot do they understand?
    I've a neater, sweeter maiden in a cleaner, greener land!
    On the road to Mandalay . . .

Ship me somewheres east of Suez, where the best is like the
      worst,
Where there aren't no Ten Commandments an' a man can raise
      a thirst;
For the temple-bells are callin', an' it's there that I would be –
By the old Moulmein Pagoda, looking lazy at the sea;
    On the road to Mandalay,
    Where the old Flotilla lay,
    With our sick beneath the awnings when we went to
      Mandalay!
    On the road to Mandalay,
    Where the flyin'-fishes play,
      An' the dawn comes up like thunder outer China 'crost
      the Bay!

['Mandalay', *Barrack-Room Ballads*]

PENANG

You in India have never seen a proper *'rickshaw*. There are about two thousand of them in Penang, and no two seem alike. They are lacquered with bold figures of dragons and horses and birds and butterflies: their shafts are of black wood bound with white metal, and so strong that the coolie sits upon them when he waits for his fare. There is only one coolie, but he is strong, and he runs just as well as six Hill-men. He ties up his pigtail, being a Cantonese, – and this is a disadvantage to sahibs who cannot speak Tamil, Malay, or Cantonese. Otherwise he might be steered like a camel.

[*From Sea to Sea*]

✖ ✖ ✖

SINGAPORE

Singapur is another Calcutta, but much more so. In the suburbs they are building rows of cheap houses; in the city they run over you and jostle you into the kennel. These are unfailing signs of commercial prosperity. India ended so long ago that I cannot even talk about the natives of the place. They are all Chinese, except where they are French or Dutch or German. England is by the uninformed supposed to own the island. The rest belongs to China and the Continent, but chiefly China. I knew I had touched the borders of the Celestial Empire when I was thoroughly impregnated with the reek of Chinese tobacco, a fine-cut, greasy, glossy weed, to whose smoke the aroma of a huqa in the cookhouse is all Rimmel's shop.

Providence conducted me along a beach, in full view of five miles of shipping, – five solid miles of masts and funnels, – to a place called Raffles Hotel, where the food is as excellent as the rooms are bad. Let the traveller take note. Feed at Raffles and sleep at the Hotel de l'Europe. I would have done this but for the apparition of two large ladies tastefully attired in bed-gowns, who sat with their feet propped on a chair. This Joseph ran; but it turned out that they were Dutch ladies from Batavia, and that that was their national costume till dinner time.

[*From Sea to Sea*]

✠ ✠ ✠

HONG KONG

WHEN YOU ARE IN the China Seas be careful to keep all your flannel-wear to hand. In an hour the steamer swung from tropical heat (including prickly) to a cold raw fog, as wet as a Scotch mist. Morning gave us a new world – somewhere between Heaven and Earth. The sea was smoked glass: reddish-grey islands lay upon it under fog-banks that hovered fifty feet above our heads. The squat sails of junks danced for an instant like autumn leaves in the breeze and disappeared, and there was no solidity in the islands against which the glassy levels splintered in snow. The steamer groaned and grunted and howled because she was so damp and miserable, and I groaned also because the guide-book said that Hong-Kong had the finest harbour in the world, and I could not see two hundred yards in any direction. Yet this ghost-like in-gliding through the belted fog was livelily mysterious, and became more so when the movement of the air vouchsafed us a glimpse of a warehouse and a derrick, both apparently close aboard, and behind them the shoulder of a mountain. [. . .]

All Hong-Kong is built on the sea-face; the rest is fog. One muddy road runs for ever in front of a line of houses which are partly Chowringhee and partly Rotherhithe. You live in the houses, and when wearied of this, walk across the road and drop into the sea, if you can find a square foot of unencumbered water. So vast is the accumulation of country shipping, and such is its dirtiness as it rubs against the bund, that the superior inhabitants are compelled to hang their boats from davits above the common craft, who are greatly disturbed by a multitude of steam-launches. These ply for amusement and the pleasure of whistling, and are held in such small esteem that every hotel owns one, and the others are masterless. Beyond the launches lie more steamers than the eye can count, and four out of five of these belong to Us. I was proud when I saw the shipping at Singapur, but I swell with patriotism as I watch the fleets of Hong-Kong from the balcony of the Victoria Hotel. I can almost spit into the water; but many mariners stand below and they are a strong breed.

[*From Sea to Sea*]

✻ ✻ ✻

CHINA

NEITHER AT PENANG, SINGAPUR, nor this place have I seen a single Chinaman asleep while daylight lasted. Nor have I seen twenty men who were obviously loafing. All were going to some definite end – if it were only like the coolie on the wharf, to steal wood from the scaffolding of a half-built house. In his own land, I believe, the Chinaman is treated with a certain amount of carelessness, not to say ferocity. Where he hides his love of Art, the Heaven that made him out of the yellow earth that holds so much iron only knows. His love is for little things, or else why should he get quaint pendants for his pipe, and at the backmost back of his shop build up for himself a bowerbird's collection of odds and ends, every one of which has beauty if you hold it sufficiently close to the eye. It grieves me that I cannot account for the ideas of a few hundred million men in a few hours. This much, however, seems certain. If we had control over as many Chinamen as we have natives of India, and had given them one tithe of the cosseting, the painful pushing forward, and studious, even nervous, regard of their interests and aspirations that we have given to India, we should long ago have been expelled from, or have reaped the reward of, the richest land on the face of the earth.

[*From Sea to Sea*]

✻ ✻ ✻

CANTON

Aʜ Cᴜᴍ ʟᴇᴅ ᴜs to the Potter's Field, where the executions take place. The Chinese slay by the hundred, and far be it from me to say that such generosity of bloodshed is cruel. They could afford to execute in Canton alone at the rate of ten thousand a year without disturbing the steady flow of population. An executioner who happened to be wandering about – perhaps in search of employment – offered us a sword under guarantee that it had cut off many heads. 'Keep it,' I said. 'Keep it, and let the good work go on. My friend, you cannot execute too freely in this land. You are blessed, I apprehend, with a purely literary bureaucracy recruited – correct me if I am wrong – from all social strata, more especially those in which the idea of cold-blooded cruelty has, as it were, become embedded. Now, when to inherited devildom is superadded a purely literary education of grim and formal tendencies, the result, my evil-looking friend, – the result, I repeat, – is a state of affairs which is faintly indicated in the Little Pilgrim's account of the Hell of Selfishness. You, I presume, have not yet read the works of the Little Pilgrim.'

'He looks as if he was going to cut at you with that sword,' said the Professor. 'Come away and see the Temple of Horrors.'

That was a sort of Chinese Madame Tussaud's – lifelike models of men being brayed in mortars, sliced, fried, toasted, stuffed, and variously bedevilled – that made me sick and unhappy. But the Chinese are merciful even in their tortures. When a man is ground in a mill, he is, according to the models, popped in head first. This is hard on the crowd who are waiting to see the fun, but it saves trouble to the executioners. A half-ground man has to be carefully watched, or else he wriggles out of his place. To crown all, we went to the prison, which was a pest-house in a back street. The Professor shuddered. 'It's all right,' I said. 'The people who sent the prisoners here don't care. The men themselves look hideously miserable, but I suppose they don't care, and goodness knows I don't care. They are only Chinamen. If they treat each other like dogs, why should we regard 'em as human beings? Let 'em rot. I want to get back to the steamer. I want to get under the guns of Hong-Kong. Phew!'

✖ ✖ ✖

JAPAN

A LAPIS-LAZULI COLOURED LOCOMOTIVE which, by accident, had a mixed train attached to it happened to loaf up to the platform just then, and we entered a first-class English compartment. There was no stupid double roof, window shade, or abortive thermantidote. It was a London and Southwestern carriage. Osaka is about eighteen miles from Kobé, and stands at the head of the bay of Osaka. The train is allowed to go as fast as fifteen miles an hour and to play at the stations all along the line. You must know that the line runs between the hills and the shore, and the drainage-fall is a great deal steeper than anything we have between Saharunpur and Umballa. The rivers and the hill torrents come down straight from the hills on raised beds of their own formation, which beds again have to be bunded and spanned with girder bridges or – here, perhaps, I may be wrong – tunnelled.

The stations are black-tiled, red-walled, and concrete-floored, and all the plant from signal levers to goods-truck is English. The official colour of the bridges is a yellow-brown most like unto a faded chrysanthemum. The uniform of the ticket-collectors is a peaked forage cap with gold lines, black frock-coat with brass buttons, very long in the skirt, trousers with black mohair braid, and buttoned kid boots. You cannot be rude to a man in such raiment.

But the countryside was the thing that made us open our eyes. Imagine a land of rich black soil, very heavily manured, and worked by the spade and hoe almost exclusively, and if you split your field (of vision) into half-acre plots, you will get a notion of the raw material the cultivator works on. But all I can write will give you no notion of the wantonness of neatness visible in the fields; of the elaborate system of irrigation, and the mathematical precision of the planting. There was no mixing of crops, no waste of boundary in footpath, and no difference of value in the land. The water stood everywhere within ten feet of the surface, as the well-sweeps attested. On the slopes of the foothills each drop between the levels was neatly riveted with unmortared stones, and the edges of the water-cuts were faced in like manner. The young rice was transplanted very much as draughts are laid on the board; the tea might have been cropped garden box; and between the lines of the mustard the water lay in the drills as in a wooden trough, while the purple of the beans ran up to the mustard and stopped as though cut with a rule.

On the seaboard we saw an almost continuous line of towns variegated with factory chimneys; inland, the crazy-quilt of green, dark-green and gold. Even in the rain the view was lovely, and exactly as Japanese pictures had led me to hope for. Only one drawback occurred to the Professor and myself at the same time. Crops don't grow to the full limit of the seed on heavily worked ground dotted with villages except at a price.

[*From Sea to Sea*]

✳ ✳ ✳

I HAVE SEEN ONE sort of work among the Japanese, but it was not the kind that makes crops. It was purely artistic. A ward of the city of Kioto is devoted to manufactures. A manufacturer in this part of the world does not hang out a sign. He may be known in Paris and New York: that is the concern of the two cities. The Englishman who wishes to find his establishment in Kioto has to hunt for him up and down slums with the aid of a guide. I have seen three manufactories. The first was of porcelain-ware, the second of *cloisonnée*, and the third of lacquer, inlay, and bronzes. The first was behind black wooden palings, and for external appearance might just as well have been a tripe-shop. Inside sat the manager opposite a tiny garden, four feet square, in which a papery-looking palm grew out of a coarse stoneware pot and overshadowed a dwarfed pine. The rest of the room was filled with pottery waiting to be packed – modern Satsuma for the most part, the sort of thing you buy at an auction.

'This made send Europe – India – America,' said the manager calmly. 'You come to see?'

He took us along a verandah of polished wood to the kilns, to the clay vats, and the yards where the tiny 'saggers' were awaiting their complement of pottery. There are differences many and technical between Japanese and Burslem pottery in the making, but these are of no consequence. In the moulding house, where they were making the bodies of Satsuma vases, the wheels, all worked by hand, ran true as a hair. The potter sat on a clean mat with his tea-things at his side. When he had turned out a vase-body he saw that it was good, nodded appreciatively to himself, and poured out some tea ere starting the next one. The potters lived close to the kilns and had nothing pretty to look at. It was different in the painting rooms. Here in a cabinet-like house sat the men, women, and boys who painted the designs on the vases after the first firing. That all their arrangements were scrupulously neat is only saying that they were Japanese; that their surroundings were fair and proper is only saying that they were artists. A sprig of a cherry-blossom stood out defiantly against the black of the garden paling; a gnarled pine cut the blue of the sky with its spiky splinters as it lifted itself above the paling, and in a little pond the iris and the horsetail nodded to the wind. The workers when at fault had only to lift their eyes, and Nature herself would graciously supply the missing link of a design. Somewhere in dirty England men dream of craftsmen working under conditions which shall help and not stifle the half-formed thought. They even form guilds and write semi-rhythmical prayers to Time and Chance and all the other gods that they worship, to bring about the desired end. Would they have their dream realised, let them see how they make pottery in Japan, each man sitting on a snowy mat with loveliness of line and colour within arm's length of him, while with downcast eyes he splashes in the conventional diaper of a Satsuma vase as fast as he can! The Barbarians want Satsuma and they shall have it, if it has to be made in Kioto one piece per twenty minutes. So much for the baser forms of the craft.

[*From Sea to Sea*]

✠ ✠ ✠

THERE ARE WAYS AND ways of entering Japan. The best is to descend upon it from America and the Pacific – from the barbarians and the deep sea. Coming from the East, the blaze of India and the insolent tropical vegetation of Singapore dull the eye to half-colours and little tones. It is at Bombay that the smell of All Asia boards the ship miles off shore, and holds the passenger's nose till he is clear of Asia again. That is a violent, and aggressive smell, apt to prejudice the stranger, but kin none the less to the gentle and insinuating flavour that stole across the light airs of the daybreak when the fairy boat went to shore – a smell of very clean new wood; split bamboo, wood-smoke, damp earth, and the things that people who are not white people eat – a homelike and comforting smell. Then followed on shore the sound of an Eastern tongue, that is beautiful or not as you happen to know it. The Western races have many languages, but a crowd of Europeans heard through closed doors talk with the Western pitch and cadence. So it is with the East. A line of jinrickshaw coolies sat in the sun discoursing to each other, and it was as though they were welcoming a return in speech that the listener must know as well as English. They talked and they talked, but the ghosts of familiar words would not grow any clearer till presently the Smell came down the open streets again, saying that this was the East where nothing matters, and trifles old as the Tower of Babel mattered less than nothing, and that there were old acquaintances waiting at every corner beyond the township. Great is the Smell of the East! Railways, telegraphs, docks, and gunboats cannot banish it, and it will endure till the railways are dead. He who has not smelt that smell has never lived.

[*From Tideway to Tideway*]

NAGASAKI

THERE WAS A YELLOW-SHOT greenness upon the hills round
Nagasaki different, so my willing mind was disposed to believe,
from the green of other lands. It was the green of a Japanese
screen, and the pines were screen pines. The city itself hardly
showed from the crowded harbour. It lay low among the hills,
and its business face – a grimy bund – was sloppy and deserted.
Business, I was rejoiced to learn, was at a low ebb in Nagasaki.
The Japanese should have no concern with business. Close to
one of the still wharves lay a ship of the Bad People; a Russian
steamer down from Vladivostok. Her decks were cumbered with
raffle of all kinds; her rigging was as frowsy and draggled as the
hair of a lodging-house slavey, and her sides were filthy . . .

If you look for extravagance of colour, for flaming shop-fronts
and glaring lanterns, you shall find none of these things in the
narrow stone-paved streets of Nagasaki. But if you desire details
of house construction, glimpses of perfect cleanliness, rare taste,
and perfect subordination of the thing made to the needs of the
maker, you shall find all you seek and more. All the roofs are
dull lead colour, being shingled or tiled, and all the house fronts
are of the colour of the wood God made. There is neither smoke
nor haze, and in the clear light of a clouded sky I could see down
the narrowest alleyway as into the interior of a cabinet.

The books have long ago told you how a Japanese house is
constructed, chiefly of sliding screens and paper partitions, and
everybody knows the story of the burglar of Tokio who burgled
with a pair of scissors for jimmy and centre-bit and stole the
Consul's trousers. But all the telling in print will never make
you understand the exquisite finish of a tenement that you could
kick in with your foot and pound to match-wood with your fists.
Behold a *bunnia's* shop. He sells rice and chillies and dried fish
and wooden scoops made of bamboo. The front of his shop is
very solid. It is made of half-inch battens nailed side by side. Not
one of the battens is broken; and each one is foursquare perfectly.
Feeling ashamed of himself for this surly barring up of his house,
he fills one-half the frontage with oiled paper stretched upon
quarter-inch framing. Not a single square of oil paper has a

hole in it, and not one of the squares, which in more uncivilised countries would hold a pane of glass if strong enough, is out of line. And the *bunnia*, clothed in a blue dressing-gown, with thick white stockings on his feet, sits behind, not among his wares, on a pale gold-coloured mat of soft rice straw bound with black list at the edges. This mat is two inches thick, three feet wide and six long. You might, if you were a sufficient pig, eat your dinner off any portion of it. The *bunnia* lies with one wadded blue arm round a big brazier of hammered brass on which is faintly delineated in incised lines a very terrible dragon. The brazier is full of charcoal ash, but there is no ash on the mat. By the *bunnia's* side is a pouch of green leather tied with a red silk cord, holding tobacco cut fine as cotton. He fills a long black and red lacquered pipe, lights it at the charcoal in the brazier, takes two whiffs, and the pipe is empty. Still there is no speck on the mat. Behind the *bunnia* is a shadow-screen of bead and bamboo. This veils a room floored with pale gold and roofed with panels of grained cedar. There is nothing in the room save a blood-red blanket laid out smoothly as a sheet of paper. Beyond the room is a passage of polished wood, so polished that it gives back the reflections of the white paper wall. At the end of the passage and clearly visible to this unique *bunnia* is a dwarfed pine two feet high in a green glazed pot, and by its side is a branch of azalea, blood-red as the blanket, set in a pale grey cracklepot. The *bunnia* has put it there for his own pleasure, for the delight of his eyes, because he loves it. The white man has nothing whatever to do with his tastes, and he keeps his house specklessly pure because he likes cleanliness and knows it is artistic. What shall we say to such a *bunnia*? [. . .]

We could not go beyond this courtyard because a label said, 'No admittance,' and thus all we saw of the temple was rich-brown high roofs of blackened thatch, breaking back and back in wave and undulation till they were lost in the foliage. The Japanese play with thatch as men play with modelling clay; but how their light underpinnings can carry the weight of the roof is a mystery to the lay eye.

We went down the steps to tiffin, and a half-formed resolve was shaping itself in my heart the while. Burma was a very nice place, but they eat *gnapi* there, and there were smells, and after all, the girls weren't so pretty as some others—

'You must take off your boots,' said Y-Tokai.

I assure you there is no dignity in sitting down on the steps of a tea-house and struggling with muddy boots. And it is impossible to be polite in your stockinged feet when the floor under you is as smooth as glass and a pretty girl wants to know where you would like tiffin. Take at least one pair of beautiful socks with you when you come this way. Get them made of embroidered *sambhur* skin, of silk if you like, but do not stand as I did in cheap striped brown things with a darn at the heel, and try to talk to a tea-girl.

They led us – three of them, and all fresh and pretty – into a room furnished with a golden-brown bearskin. The *tokonoma*, recess aforementioned, held one scroll-picture of bats wheeling in the twilight, a bamboo flower-holder, and yellow flowers. The ceiling was of panelled wood, with the exception of one strip at the side nearest the window, and this was made of plaited shavings of cedar-wood, marked off from the rest of the ceiling by a wine-brown bamboo so polished that it might have been lacquered. A touch of the hand sent one side of the room flying back, and we entered a really large room with another *tokonoma* framed on one side by eight or ten feet of an unknown wood bearing the same grain as a 'Penang lawyer,' and above by a stick of unbarked tree set there purely because it was curiously mottled. In this second *tokonoma* was a pearl-grey vase, and that was all. Two sides of the room were of oiled paper, and the joints of the beams were covered by the brazen images of crabs, half life-size. Save for the sill of the *tokonoma*, which was black lacquer, every inch of wood in the place was natural grain without flaw. Outside lay the garden, fringed with a hedge of dwarf-pines and adorned with a tiny pond, water-smoothed stones sunk in the soil, and a blossoming cherry tree.

They left us alone in this paradise of cleanliness and beauty, and being only a shameless Englishman without his boots – a white man is always degraded when he goes barefoot – I wandered round the wall, trying all the screens. It was only when I stopped to examine the sunk catch of a screen that I saw it was a plaque of inlay-work representing two white cranes feeding on fish. The whole was about three inches square and in the ordinary course of events would never be looked at. The screens are a cupboard in which all the lamps and candlesticks and pillows and sleeping-bags of the household seemed to be stored. An Oriental nation that can fill a cupboard tidily is a nation to bow down to. Upstairs I went by a staircase of grained wood and lacquer into rooms of rarest device with circular windows that opened on nothing, and so were filled with bamboo tracery for the delight of the eye. The passages floored with dark wood shone like ice, and I was ashamed.

[. . .] The Professor opened his eyes a little, but said no word. The chopsticks demanded all his attention, and the return of the girls took up the rest. O-Toyo, ebon-haired, rosy-cheeked, and made throughout of delicate porcelain, laughed at me because I devoured all the mustard-sauce that had been served with my raw fish, and wept copiously till she gave me *saki* from a lordly bottle about four inches high. If you took some very thin hock, and tried to mull it and forgot all about the brew till it was half cold, you would get *saki*. I had mine in a saucer so tiny that I was bold to have it filled eight or ten times and loved O-Toyo none the less at the end.

After raw fish and mustard-sauce came some other sort of fish cooked with pickled radishes, and very slippery on the chopsticks. The girls knelt in a semicircle and shrieked with delight at the Professor's clumsiness, for indeed it was not I that nearly upset the dinner table in a vain attempt' to recline gracefully. After the bamboo-shoots came a basin of white beans in sweet sauce – very tasty indeed. Try to convey beans to your mouth with a pair of wooden knitting-needles and see what happens. Some chicken cunningly boiled with turnips, and a bowlful of snow-white boneless fish and a pile of rice, concluded the meal. I have forgotten one or two of the courses, but when O-Toyo handed me the tiny lacquered Japanese pipe full of hay-like tobacco, I counted nine dishes in the lacquer stand – each dish representing a course. Then O-Toyo and I smoked by alternate pipefuls.

My very respectable friends at all the clubs and messes, have you ever after a good tiffin lolled on cushions and smoked, with one pretty girl to fill your pipe and four to admire you in an unknown tongue? You do not know what life is. I looked round me at that faultless room, at the dwarf-pines and creamy cherry blossoms without, at O-Toyo bubbling with laughter because I blew smoke through my nose, and at the ring of *Mikado* maidens over against the golden-brown bearskin rug. Here was colour, form, food, comfort, and beauty enough for half a year's contemplation. I would not be a Burman any more. I would be a Japanese – always with O-Toyo of course – in a cabinet-work house on a camphor-scented hillside.

[*From Sea to Sea*]

✠ ✠ ✠

TOKYO

HAVING THOROUGHLY SETTLED THE military side of the nation exactly as my Japanese friend at the beginning of this letter settled Us, – on the strength of two hundred men caught at random, – I devoted myself to a consideration of Tokio. I am wearied of temples. Their monotony of splendour makes my head ache. You also will weary of temples unless you are an artist, and then you will be disgusted with yourself. Some folk say that Tokio covers an area equal to London. Some folk say that it is not more than ten miles long and eight miles broad. There are a good many ways of solving the question. I found a tea-garden situated on a green plateau far up a flight of steps, with pretty girls smiling on every step. From this elevation I looked forth over the city, and it stretched away from the sea, as far as the eye could reach – one grey expanse of packed house-roof, the perspective marked by numberless factory chimneys. Then I went several miles away and found a park, another eminence, and some more tea-girls prettier than the last; and, looking again, the city stretched out in a new direction as far as the eye could reach. Taking the scope of the eye on a clear day at eighteen miles, I make Tokio thirty-six miles long by thirty-six miles broad exactly; and there may be some more which I missed. The place roared with life through all its quarters. Double lines of trams ran down the main streets for mile on mile, rows of omnibuses stood at the principal railway station, and the 'Compagnie General des Omnibus de Tokio' paraded the streets with gold and vermilion cars. All the trams were full, all the private and public omnibuses were full, and the streets were full of 'rickshaws. From the seashore to the shady green park, from the park to the dim distance, the land pullulated with people.

Here you saw how western civilisation had eaten into them. Every tenth man was attired in Europe clothes from hat to boots. It is a queer race. It can parody every type of humanity to be met in a large English town. Fat and prosperous merchant with mutton-chop whiskers; mild-eyed, long-haired professor of science, his clothes baggy about him; schoolboy in Eton jacket, broadcloth trousers; young clerk, member of the Clapham Athletic Club, in tennis flannels; artisans in sorely worn tweeds; top-hatted lawyer with clean-shaven upper lip and black leather bag; sailor out of work; and counter-jumper; all these and many, many more you shall find in the streets of Tokio in half an hour's walk. But when you come to speak to the imitation, behold it can only talk Japanese. You touch it, and it is not what you thought. I fluctuated down the streets addressing myself to the most English-looking folk I saw. They were polite with a graciousness that in no way accorded with their raiment, but they knew not a word of my tongue. One small boy in the uniform of the Naval College said suddenly: 'I spik Englees,' and collapsed. The rest of the people in our clothes poured their own vernacular upon my head. Yet the shop-signs were English, the tramway under my feet was English gauge, the commodities sold were English, and the notices on the streets were in English. It was like walking in a dream. I reflected. Far away from Tokio and off the line of rail I had met men like these men in the streets. Perfectly dressed Englishmen to the outer eye, but dumb. The country must be full of their likes.

[*From Sea to Sea*]

🕸 🕸 🕸

KAMAKURA

THIS THAT FOLLOWS HAPPENED on the coast twenty miles through the fields from Yokohama, at Kamakura, that is to say, where the great bronze Buddha sits facing the sea to hear the centuries go by. He has been described again and again – his majesty, his aloofness, and every one of his dimensions, the smoky little shrine within him, and the plumed hill that makes the background to his throne. For that reason he remains, as he remained from the beginning, beyond all hope of description – as it might be, a visible god sitting in the garden of a world made new. They sell photographs of him with tourists standing on his thumb nail, and, apparently, any brute of any gender can scrawl his or its ignoble name over the inside of the massive bronze plates that build him up. Think for a moment of the indignity and the insult! Imagine the ancient, orderly gardens with their clipped trees, shorn turf, and silent ponds smoking in the mist that the hot sun soaks up after rain, and the green-bronze image of the Teacher of the Law wavering there as it half seems through incense clouds. The earth is all one censer, and myriads of frogs are making the haze ring. It is too warm to do more than to sit on a stone and watch the eyes that, having seen all things, see no more – the down-dropped eyes, the forward droop of the head, and the colossal simplicity of the folds of the robe over arm and knee. Thus, and in no other fashion, did Buddha sit in the old days when Ananda asked questions and the dreamer began to dream of the lives that lay behind him ere the lips moved, and as the Chronicles say: 'He told a tale.' This would be the way he began, for dreamers in the East tell something the same sort of tales to-day: 'Long ago when Devadatta was King of Benares, there lived a virtuous elephant, a reprobate ox, and a King without understanding.' And the tale would end, after the moral had been drawn for Ananda's benefit: 'Now, the reprobate ox was such an one, and the King was such another, but the virtuous elephant was I, myself, Ananda.' Thus, then, he told the tales in the bamboo grove, and the bamboo grove is there to-day. Little blue and gray and slate robed figures pass under its shadow, buy two or three joss-sticks, disappear into the shrine, that is, the body of the god, come out smiling, and drift away through the shrubberies. A fat carp in a pond sucks at a fallen leaf with just the sound of a wicked little worldly kiss. Then the earth steams, and steams in silence, and a gorgeous butterfly, full six inches from wing to wing, cuts through the steam in a zigzag of colour and flickers up to the forehead of the god. And Buddha said that a man must look on everything as illusion – even light and colour – the time-worn bronze of metal against blue-green of pine and pale emerald of bamboo – the lemon sash of the girl in the cinnamon dress, with coral pins in her hair, leaning against a block of weather-bleached stone – and, last, the spray of blood-red azalea that stands on the pale gold mats of the tea-house beneath the honey-coloured thatch. To overcome desire and covetousness of mere gold, which is often very vilely designed, that is conceivable; but why must a man give up the delight of the eye, colour that rejoices, light that cheers, and line that satisfies the innermost deeps of the heart? Ah, if the Bodhisat had only seen his own image!

[*From Tideway to Tideway*]

✠ ✠ ✠

'And there is a Japanese idol at Kamakura'

O YE WHO TREAD the Narrow Way
By Tophet-flare to judgment Day,
Be gentle when 'the heathen' pray
    To Buddha at Kamakura!

To him the Way, the Law, apart,
Whom Maya held beneath her heart,
Ananda's Lord, the Bodhisat,
    The Buddha of Kamakura.

For though he neither burns nor sees,
Nor hears ye thank your Deities,

Ye have not sinned with such as these,
　His children at Kamakura,

Yet spare us still the Western joke
When joss-sticks turn to scented smoke
The little sins of little folk
　That worship at Kamakura –

The grey-robed, gay-sashed butterflies
That flit beneath the Master's eyes.
He is beyond the Mysteries
　But loves them at Kamakura.

And whoso will, from Pride released,
Contemning neither creed nor priest,
May feel the Soul of all the East
　About him at Kamakura.

Yea, every tale Ananda heard,
Of birth as fish or beast or bird,
While yet in lives the Master stirred,
　The warm wind brings Kamakura.

Till drowsy eyelids seem to see
A-flower 'neath her golden htee
The Shwe-Dagon flare easterly
　From Burmah to Kamakura,

And down the loaded air there comes
The thunder of Thibetan drums,
And droned – 'Om mane padme hums' –
　A world's-width from Kamakura.

Yet Brahmans rule Benares still,
Buddh-Gaya's ruins pit the hill,
And beef-fed zealots threaten ill
　To Buddha and Kamakura.

A tourist-show, a legend told,
A rusting bulk of bronze and gold,
So much, and scarce so much, ye hold
    The meaning of Kamakura?

But when the morning prayer is prayed,
Think, ere ye pass to strife and trade,
Is God in human image made
    No nearer than Kamakura?

['Buddha at Kamakura', *The Five Nations*]

᧭ 3 ᧳

NORTH AMERICA

Beautiful Land of the Masses

San Francisco – Oakland – Vancouver – Livingston – Yellowstone – Salt Lake City – Chicago – Vermont – Mount Monadnock – St Paul – New York – Canada – Quebec – From Calgary to the Pacific – The Rocky Mountains.

The United States proved an eye-opener for the young Kipling. He knew something of the country because he travelled there on the SS *City of Peking* with Alec and Edmonia (Ted) Hill, friends from Allahabad, and Mrs Hill was American. But even before first arriving there in May 1889 he had decided he did not like Yankee-style mass culture and democracy. 'I love not the Americans in bulk,' he wrote to his Aunt Georgie (Georgina Burne-Jones) from San Francisco. 'They spit even as in the time of Dickens and their speech is not sweet to listen to – 'specially the women's.' On landing in San Francisco he was taken aback by the fuss the American press made of him, though he soon warmed to the city's air of 'recklessness'.

From there he more or less contentedly made his way up the west coast to Vancouver, where he bought a plot of land, then through the Rockies to Livingston and Yellowstone National Park, and on to Chicago and New England. All the while he continued to regale readers of the *Pioneer* with his observations in articles, later collected in *From Sea to Sea*.

Despite occasional pleasures, such as fishing in Oregon, Kipling was disdainful about many of the places he visited. At Yellowstone, warming to an old theme, he railed against an influx of tourists – a subject he touched on not only in the *Pioneer* but also in a letter to Edmonia Hill. On reaching Chicago, he was dismissive of its rampant materialism, which reminded him of Calcutta, and even more shocked by the enthusiastic way it went about its major industry – the slaughter of animals.

Once married to the American Caroline Balestier in January 1892, he felt well disposed enough to her country to agree to live in her hometown of Brattleboro', Vermont. From 'Naulakha', the house he built there, he could see the imposing Mount Monadnock in the neighbouring state of New Hampshire. He also wrote 'Leaves from a Winter Notebook', a lyrical account of the seasons – and particularly the long winters – in his new abode.

Occasionally he ventured further afield in the United States. On his honeymoon trip to Japan, for example, he travelled via St Paul, Minnesota. By the time he paid his first post-matrimonial visit to England in 1894, he was, as he wrote to his fellow writer Robert Barr, feeling quite homesick for the familiar heat and sounds of New York.

North of the border, Kipling admired Canada and the way its people applied themselves to the development of their country. He paid two main visits – in 1892 (as part of his honeymoon) and in 1907 when, as guest of the Canadian Pacific Railway, he travelled through the country encouraging support for the empire. He wrote about his experiences in 1892 in his collection *From Tideway to Tideway* and about those fifteen years later in *Letters to the Family*.

SAN FRANCISCO

SAN FRANCISCO IS A mad city – inhabited for the most part by perfectly insane people whose women are of a remarkable beauty. When the *City of Peking* steamed through the Golden Gate I saw with great joy that the block-house which guarded the mouth of the 'finest harbour in the world, Sir,' could be silenced by two gunboats from Hong-Kong with safety, comfort, and despatch. [. . .]

There were no more incidents till I reached the Palace Hotel, a seven-storeyed warren of humanity with a thousand rooms in it. All the travel-books will tell you about hotel arrangements in this country. They should be seen to be appreciated. Understand clearly – and this letter is written after a thousand miles of experiences – that money will not buy you service in the West.

When the hotel clerk – the man who awards your room to you and who is supposed to give you information – when that resplendent individual stoops to attend to your wants, he does so whistling or humming, or picking his teeth, or pauses to converse with someone he knows. These performances, I gather, are to impress upon you that he is a free man and your equal. From his general appearance and the size of his diamonds he ought to be your superior. There is no necessity for this swaggering self-consciousness of freedom. Business is business, and the man who is paid to attend to a man might reasonably devote his whole attention to the job.

In a vast marble-paved hall under the glare of an electric light sat forty or fifty men; and for their use and amusement were provided spittoons of infinite capacity and generous gape. Most of the men wore frock-coats and top-hats, – the things that we in India put on at a wedding breakfast if we possessed them, – but they all spat. They spat on principle. The spittoons were on the staircases, in each bedroom – yea, and in chambers even more sacred than these. They chased one into retirement, but they blossomed in chiefest splendour round the Bar, and they were all used, every reeking one of 'em.

[*From Sea to Sea*]

✻ ✻ ✻

OAKLAND

THE OAKLAND RAILWAY TERMINUS, whence all the main lines start, does not own anything approaching to a platform. A yard with a dozen or more tracks is roughly asphalted, and the traveller laden with handbags skips merrily across the metals in search of his own particular train. The bells of half a dozen shunting engines are tolling suggestively in his ears. If he is run down, so much the worse for him. 'When the bell rings, look out for the locomotive.' Long use has made the nation familiar and even contemptuous towards trains to an extent which God never intended. Women who in England would gather up their skirts and scud timorously over a level crossing in the country, here talk dress and babies under the very nose of the cow-catcher, and little children dally with the moving car in a manner horrible to behold. We pulled out at the wholly insignificant speed of twenty-five miles an hour through the streets of a suburb of fifty thousand, and in our progress among the carts and the children and the shop fronts slew nobody; at which I was not a little disappointed.

[*From Sea to Sea*]

VANCOUVER

VANCOUVER THREE YEARS AGO was swept off by fire in sixteen minutes, and only one house was left standing. To-day it has a population of fourteen thousand people, and builds its houses out of brick with dressed granite fronts. But a great sleepiness lies on Vancouver as compared with an American town: men don't fly up and down the streets telling lies, and the spittoons in the delightfully comfortable hotel are unused; the baths are free and their doors are unlocked. You do not have to dig up the hotel clerk when you want to bathe, which shows the inferiority of Vancouver. An American bade me notice the absence of bustle, and was alarmed when in a loud and audible voice I thanked God for it. 'Give me granite-hewn granite and peace,' quoth I, 'and keep your deal boards and bustle for yourselves.'

The Canadian Pacific terminus is not a very gorgeous place as yet, but you can be shot directly from the window of the train into the liner that will take you in fourteen days from Vancouver to Yokohama. The *Parthia*, of some five thousand tons, was at her berth when I came, and the sight of the ex-Cunard on what seemed to be a little lake was curious. Except for certain currents which are not much mentioned, but which make the entrance rather unpleasant for sailing-boats, Vancouver possesses an almost perfect harbour. The town is built all round and about the harbour, and young as it is, its streets are better than those of western America. Moreover, the old flag waves over some of the buildings, and this is cheering to the soul. The place is full of Englishmen who speak the English tongue correctly and with clearness, avoiding more blasphemy than is necessary, and taking a respectable length of time to getting outside their drinks. These advantages and others that I have heard about, such as the construction of elaborate workshops and the like by the Canadian Pacific in the near future, moved me to invest in real estate. He that sold it me was a delightful English Boy who, having tried for the Army and failed, had somehow meandered into a real-estate office, where he was doing well. I couldn't have bought it from an American. He would have overstated the case and proved me the possessor of the original Eden. All the Boy said was: 'I give you my word it isn't on a cliff or under water, and before long the town ought to move out that way. I'd advise you to take it.' And I took it as easily as a man buys a piece of tobacco. *Me voici*, owner of some four hundred well-developed pines, a few thousand tons of granite scattered in blocks at the roots of the pines, and a sprinkling of earth. That's a townlot in Vancouver. You or your agent hold to it till property rises, then sell out and buy more land further out of town and repeat the process. I do not quite see how this sort of thing helps the growth of a town, but the English Boy says that it is the 'essence of speculation,' so it must be all right. But I wish there were fewer pines and rather less granite on my ground.

[*From Sea to Sea*]

✠ ✠ ✠

LIVINGSTON

LIVINGSTONE IS A TOWN of two thousand people, and the junction for the little side-line that takes you to the Yellowstone National Park. It lies in a fold of the prairie, and behind it is the Yellowstone River and the gate of the mountains through which the river flows. There is one street in the town, where the cowboy's pony and the little foal of the brood-mare in the buggy rest contentedly in the blinding sunshine while the cowboy gets himself shaved at the only other barber's shop, and swaps lies at the bar. I exhausted the town, including the saloons, in ten minutes, and got away on the rolling grass downs where I threw myself to rest. Directly under the hill I was on, swept a drove of horses in charge of two mounted men. That was a picture I shall not soon forget. A light haze of dust went up from the hoof-trodden green, scarcely veiling the unfettered devilries of three hundred horses who very much wanted to stop and graze. 'Yow! Yow! Yow!' yapped the mounted men in chorus like coyotes. The column moved forward at a trot, divided as it met a hillock and scattered into fan shape all among the suburbs of Livingstone. I heard the 'snick' of a stock-whip, half a dozen 'Yow, yows,' and the mob had come together again, and, with neighing and whickering and squealing and a great deal of kicking on the part of the youngsters, rolled like a wave of brown water toward the uplands.

I was within twenty feet of the leader, a grey stallion – lord of many brood-mares all deeply concerned for the welfare of their fuzzy foals. A cream-coloured beast – I knew him at once for the bad character of the troop – broke back, taking with him some frivolous fillies. I heard the snick of the whips somewhere in the dust, and the fillies came back at a canter, very shocked and indignant. On the heels of the last rode both the stockmen – picturesque ruffians who wanted to know 'what in hell' I was doing there, waved their hats, and sped down the slope after their charges. When the noise of the troop had died there came a wonderful silence on all the prairie – that silence, they say, which enters into the heart of the old-time hunter and trapper and marks him off from the rest of his race. The town disappeared in the darkness, and a very young moon showed herself over a baldheaded, snow-flecked peak. Then the Yellowstone, hidden by the water-willows, lifted up its voice and sang a little song to the mountains, and an old horse that had crept up in the dusk breathed inquiringly on the back of my neck. When I reached the hotel I found all manner of preparation under way for the 4th of July, and a drunken man with a Winchester rifle over his shoulder patrolling the sidewalk. I do not think he wanted any one. He carried the gun as other folk carry walking sticks. None the less I avoided the direct line of fire and listened to the blasphemies of miners and stockmen till far into the night. In every bar-room lay a copy of the local paper, and every copy impressed it upon the inhabitants of Livingstone that they were the best, finest, bravest, richest, and most progressive town of the most progressive nation under Heaven; even as the Tacoma and Portland papers had belauded their readers. And yet, all my purblind eyes could see was a grubby little hamlet full of men without clean collars and perfectly unable to get through one sentence unadorned by three oaths. They raise horses and minerals round and about Livingstone, but they behave as though they raised cherubims with diamonds in their wings.

[*From Sea to Sea*]

✠ ✠ ✠

YELLOWSTONE NATIONAL PARK

To-day I am in the Yellowstone Park, and I wish I were dead.
The train halted at Cinnabar station, and we were decanted,
a howling crowd of us, into stages, variously horsed, for the
eight-mile drive to the first spectacle of the Park – a place called
the Mammoth Hot Springs. 'What means this eager, anxious
throng?' I asked the driver. 'You've struck one of Rayment's
excursion parties – that's all – a crowd of creator-condemned
fools mostly. Aren't you one of 'em?' 'No,' I said. 'May I sit up
here with you, great chief and man with a golden tongue? I do
not know Mister Rayment. I belong to T. Cook and Son.' The other
person, from the quality of the material he handles, must be the
son of a sea-cook. He collects masses of Down-Easters from the
New England States and elsewhere and hurls them across the
continent and into the Yellowstone Park on tour. A brake-load
of Cook's Continental tourists trapezing through Paris (I've seen
'em) are angels of light compared to the Rayment trippers. It is
not the ghastly vulgarity, the oozing, rampant Bessemer-steel
self-sufficiency and ignorance of the men that revolts me, so
much as the display of these same qualities in the women-folk. I
saw a new type in the coach, and all my dreams of a better and
more perfect East died away. 'Are these – um – persons here any
sort of persons in their own places?' I asked a shepherd who
appeared to be herding them.

'Why, certainly. They include very many prominent and
representative citizens from seven States of the Union, and most
of them are wealthy. Yes, *sir*. Representative and prominent.'

[. . .] *En route* we passed other carriages full of trippers, who
had done their appointed five days in the Park, and yelped at
us fraternally as they disappeared in clouds of red dust. When
we struck the Mammoth Hot Spring Hotel – a huge yellow barn
– a sign-board informed us that the altitude was six thousand
two hundred feet. The Park is just a howling wilderness of three
thousand square miles, full of all imaginable freaks of a fiery

nature. An hotel company, assisted by the Secretary of State for the Interior, appears to control it; there are hotels at all the points of interest, guide-books, stalls for the sale of minerals, and so forth, after the model of Swiss summer places.

The tourists – may their master die an evil death at the hand of a mad locomotive! – poured into that place with a joyful whoop, and, scarce washing the dust from themselves, began to celebrate the 4th of July. They called it 'patriotic exercises'; elected a clergyman of their own faith as president, and, sitting on the landing of the first floor, began to make speeches and read the Declaration of Independence. The clergyman rose up and told them they were the greatest, freest, sublimest, most chivalrous, and richest people on the face of the earth, and they all said Amen. Another clergyman asserted in the words of the Declaration that all men were created equal, and equally entitled to Life, Liberty, and the pursuit of Happiness. I should like to know whether the wild and woolly West recognises this first right as freely as the grantors intended. The clergyman then bade the world note that the tourists included representatives of seven of the New England States whereat I felt deeply sorry for the New England States in their latter days. He opined that this running to and fro upon the earth, under the auspices of the excellent Rayment, would draw America more closely together, especially when the Westerners remembered the perils that they of the East had surmounted by rail and river. At duly appointed intervals the congregation sang 'My country, 'tis of thee' to the tune of 'God Save the Queen' (here they did not stand up) and the 'Star-Spangled Banner' (here they did), winding up the exercise with some doggerel of their own composition to the tune of 'John Brown's Body,' movingly setting forth the perils before alluded to. They then adjourned to the verandahs and watched fire-crackers of the feeblest, exploding one by one, for several hours.

[*From Sea to Sea*]

❁   ❁   ❁

I CAN'T DESCRIBE THE things I have seen. They were beyond description. Ask any one of your friends who have been to the Yellowstone and they will tell you of mountains that roared and smoked like boilers under pressure; of pink and blue and green formations as wild as anything that ever scene-painter put on to a theatre for a background to a ballet of fairies. I spent one happy evening all alone by the banks of a river watching a couple of beaver eating their evening meal. They were real live wild beaver, just as tame as rabbits and they owned a real dam and a veritable beaver Lodge of trimmed sticks. Then I felt that I had really travelled. As soon as I get back the use of my eyes and get rid of a foul headache in the back of my head I'll sit down and try to describe it for the Pioneer – and then you'll know; but at present I am only just equal to writing a line to you to tell you I am alive and well. The trip all round the park was an awfully lonesome one. There were crowds of excursionists and they all made up parties and ran about and shrieked – all but me. I didn't want a party, so I stood out and sulked. As a park, your big wilderness is a failure. I don't like having to drive 150 miles in a buggy to get even a small idea of its many wonders; and I don't like having to sleep in tents when the weather is freezing. On the 8th of July in the Yellowstone Park the water in my ewer froze nearly half an inch. It was awful cold for I had to lie out in a single fold tent and be thankful that I could get it. But the bother was worth the reward of looking down the Can[y]on – from inspiration point – 1700 feet sheer into the Roaring Yellowstone below. I shall never be able to describe it accurately.

[Letter to Edmonia Hill, 10 July 1889]

SALT LAKE CITY

A SWEET VIEW, ISN'T IT?

All the beauty of the valley could not make me forget it. But the valley is very fair. Bench after bench of land, flat as a table against the flanks of the ringing hills, marks where the Salt Lake rested for a while as it sunk from an inland sea to a lake fifty miles long and thirty broad. Before long the benches will be covered with houses. At present these are hidden among the green trees on the dead flat of the valley. You have read a hundred times how the streets of Salt Lake City are very broad, furnished with rows of shade trees and gutters of fresh water. This is true, but I struck the town in a season of great drouth – that same drouth which is playing havoc with the herds of Montana. The trees were limp, and the rills of sparkling water that one reads about were represented by dusty, paved courses. Main Street appears to be inhabited by the commercial Gentile, who has made of it a busy, bustling thoroughfare, and, in the eye of the sun, swigs the ungodly lager and smokes the improper cigar all day long. For which I like him. At the head of Main Street stand the lions of the place; the Temple and the Tabernacle, the Tithing House, and the houses of Brigham Young, whose portrait is on sale in most of the booksellers' shops. Incidentally it may be mentioned that the late Amir of Utah does not unremotely resemble His Highness the Amir of Afghanistan, whom these fortunate eyes have seen. And I have no desire to fall into the hands of the Amir. The first thing to be seen was, of course, the Temple, the outward exponent of a creed. Armed with a copy of the Book of Mormon, for better comprehension, I went to form rash opinions. Some day the Temple will be finished. It was begun only thirty years ago, and up to date rather more than three million dollars and a half have been expended in its granite bulk. The walls are ten feet thick; the edifice itself is about a hundred feet high; and its towers will be nearly two hundred. And that is all there is of it, unless you choose to inspect more closely; always reading the Book of Mormon as you walk. Then the wondrous puerility, of what I suppose we must call the design, becomes apparent. These men, directly inspired from on High, heaped stone on stone and pillar on pillar, without achieving either dignity, relief, or interest. There is, over the main door, some pitiful scratching in stone representing the all-seeing eye, the Masonic grip, the sun, moon, and stars, and, perhaps, other skittles. The flatness and meanness of the thing almost makes you weep when you look at the magnificent granite in blocks strewn abroad, and think of the art that three million dollars might have called in to the aid of the church. It is as though a child had said: 'Let us draw a great, big, fine house – finer than any house that ever was,' – and in that desire had laboriously smudged along with a ruler and pencil, piling meaningless straight lines on compass-drawn curves, with his tongue following every movement of the inept hand.

[*From Sea to Sea*]

✠ ✠ ✠

CHICAGO

I have struck a city, a real city, and they call it Chicago. The other places do not count. San Francisco was a pleasure-resort as well as a city, and Salt Lake was a phenomenon. This place is the first American city I have encountered. It holds rather more than a million people with bodies, and stands on the same sort of soil as Calcutta. Having seen it, I urgently desire never to see it again. It is inhabited by savages. Its water is the water of the Hughli, and its air is dirt. Also it says that it is the 'boss' town of America.

I do not believe that it has anything to do with this country. They told me to go to the Palmer House, which is a gilded and mirrored rabbit-warren, and there I found a huge hall of tessellated marble, crammed with people talking about money and spitting about everywhere. Other barbarians charged in and out of this inferno with letters and telegrams in their hands, and yet others shouted at each other. A man who had drunk quite as much as was good for him told me that this was 'the finest hotel in the finest city on God Almighty's earth.' By the way, when an

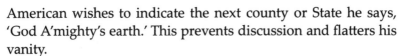

American wishes to indicate the next county or State he says, 'God A'mighty's earth.' This prevents discussion and flatters his vanity.

Then I went out into the streets, which are long and flat and without end. And verily it is not a good thing to live in the East for any length of time. Your ideas grow to clash with those held by every right-thinking white man. I looked down interminable vistas flanked with nine, ten, and fifteen storeyed houses, and crowded with men and women, and the show impressed me with a great horror. Except in London – and I have forgotten what London is like – I had never seen so many white people together, and never such a collection of miserables. There was no colour in the street and no beauty – only a maze of wire-ropes overhead and dirty stone flagging underfoot. A cab-driver volunteered to show me the glory of the town for so much an hour, and with him I wandered far. He conceived that all this turmoil and squash was a thing to be reverently admired; that it was good to huddle men together in fifteen layers, one atop of the other, and to dig holes in the ground for offices. He said that Chicago was a live town, and that all the creatures hurrying by me were engaged in business. That is to say, they were trying to make some money, that they might not die through lack of food to put into their bellies. He took me to canals, black as ink, and filled with untold abominations, and bade me watch the stream of traffic across the bridges. He then took me into a saloon, and, while I drank, made me note that the floor was covered with coins sunk into cement. A Hottentot would not have been guilty of this sort of barbarism. The coins made an effect pretty enough, but the man who put them there had no thought to beauty, and therefore he was a savage. Then my cab-driver showed me business-blocks, gay with signs and studded with fantastic and absurd advertisements of goods, and looking down the long street so adorned it was as though each vendor stood at his door howling: 'For the sake of money, employ or buy of *me* and me only!' Have you ever seen a crowd at our famine-relief distributions? You know then how men leap into the air, stretching out their arms above the crowd in the hope of being seen; while the women dolorously slap the stomachs of their children and whimper. I had sooner watch famine-relief than the white man engaged in what he calls legitimate competition. The one I understand. The other makes me ill. And the cabman said that these things were the proof of progress; and by that I knew he had been reading his newspaper, as every intelligent American should. The papers tell their readers in language fitted to their comprehension that the snarling together of telegraph wires, the heaving up of houses, and the making of money is progress.

I spent ten hours in that huge wilderness, wandering through scores of miles of these terrible streets, and jostling some few hundred thousand of these terrible people who talked money through their noses. The cabman left me: but after a while I picked up another man who was full of figures, and into my ears he poured them as occasion required or the big blank factories suggested. Here they turned out so many hundred thousand dollars' worth of such and such an article; there so many million other things; this house was worth so many million dollars; that one so many million more or less. It was like listening to a child babbling of its hoard of shells. It was like watching a fool playing with buttons. But I was expected to do more than listen or watch. He demanded that I should admire; and the utmost that I could say was: 'Are these things so? Then I am very sorry for you.' That made him angry, and he said that insular envy made me unresponsive. So you see I could not make him understand. [. . .]

I went off to see cattle killed by way of clearing my head, which, as you will perceive, was getting muddled. They say every Englishman goes to the Chicago stock-yards. You shall find them about six miles from the city; and once having seen them will never forget the sight. As far as the eye can reach stretches a township of cattle-pens, cunningly divided into blocks so that the animals of any pen can be speedily driven out close to an inclined timber path which leads to an elevated covered way straddling high above the pens. These viaducts are two-storeyed. On the upper story tramp the doomed cattle, stolidly for the most part. On the lower, with a scuffling of sharp hooves and multitudinous yells, run the pigs. The same end is appointed for each. Thus you will see the gangs of cattle waiting their turn – as they wait sometimes for days and they need not be distressed by the sight of their fellows running about in the fear of death. All they know is that a man on horseback causes their next-door neighbours to move by means of a whip. Certain bars and fences are unshipped, and, behold, that crowd have gone up the mouth of a sloping tunnel and return no more. It is different with the pigs. They shriek back the news of the exodus to their friends, and a hundred pens skirl responsive. It was to the pigs I first addressed myself. Selecting a viaduct which was full of them, as I could hear though I could not see, I marked a sombre building whereto it ran, and went there, not unalarmed by stray cattle who had managed to escape from their proper quarters. A pleasant smell of brine warned me of what was coming. I entered the factory and found it full of pork in barrels, and on another storey more pork unbarrelled, and in a huge room, the halves of swine for whose use great lumps of ice were being pitched in at the window. That room was the mortuary chamber where the pigs lie for a little while in state ere they begin their progress through such passages as kings may sometimes travel. Turning a corner and not noting an overhead arrangement of greased rail, wheel, and pulley, I ran into the arms of four eviscerated carcasses, all pure white and of a human aspect, being pushed by a man clad in vehement red. When I leaped aside, the floor was slippery under me. There was a flavour of farmyard in my nostrils and the shouting of a multitude in my ears. But there was no joy in that shouting. Twelve men stood in two lines – six a-side. Between them and overhead ran the railway of death that had nearly shunted me through the window. Each man carried a knife, the sleeves of his shirt were cut off at the elbows, and from bosom to heel he was blood-red. The atmosphere was stifling as a night in the Rains, by reason of the steam and the crowd. I climbed to the beginning of things and, perched upon a narrow beam, overlooked very nearly all the pigs ever bred in Wisconsin. They had just been shot out of the mouth of the viaduct and huddled together in a large pen. Thence they were flicked persuasively, a few at a time, into a smaller chamber, and there a man fixed tackle on their hinder legs so that they rose in the air suspended from the railway of death. Oh! it was then they shrieked and called on their mothers and made promises of amendment, till the tackle-man punted them in their backs, and they slid head down into a brick-floored passage, very like a big kitchen sink that was blood-red. There awaited them a red man with a knife which he passed jauntily through their throats, and the full-voiced shriek became a sputter, and then a fall as of heavy tropical rain. The red man who was backed against the passage wall stood clear of the wildly kicking hooves and passed his hand over his eyes, not from any feeling of compassion, but because the spurted blood was in his eyes, and he had barely time to stick the next arrival. Then that first stuck swine dropped, still kicking, into a great vat of boiling water, and spoke no more words, but wallowed in obedience to some unseen machinery, and presently came forth at the lower end of the vat and was heaved on the blades of a blunt paddle-wheel-thing which said, 'Hough! Hough! Hough!' and skelped all the hair off him except what little a couple of men with knives could remove. Then he was again hitched by the heels to that sad railway and passed down the line of the twelve men – each man with a knife – leaving with each man a certain amount of his individuality which was taken away in a wheelbarrow, and when he reached the last man he was very beautiful to behold, but immensely unstuffed and limp. Preponderance of individuality was ever a bar to foreign travel. That pig could have been in no case to visit you in India had he not parted with some of his most cherished notions.

The dissecting part impressed me not so much as the slaying. They were so excessively alive, these pigs. And then they were so excessively dead, and the man in the dripping, clammy, hot passage did not seem to care, and ere the blood of such an one had ceased to foam on the floor, such another, and four friends with him, had shrieked and died. But a pig is only the Unclean animal – forbidden by the Prophet.

I was destined to make rather a queer discovery when I went over to the cattle-slaughter. All the buildings here were on a much larger scale, and there was no sound of trouble, but I could smell the salt reek of blood before I set foot in the place.

The cattle did not come directly through the viaduct as the pigs had done. They debouched into a yard by the hundred, and they were big red brutes carrying much flesh. In the centre of that yard stood a red Texan steer with a head stall on his wicked head. No man controlled him. He was, so to speak, picking his teeth and whistling in an open byre of his own when the cattle arrived. As soon as the first one had fearfully quitted the viaduct, this red devil put his hands in his pockets and slouched across the yard, no man guiding him. Then he lowed something to the effect that he was the regularly appointed guide of the establishment and would show them round. They were country folk, but they knew how to behave; and so followed Judas some hundred strong, patiently, and with a look of bland wonder in their faces. I saw his broad back jogging in advance of them, up a lime-washed incline where I was forbidden to follow. Then a door shut, and in a minute back came Judas with the air of a virtuous plough-bullock and took up his place in his byre. Somebody laughed across the yard, but I heard no sound of cattle from the big brick building into which the mob had disappeared. Only Judas chewed the cud with a malignant satisfaction, and so I knew there was trouble, and ran round to the front of the factory and so entered and stood aghast.

Who takes count of the prejudices which we absorb through the skin by way of our surroundings? It was not the spectacle that impressed me. The first thought that almost spoke itself aloud was: 'They are killing kine'; and it was a shock. The pigs were nobody's concern, but cattle – the brothers of the Cow, the Sacred Cow – were quite otherwise. The next time an M.P. tells me that India either Sultanises or Brahminises a man, I shall believe about half what he says. It is unpleasant to watch the slaughter of cattle when one has laughed at the notion for a few years. I could not see actually what was done in the first instance, because the row of stalls in which they lay was separated from me by fifty impassable feet of butchers and slung carcasses. All I know is that men swung open the doors of a stall as occasion required, and there lay two steers already stunned, and breathing heavily. These two they pole-axed, and half raising them by tackle they cut their throats. Two men skinned each carcass, somebody cut off the head, and in half a minute more the overhead rail carried two sides of beef to their appointed place. There was clamour enough in the operating-room, but from the waiting cattle, invisible on the other side of the line of pens, never a sound. They went to their death, trusting Judas, without a word. They were slain at the rate of five a minute, and if the pig men were spattered with blood, the cow butchers were bathed in it. The blood ran in muttering gutters. There was no place for hand or foot that was not coated with thicknesses of dried blood, and the stench of it in the nostrils bred fear.

And then the same merciful Providence that has showered good things on my path throughout sent me an embodiment of the city of Chicago, so that I might remember it forever. Women come sometimes to see the slaughter, as they would come to see the slaughter of men. And there entered that vermilion hall a young woman of large mould, with brilliantly scarlet lips, and heavy eye-brows, and dark hair that came in a 'widow's peak' on the forehead. She was well and healthy and alive, and she was dressed in flaming red and black, and her feet (know you that the feet of American women are like unto the feet of fairies?) her feet, I say, were cased in red leather shoes. She stood in a patch of sunlight, the red blood under her shoes, the vivid carcasses stacked round her, a bullock bleeding its life away not six feet away from her, and, the death-factory roaring all round her. She looked curiously, with hard, bold eyes, and was not ashamed.

Then said I: 'This is a special Sending. I have seen the City of Chicago.' And I went away to get peace and rest.

[*From Sea to Sea*]

VERMONT

WE HAD WALKED ABREAST of the year from the very beginning, and that was when the first blood-root came up between the patches of April snow, while yet the big drift at the bottom of the meadow held fast. In the shadow of the woods and under the blown pine-needles, clots of snow lay till far into May, but neither the season nor the flowers took any note of them, and, before we were well sure Winter had gone, the lackeys of my Lord Baltimore in their new liveries came to tell us that Summer was in the valley, and please might they nest at the bottom of the garden?

Followed, Summer, angry, fidgety, and nervous, with the corn and tobacco to ripen in five short months, the pastures to reclothe, and the fallen leaves to hide away under new carpets. Suddenly, in the middle of her work, on a stuffy-still July day, she called a wind out of the Northwest, a wind blown under an arch of steel-bellied clouds, a wicked bitter wind with a lacing of hail to it, a wind that came and was gone in less than ten minutes, but blocked the roads with fallen trees, toppled over a barn, and – blew potatoes out of the ground! When that was done, a white cloud shaped like a dumb-bell whirled down the valley across the evening blue, roaring and twisting and twisting and roaring all alone by itself. A West Indian hurricane could not have been quicker on its feet than our little cyclone, and when the house rose a-tiptoe, like a cockerel in act to crow, and a sixty-foot elm went by the board, and that which had been a dusty road became a roaring torrent all in three minutes, we felt that the New England summer had creole blood in her veins. She went away, red-faced and angry to the last, slamming all the doors of the hills behind her, and Autumn, who is a lady, took charge.

No pen can describe the turning of the leaves – the insurrection of the tree-people against the waning year. A little maple began it, flaming blood-red of a sudden where he stood against the dark green of a pine-belt. Next morning there was an answering signal from the swamp where the sumacs grow. Three days later, the hill-sides as far as the eye could range were afire, and the roads paved, with crimson and gold. Then a wet wind blew, and ruined all the uniforms of that gorgeous army; and the oaks, who had held themselves in reserve, buckled on their dull and bronzed cuirasses and stood it out stiffly to the last blown leaf, till nothing remained but pencil-shading of bare boughs, and one could see into the most private heart of the woods.

Frost may be looked for till the middle of May and after the middle of September, so Summer has little time for enamel-work or leaf-embroidery. Her sisters bring the gifts – Spring, wind-flowers, Solomon's-seal, Dutchman's-breeches, Quaker-ladies, and trailing arbutus, that smells as divinely as the true May. Autumn has golden-rod and all the tribe of asters, pink, lilac, and creamy white, by the double armful. When these go the curtain comes down, and whatever Powers shift the scenery behind, work without noise. In tropic lands you can hear the play of growth and decay at the back of the night-silences. Even in England the tides of the winter air have a set and a purpose; but here they are dumb altogether. The very last piece of bench-work this season was the trailed end of a blackberry-vine, most daringly conventionalised in hammered iron, flung down on the frosty grass an instant before people came to look. The blue bloom of the furnace was still dying along the central rib, and the side-sprays were cherry red, even as they had been lifted from the charcoal. It was a detail, evidently, of some invisible gate in the woods; but we never found that workman, though he had left the mark of his cloven foot as plainly as any strayed deer. In a week the heavy frosts with scythes and hammers had slashed and knocked down all the road-side growth and the kindly bushes that veil the drop off the unfenced track.

There the seasons stopped awhile. Autumn was gone, Winter was not. We had Time dealt out to us – mere, clear, fresh Time – grace-days to enjoy. The white wooden farm-houses were banked round two feet deep with dried leaves or earth, and the choppers went out to get ready next year's stores of wood. Now, chopping is an art, and the chopper in all respects an artist. He makes his own axe-helve, and for each man there is but one perfect piece of wood in all the world. This he never finds, but the likest substitute is trimmed and balanced and poised to that ideal. One man I know has evolved very nearly the weapon of Umslopogaas. It is almost straight, lapped at the butt with leather, amazingly springy, and carries a two-edged blade for splitting and chopping. If his Demon be with him – and what artist can answer for all his moods? – he will cause a tree to fall upon any stick or stone that you choose, uphill or down, to the right or to the left. Artist-like, however, he explains that that is nothing. Any fool can play with a tree in the open, but it needs the craftsman to bring a tree down in thick timber and do no harm. To see an eighty-foot maple, four feet in the butt, dropped, deftly as a fly is cast, in the only place where it will not outrage the feelings and swipe off the tops of fifty juniors, is a revelation. White pine, hemlock, and spruce share this country with maples, black and white birches, and beech. Maple seems to have few preferences, and the white birches straggle and shiver on the outskirts of every camp; but the pines hold together in solid regiments, sending out skirmishers to invade a neglected pasture on the first opportunity. There is no overcoat warmer than the pines in a gale when the woods for miles round are singing like cathedral organs, and the first snow of the year powders the rock-ledges.

The mosses and lichens, green, sulphur, and amber, stud the copper floor of needles, where the feathery ground-pine runs aimlessly to and fro along the ground, spelling out broken words of half-forgotten charms. There are checker-berries on the outskirts of the wood, where the partridge (he is a ruffed grouse really) dines, and by the deserted logging-roads toadstools of all colours sprout on the decayed stumps. Wherever a green or blue rock lifts from the hillside, the needles have been packed and matted round its base, till, when the sunshine catches them, stone and setting together look no meaner than turquoise in dead gold. The woods are full of colour, belts and blotches of it, the colours of the savage – red, yellow, and blue. Yet in their lodges there is very little life, for the wood-people do not readily go into the shadows. The squirrels have their business among the beeches and hickories by the road-side, where they can watch the traffic and talk. We have no gray ones hereabouts (they are good to eat and suffer for it), but five reds live in a hickory hard by, and no weather puts them to sleep. The wood-chuck, a marmot and a strategist, makes his burrow in the middle of a field, where he must see you ere you see him. Now and again a dog manages to cut him off his base, and the battle is worth crossing fields to watch. But the wood-chuck turned in long ago, and will not be out till April. The coon lives – well, no one seems to know particularly where Brer Coon lives, but when the Hunter's Moon is large and full he descends into the corn-lands, and men chase him with dogs for his fur, which makes the finest kind of overcoat, and his flesh, which tastes like chicken. He cries at night sorrowfully as though a child were lost.

They seem to kill, for one reason or other, everything that moves in this land. Hawks, of course; eagles for their rarity; foxes for their pelts; red-shouldered blackbirds and Baltimore orioles because they are pretty, and the other small things for sport – French fashion. You can get a rifle of a kind for twelve shillings, and if your neighbour be fool enough to post notices forbidding 'hunting' and fishing, you naturally seek his woods. So the country is very silent and unalive.

There are, however, bears within a few miles, as you will see from this notice, picked up at the local tobacconist's:

JOHNNY GET YOUR GUN! BEAR HUNT!
As bears are too numerous in the town of Peltyville Corners, Vt., the hunters of the surrounding towns are invited to participate in a grand hunt to be held on Blue Mountains in the town of Peltyville Corners, Vt., Wednesday, Nov. 8th, if pleasant. If not, first fine day. Come one, come all!

They went, but it was the bear that would not participate. The notice was printed at somebody's Electric Print Establishment. Queer mixture, isn't it?

[. . .] In January or February come the great ice-storms, when every branch, blade, and trunk is coated with frozen rain, so that you can touch nothing truly. The spikes of the pines are sunk into pear-shaped crystals, and each fence-post is miraculously hilted with diamonds. If you bend a twig, the icing cracks like varnish, and a half-inch branch snaps off at the lightest tap. If wind and sun open the day together, the eye cannot look steadily at the splendour of this jewelry. The woods are full of the clatter of arms; the ringing of bucks' horns in flight; the stampede of mailed feet up and down the glades; and a great dust of battle is puffed out into the open, till the last of the ice is beaten away and the cleared branches take up their regular chant.

Again the mercury drops twenty and more below zero, and the very trees swoon. The snow turns to French chalk, squeaking under the heel, and their breath cloaks the oxen in rime. At night a tree's heart will break in him with a groan. According to the books, the frost has split something, but it is a fearful sound, this grunt as of a man stunned.

Winter that is winter in earnest does not allow cattle and horses to play about the fields, so everything comes home; and since no share can break ground to any profit for some five months, there would seem to be very little to do. As a matter of fact, country interests at all seasons are extensive and peculiar, and the day is not long enough for them when you take out that time which a self-respecting man needs to turn himself round in. Consider! The solid undisturbed hours stand about one like ramparts. At a certain time the sun will rise. At another hour, equally certain, he will set. This much we know. Why, in the name of Reason, therefore, should we vex ourselves with vain exertions? An occasional visitor from the Cities of the Plains comes up panting to do things. He is set down to listen to the normal beat of his own heart – a sound that very few men have heard. In a few days, when the lather of impatience has dried off, he ceases to talk of 'getting there' or 'being left.' He does not desire to accomplish matters 'right away,' nor does he look at his watch from force of habit, but keeps it where it should be – in his stomach. At the last he goes back to his beleaguered city, unwillingly, partially civilised, soon to be resavaged by the clash of a thousand wars whose echo does not reach here.

The air which kills germs dries out the very newspapers. They might be of to-morrow or a hundred years ago. They have nothing to do with to-day – the long, full, sunlit to-day. Our interests are not on the same scale as theirs, perhaps, but much more complex. The movement of a foreign power – an alien sleigh on this Pontic shore – must be explained and accounted for, or this public's heart will burst with unsatisfied curiosity. If it be Buck

Davis, with the white mare that he traded his colt for, and the practically new sleigh-robe that he bought at the Sewell auction, why does Buck Davis, who lives on the river flats, cross our hills, unless Murder Hollow be blockaded with snow, or unless he has turkeys for sale? But Buck Davis with turkeys would surely have stopped here, unless he were selling a large stock in town. A wail from the sacking at the back of the sleigh tells the tale. It is a winter calf, and Buck Davis is going to sell it for one dollar to the Boston Market where it will be turned into potted chicken. This leaves the mystery of his change of route unexplained. After two days' sitting on tenter-hooks it is discovered, obliquely, that Buck went to pay a door-yard call on Orson Butler, who lives on the saeter where the wind and the bald granite scaurs fight it out together. Kirk Demming had brought Orson news of a fox at the back of Black Mountain, and Orson's eldest son, going to Murder Hollow with wood for the new barn floor that the widow Amidon is laying down, told Buck that he might as well come round to talk to his father about the pig. But old man Butler meant fox-hunting from the first, and what he wanted to do was to borrow Buck's dog, who had been duly brought over with the calf, and left on the mountain. No old man Butler did not go hunting alone, but waited till Buck came back from town. Buck sold the calf for a dollar and a quarter and not for seventy-five cents as was falsely asserted by interested parties. Then the two went after the fox together. This much learned, everybody breathes freely, if life has not been complicated in the meantime by more strange counter-marchings.

Five or six sleighs a day we can understand, if we know why they are abroad; but any metropolitan rush of traffic disturbs and excites.

['Leaves from a Winter Notebook', *From Tideway to Tideway*]

❈　❈　❈

MOUNT MONADNOCK

AFTER THE GLOOM OF gray Atlantic weather, our ship came to America in a flood of winter sunshine that made unaccustomed eyelids blink, and the New Yorker, who is nothing if not modest, said, 'This isn't a sample of our really fine days. Wait until such and such times come, or go to such and a such a quarter of the city.' We were content, and more than content, to drift aimlessly up and down the brilliant streets, wondering a little why the finest light should be wasted on the worst pavements in the world; to walk round and round Madison Square, because that was full of beautifully dressed babies playing counting-out games, or to gaze reverently at the broad-shouldered, pug-nosed Irish New York policemen. Wherever we went there was the sun, lavish and unstinted, working nine hours a day, with the colour and the clean-cut lines of perspective that he makes. That anyone should dare to call this climate muggy, yea, even 'subtropical,' was a shock. There came such a man, and he said, 'Go north if you want weather – weather that is weather. Go to New England.' So New York passed away upon a sunny afternoon, with her roar and rattle, her complex smells, her triply over-heated rooms, and much too energetic inhabitants, while the train went north to the lands where the snow lay. It came in one sweep – almost, it seemed, in one turn of the wheels – covering the winter-killed grass and turning the frozen ponds that looked so white under the shadow of lean trees into pools of ink.

As the light closed in, a little wooden town, white, cloaked, and dumb, slid past the windows, and the strong light of the car lamps fell upon a sleigh (the driver furred and muffled to his nose) turning the corner of a street. Now the sleigh of a picture-book, however well one knows it, is altogether different from the thing in real life, a means of conveyance at a journey's end; but it is well not to be over-curious in the matter, for the same American who has been telling you at length how he once followed a kilted Scots soldier from Chelsea to the Tower, out of pure wonder and curiosity at his bare knees and sporran, will laugh at your interest in 'just a cutter.'

The staff of the train – surely the great American nation

would be lost if deprived of the ennobling society of brakeman, conductor, Pullman-car conductor, negro porter, and newsboy – told pleasant tales, as they spread themselves at ease in the smoking compartments, of snowings up the line to Montreal, of desperate attacks – four engines together and a snow-plough in front – on drifts thirty feet high, and the pleasures of walking along the tops of goods wagons to brake a train, with the thermometer thirty below freezing. 'It comes cheaper to kill men that way than to put air-brakes on freight-cars,' said the brakeman.

Thirty below freezing! It was inconceivable till one stepped out into it at midnight, and the first shock of that clear, still air took away the breath as does a plunge into sea-water. A walrus sitting on a woolpack was our host in his sleigh, and he wrapped us in hairy goatskin coats, caps that came down over the ears, buffalo robes and blankets, and yet more buffalo robes till we, too, looked like walruses and moved almost as gracefully. The night was as keen as the edge of a newly-ground sword; breath froze on the coat-lapels in snow; the nose became without sensation, and the eyes wept bitterly because the horses were in a hurry to get home; and whirling through air at zero brings tears. But for the jingle of the sleigh-bells the ride might have taken place in a dream, for there was no sound of hoofs upon the snow, the runners sighed a little now and again as they glided over an inequality, and all the sheeted hills round about were as dumb as death. Only the Connecticut River kept up its heart and a lane of black water through the packed ice; we could hear the stream worrying round the heels of its small bergs. Elsewhere there was nothing but snow under the moon – snow drifted to the level of the stone fences or curling over their tops in a lip of frosted silver; snow banked high on either side of the road, or lying heavy on the pines and the hemlocks in the woods, where the air seemed, by comparison, as warm as a conservatory. It was beautiful beyond expression, Nature's boldest sketch in black and white, done with a Japanese disregard of perspective, and daringly altered from time to time by the restless pencils of the moon.

In the morning the other side of the picture was revealed in the colours of the sunlight. There was never a cloud in the sky that rested on the snow-line of the horizon as a sapphire on white velvet. Hills of pure white, or speckled and furred with woods, rose up above the solid white levels of the fields, and the sun rioted over their embroideries till the eyes ached. Here and there on the exposed slopes the day's warmth – the thermometer was nearly forty degrees – and the night's cold had made a bald and shining crust upon the snow; but the most part was soft powdered stuff, ready to catch the light on a thousand crystals and multiply it sevenfold. Through this magnificence, and thinking nothing of it, a wood-sledge drawn by two shaggy red steers, the unbarked logs diamond-dusted with snow, shouldered down the road in a cloud of frosty breath. It is the mark of inexperience in this section of the country to confound a sleigh which you use for riding with the sledge that is devoted to heavy work; and it is, I believe, a still greater sign of worthlessness to think that oxen are driven, as they are in most places, by scientific twisting of the tail. The driver with red mittens on his hands, felt overstockings that come up to his knees, and, perhaps, a silvery-gray coon-skin coat on his back, walks beside, crying, 'Gee, haw!' even as is written in American stories. And the speech of the driver explains many things in regard to the dialect story, which at its best is an infliction to many. Now that I have heard the long, unhurried drawl of Vermont, my wonder is, not that the New England tales should be printed in what, for the sake of argument, we will call English and its type, but rather that they should not have appeared in Swedish or Russian. Our alphabet is too limited. This part of the country belongs by laws unknown to the United States, but which obtain all the world over, to the New England story and the ladies who write it. You feel this in the air as soon as you see the white-painted wooden houses left out in the snow, the austere schoolhouse, and the people – the men of the farms, the women who work as hard as they with, it may be, less enjoyment of life – the other houses, well painted and quaintly roofed, that belong to Judge This, Lawyer That, and Banker Such an one; all powers in the metropolis of six thousand folk over by the railway station. More acutely still, do you realise the atmosphere when you read in the local paper announcements of 'chicken suppers' and 'church sociables' to be given by such and such a denomination, sandwiched between paragraphs of genial and friendly interest, showing that the countryside live (and without slaying each other) on terms of terrifying intimacy.

The folk of the old rock, the dwellers in the older houses, born and raised hereabouts, would not live out of the town for any consideration, and there are insane people from the South – men and women from Boston and the like – who actually build houses out in the open country, two, and even three miles from Main Street which is nearly 400 yards long, and the centre of life and population. With the strangers, more particularly if they do not buy their groceries 'in the street,' which means, and is, the town, the town has little to do; but it knows everything, and much more also, that goes on among them. Their dresses, their cattle, their views, the manners of their children, their manner towards their servants, and every other conceivable thing, is reported, digested, discussed, and rediscussed up and down Main Street. Now, the wisdom of Vermont, not being at all times equal to grasping all the problems of everybody else's life with delicacy, sometimes makes pathetic mistakes, and the town is set by the ears. You will see, therefore, that towns of a certain size do not differ materially all the world over. The talk of the men of the farms is of their farms – purchase, mortgage, and sale, recorded rights, boundary lines, and road tax. It was in the middle of New Zealand, on the edge of the Wild horse plains, that I heard this talk last, when a man and his wife, twenty miles from the nearest neighbour, sat up half the night discussing just the same things that the men talked of in Main Street, Vermont, U.S.A.

There is one man in the State who is much exercised over this place. He is a farm-hand, raised in a hamlet fifteen or twenty miles from the nearest railway, and, greatly daring, he has wandered here. The bustle and turmoil of Main Street, the new glare of the electric lights and the five-storeyed brick business block, frighten and distress him much. He has taken service on a farm well away from these delirious delights, and, says he, 'I've been offered $25 a month to work in a bakery at New York. But you don't get me to no New York, I've seen this place an' it just scares me,' His strength is in the drawing of hay and the feeding of cattle. Winter life on a farm does not mean the comparative idleness that is so much written of. Each hour seems to have its sixty minutes of work; for the cattle are housed and eat eternally; the colts must be turned out for their drink, and the ice broken for them if necessary; then ice must be stored for the summer use, and then the real work of hauling logs for firewood begins. New England depends for its fuel on the woods. The trees are 'blazed' in the autumn just before the fall of the leaf, felled later, cut into four-foot lengths, and, as soon as the friendly snow makes sledging possible, drawn down to the woodhouse. Afterwards the needs of the farm can be attended to, and a farm, like an arch, is never at rest. A little later will come maple-sugar time, when the stately maples are tapped as the sap begins to stir, and be-ringed with absurd little buckets (a cow being milked into a thimble gives some idea of the disproportion), which are emptied into cauldrons. Afterwards (this is the time of the 'sugaring-off parties') you pour the boiled syrup into tins full of fresh snow, where it hardens, and you pretend to help and become very sticky and make love, boys and girls together. Even the introduction of patent sugar evaporators has not spoiled the love-making.

There is a certain scarcity of men to make love with; not so much in towns which have their own manufactories and lie within a lover's Sabbath-day journey of New York, but in the farms and villages. The men have gone away – the young men are fighting fortune further West, and the women remain – remain for ever as women must. On the farms, when the children depart, the old man and the old woman strive to hold things together without help, and the woman's portion is work and monotony. Sometimes she goes mad to an extent which appreciably affects statistics and is put down in census reports. More often, let us hope, she dies. In the villages where the necessity for heavy work is not so urgent the women find consolation in the formation of literary clubs and circles, and so gather to themselves a great deal of wisdom in their own way. That way is not altogether lovely. They desire facts and the knowledge that they are at a certain page in a German or an Italian book before a certain time, or that they have read the proper books in a proper way. At any rate, they have something to do that seems as if they were doing something. It has been said that the New England stories are cramped and narrow. Even a far-off view of the iron-bound life whence they are drawn justifies the author. You can carve a nut in a thousand different ways by reason of the hardness of the shell.

Twenty or thirty miles across the hills, on the way to the Green Mountains, lie some finished chapters of pitiful stories – a few score abandoned farms, started in a lean land, held fiercely so long as there was any one to work them, and then left on the hill-sides. Beyond this desolation are woods where the bear and the deer still find peace, and sometimes even the beaver forgets that he is persecuted and dares to build his lodge. These things were told me by a man who loved the woods for their own sake and not for the sake of slaughter – a quiet, slow-spoken man of the West, who came across the drifts on show-shoes and refrained from laughing when I borrowed his foot-gear and tried to walk. The gigantic lawn-tennis bats strung with hide are not easy to manoeuvre. If you forget to keep the long heels down and trailing in the snow you turn over and become as a man who fails into deep water with a life-belt tied to his ankles. If you lose your balance, do not attempt to recover it, but drop, half-sitting and half-kneeling, over as large an area as possible. When you have mastered the wolf-step, can slide one shoe above the other deftly, that is to say, the sensation of paddling over a ten-foot-deep drift and taking short cuts by buried fences is worth the ankle-ache. The man from the West interpreted to me the signs on the snow, showed how a fox (this section of the country is full of foxes, and men shoot them because riding is impossible) leaves one kind of spoor, walking with circumspection as becomes a thief, and a dog, who has nothing to be ashamed of, but widens his four legs and plunges, another; how coons go to sleep for the winter and squirrels too, and how the deer on the Canada border trample down deep paths that are called yards and are caught there by inquisitive men with cameras, who hold them by their tails when the deer have blundered into deep snow, and so photograph their frightened dignity. He told me of people also – the manners and customs of New Englanders here, and how they blossom and develop in the Far West on the newer railway lines, when matters come very nearly to civil war between rival companies racing for the same cañon; how there is a country not very far away called Caledonia, populated by the Scotch, who can give points to a New Englander in a bargain, and how these same Scotch-Americans by birth, name their townships still after the cities of their thrifty race. It was all as new and delightful as the steady 'scrunch' of the snow-shoes and the dazzling silence of the hills.

Beyond the very furthest range, where the pines turn to a faint blue haze against the one solitary peak – a real mountain and not a hill – showed like a gigantic thumbnail pointing heavenward.

'And that's Monadnock,' said the man from the West; 'all the hills have Indian names. You left Wantastiquet on your right coming out of town.'

You know how it often happens that a word shuttles in and out of many years, waking all sorts of incongruous associations. I had met Monadnock on paper in a shameless parody of Emerson's style, before ever style or verse had interest for me. But the word stuck because of a rhyme, in which one was

> . . . crowned coeval
> With Monadnock's crest,
>   And my wings extended
> Touch the East and West.

Later the same word, pursued on the same principle as that blessed one Mesopotamia, led me to and through Emerson, up to his poem on the peak itself – the wise old giant 'busy with his sky affairs,' who makes us sane and sober and free from little things if we trust him. So Monadnock came to mean everything that was helpful, healing, and full of quiet, and when I saw him half across New Hampshire he did not fail. In that utter stillness a hemlock bough, overweighted with snow, came down a foot or two with a tired little sigh; the snow slid off and the little branch flew nodding back to its fellows.

For the honour of Monadnock there was made that afternoon an image of snow of Gautama Buddha, something too squat and not altogether equal on both sides, but with an imperial and reposeful waist. He faced towards the mountain, and presently some men in a wood-sledge came up the road and faced him. Now, the amazed comments of two Vermont farmers on the nature and properties of a swag-bellied god are worth hearing. They were not troubled about his race, for he was aggressively white; but rounded waists seem to be out of fashion in Vermont. At least, they said so, with rare and curious oaths.

Next day all the idleness and trifling were drowned in a snowstorm that filled the hollows of the hills with whirling blue mist, bowed the branches of the woods till you ducked, but were powdered all the same when you drove through, and wiped out the sleighing tracks. Mother Nature is beautifully tidy if you leave her alone. She rounded off every angle, broke down every scarp, and tucked the white bedclothes, till not a wrinkle remained, up to the chine of the spruces and the hemlocks that would not go to sleep.

'Now,' said the man of the West, as we were driving to the station, and alas! to New York, 'all my snow-tracks are gone; but when that snow melts, a week hence or a month hence, they'll all come up again and show where I've been.'

Curious idea, is it not? Imagine a murder committed in the lonely woods, a snowstorm that covers the tracks of the flying man before the avenger of blood has buried the body, and then, a week later, the withdrawal of the traitorous snow, revealing step by step the path Cain took – the six-inch dee-trail of his snow-shoes – each step a dark disk on the white till the very end.

There is so much, so very much to write, if it were worth while, about that queer little town by the railway station, with its life running, to all outward seeming, as smoothly as the hack-coupés on their sleigh mounting, and within disturbed by the hatreds and troubles and jealousies that vex the minds of all but the gods. For instance – no, it is better to remember the lesson Monadnock, and Emerson has said, 'Zeus hates busy-bodies and people who do too much.'

That there are such folk, a long nasal drawl across Main Street attests. A farmer is unhitching his horses from a post opposite a store. He stands with the tie-rope in his hand and gives his opinion to his neighbour and the world generally – 'But them there Andersons, they ain't got no notion of etikwette!'

[*From Tideway to Tideway*]

🞙 🞙 🞙

St Paul

YES, IT IS VERY good to get away once more and pick up the old and ever fresh business of the vagrant, loafing through new towns, learned in the manners of dogs, babies, and perambulators half the world over, and tracking the seasons by the up-growth of flowers in stranger-people's gardens. St. Paul, standing at the barn-door of the Dakota and Minnesota granaries, is all things to all men except to Minneapolis, eleven miles away, whom she hates and by whom she is patronised. She calls herself the capital of the North-West, the new North-West, and her citizens wear, not only the tall silk hat of trade, but the soft slouch of the West. She talks in another tongue than the New Yorker, and – sure sign that we are far across the continent – her papers argue with the San Francisco ones over rate wars and the competition of railway companies. St. Paul has been established many years, and if one were reckless enough to go down to the business quarters one would hear all about her and more also. But the residential parts of the town are the crown of it. In common with scores of other cities, broad-crowned suburbs – using the word in the English sense – that make the stranger jealous. You get here what you do not get in the city – well-paved or asphalted roads, planted with trees, and trim side-walks, studded with houses of individuality, not boorishly fenced off from each other, but standing each on its plot of well-kept turf running down to the pavement. It is always Sunday in these streets of a morning. The cable-car has taken the men down town to business, the children are at school, and the big dogs, three and a third to each absent child, lie nosing the winter-killed grass and wondering when the shoots will make it possible for a gentleman to take his spring medicine. In the afternoon, the children on tricycles stagger up and down the asphalt with due proportion of big dogs at each wheel; the cable-cars coming up hill begin to drop the men each at his own door – the door of the house that he builded for himself (though the architect incited him to that vile little attic tower and useless loggia), and, naturally enough, twilight brings the lovers walking two by two along the very quiet ways. You can tell from the houses almost the exact period at which they were built, whether in the jig-saw days, when it behoved respectability to use unlovely turned rails and pierced gable-ends, or during the Colonial craze, which means white paint and fluted pillars, or in the latest domestic era, a most pleasant mixture, that is, of stained shingles, hooded dormer-windows, cunning verandas, and recessed doors. Seeing these things, one begins to understand why the Americans visiting England are impressed with the old and not with the new. He is not much more than a hundred years ahead of the English in design, comfort, and economy, and (this is most important) labour-saving appliances in his house. From Newport to San Diego you will find the same thing to-day.

[*From Tideway to Tideway*]

✠ ✠ ✠

NEW YORK

A REGULAR WEATHER-BREEDER OF a day to-day – real warmth at last and it raked in me a lively desire to be back in Main Street Brattleboro Vt. U.S.A. and hear the sody water fizzing in the drug-store and discuss the outlook for the Episcopalian Church with the clerk; and get a bottle of lager in the basement of the Brooks house and hear the doctor tell yarns and have the iron-headed old farmers loaf up and jerk out: 'Bin in Yurope haint yer?' and then go home, an easy gait, through the deep white dust with the locust trees just stinking to heaven and the fire flies playing up and down the swamp road and the Katydids giving oratorios free-gratis and for nothing to the whip-poorwill and everybody sitting out in the verandah after dinner smoking Durham tobacco in a cob pipe with our feet on the verandah railings and the moon coming up behind Wantastiquet. There's one Britisher at least homesick for a section of your depraved old land and he's going, please Allah, the first week in August by the Kaiser Wilhelm and won't New York be hot just! There's a smell of horse-piss, Italian fruit-vendor, nickel-cigars; sour lager and warm car-conductor drifting down Carmine Street at this minute from Sixth Ave. which I can smell with the naked eye as I sit here. I shall go to Long Island to a friend's and eat new corn and visit 'em at the Senanhaka the first thing and I wish you were coming too.

[Letter to Robert Barr, 28 July 1894]

✠ ✠ ✠

CANADA

THEY WILL NOT RUN trains on Sunday at Montreal, and this is Wednesday. Therefore, the Canadian Pacific makes up a train for Vancouver at Winnipeg. This is worth remembering, because few people travel in that train, and you escape any rush of tourists running westward to catch the Yokohama boat. The car is your own, and with it the service of the porter. Our porter, seeing things were slack, beguiled himself with a guitar, which gave a triumphal and festive touch to the journey, ridiculously out of keeping the view. For eight-and-twenty long hours did the bored locomotive trail us through a flat and hairy land, powdered, ribbed, and speckled with snow, small snow that drives like dust-shot in the wind – the land of Assiniboia. Now and again, for no obvious reason to the outside mind, there was a town. Then the towns gave place to 'section so and so'; then there were trails of the buffalo, where he once walked in his pride; then there was a mound of white bones, supposed to belong to the said buffalo, and then the wilderness took up the tale. Some of it was good ground, but most of it seemed to have fallen by the wayside, and the tedium of it was eternal.

At twilight – an unearthly sort of twilight – there came another curious picture. Thus – a wooden town shut in among low, treeless, rolling ground, a calling river that ran unseen between scarped banks; barracks of a detachment of mounted police, a little cemetery where ex-troopers rested, a painfully formal public garden with pebble paths and foot-high fir trees, a few lines of railway buildings, white women walking up and down in the bitter cold with their bonnets off, some Indians in red blanketing with buffalo horns for sale trailing along the platform, and, not ten yards from the track, a cinnamon bear and a young grizzly standing up with extended arms in their pens and begging for food. It was strange beyond anything that this bald telling can suggest – opening a door into a new world. The only commonplace thing about the spot was its name – Medicine Hat, which struck me instantly as the only possible name such a town could carry. This is that place which later became a town; but I had seen it three years before when it was even smaller and was reached by me in a freight-car, ticket unpaid for.

That next morning brought us the Canadian Pacific Railway as one reads about it. No pen of man could do justice to the scenery there. The guide-books struggle desperately with descriptions, adapted for summer reading, of rushing cascades, lichened rocks, waving pines, and snow-capped mountains; but in April these things are not there. The place is locked up – dead as a frozen corpse. The mountain torrent is a boss of palest emerald ice against the dazzle of the snow; the pine-stumps are capped and hooded with gigantic mushrooms of snow; the rocks are overlaid five feet deep; the rocks, the fallen trees, and the lichens together, and the dumb white lips curl up to the track cut in the side of the mountain, and grin there fanged with gigantic icicles. You may listen in vain when the train stops for the least sign of breath or power among the hills. The snow has smothered the rivers, and the great looping trestles run over what might be a lather of suds in a huge wash-tub. The old snow near by is blackened and smirched with the smoke of locomotives, and its dulness is grateful to aching eyes.

[*From Tideway to Tideway*]

✴ ✴ ✴

QUEBEC

THE ST. LAWRENCE ON the last day of the voyage played up nobly. The maples along its banks had turned – blood red and splendid as the banners of lost youth. Even the oak is not more of a national tree than the maple, and the sight of its welcome made the folks aboard still more happy. A dry wind brought along all the clean smell of their Continent-mixed odours of sawn lumber, virgin earth, and wood-smoke; and they snuffed it, and their eyes softened as they identified point after point along their own beloved River – places where they played and fished and amused themselves in holiday time. It must be pleasant to have a country of one's very own to show off. Understand, they did not in any way boast, shout, squeak, or exclaim, these even-voiced returned men and women. They were simply and unfeignedly glad to see home again, and they said: 'Isn't it lovely? Don't you think it's beautiful? We love it.'

At Quebec there is a sort of place, much infested by locomotives, like a coal-chute, whence rise the heights that Wolfe's men scaled on their way to the Plains of Abraham. Perhaps of all the tide-marks in all our lands the affair of Quebec touches the heart and the eye more nearly than any other. Everything meets there; France, the jealous partner of England's glory by land and sea for eight hundred years; England, bewildered as usual, but for a wonder not openly opposing Pitt, who knew; those other people, destined to break from England as soon as the French peril was removed; Montcalm himself, doomed and resolute; Wolfe, the inevitable trained workman appointed for the finish; and somewhere in the background one James Cook, master of H.M.S. *Mercury*, making beautiful and delicate charts of the St. Lawrence River.

For these reasons the Plains of Abraham are crowned with all sorts of beautiful things – including a jail and a factory. Montcalm's left wing is marked by the jail, and Wolfe's right by the factory. There is, happily, now a movement on foot to abolish these adornments and turn the battle-field and its surroundings into a park, which by nature and association would be one of the most beautiful in our world.

Yet, in spite of jails on the one side and convents on the other and the thin black wreck of the Quebec Railway Bridge, lying like a dumped car-load of tin cans in the river, the Eastern Gate to Canada is noble with a dignity beyond words. We saw it very early, when the under sides of the clouds turned chilly pink over a high-piled, brooding, dusky-purple city. Just at the point of dawn, what looked like the Sultan Harun-al-Raschid's own private shallop, all spangled with coloured lights, stole across the iron-grey water, and disappeared into the darkness of a slip. She came out again in three minutes, but the full day had come too; so she snapped off her masthead, steering and cabin electrics, and turned into a dingy white ferryboat, full of cold passengers.

[*Letters to the Family*]

✻ ✻ ✻

CALGARY TO THE PACIFIC

THE PRAIRIE PROPER ENDS at Calgary, among the cattle-ranches, mills, breweries, and three million acre irrigation works. The river that floats timber to the town from the mountains does not slide nor rustle like Prairie rivers, but brawls across bars of blue pebbles, and a greenish tinge in its water hints of the snows.

What I saw of Calgary was crowded into one lively half-hour (motors were invented to run about new cities). What I heard I picked up, oddly enough, weeks later, from a young Dane in the North Sea. He was qualmish, but his Saga of triumph upheld him.

'Three years ago I come to Canada by steerage – third class. And I have the language to learn. Look at me! I have now my own dairy business, in Calgary, and – look at me! – my own half section, that is, three hundred and twenty acres. All my land which is mine! And now I come home, first class, for Christmas here in Denmark, and I shall take out back with me, some friends of mine which are farmers, to farm on those irrigated lands near by Calgary. Oh, I tell you there is nothing wrong with Canada for a man which works.'

'And will your friends go?' I inquired.

'You bet they will. It is all arranged already. I bet they get ready to go now already; and in three years they will come back for Christmas here in Denmark, first class like me.'

'Then you think Calgary is going ahead?'

'You bet! We are only at the beginning of things. Look at me! Chickens? I raise chickens also in Calgary,' etc., etc.

After all this pageant of unrelieved material prosperity, it was a rest to get to the stillness of the big foothills, though they, too, had been in-spanned for the work of civilisation. The timber off their sides was ducking and pitch-poling down their swift streams, to be sawn into house-stuff for all the world. The woodwork of a purely English villa may come from as many Imperial sources as its owner's income.

The train crept, whistling to keep its heart up, through the winding gateways of the hills, till it presented itself, very humbly, before the true mountains, the not so Little Brothers to the Himalayas. Mountains of the pine-cloaked, snow-capped breed are unchristian things.

Men mine into the flanks of some of them, and trust to modern science to pull them through. Not long ago, a mountain kneeled on a little mining village as an angry elephant kneels; but it did not get up again, and the half of that camp was no more seen on earth. The other half still stands – uninhabited. The 'heathen in his blindness' would have made arrangements with the Genius of the Place before he ever drove a pick there. As a learned scholar of a little-known university once observed to an engineer officer on the Himalaya–Tibet Road – 'You white men gain nothing by not noticing what you cannot see. You fall off the road, or the road falls on you, and you die, and you think it all an accident. How much wiser it was when we were allowed to sacrifice a man officially, sir, before making bridges or other public works. Then the local gods were officially recognised, sir, and did not give any more trouble, and the local workmen, sir, were much pleased with these precautions.'

There are many local gods on the road through the Rockies: old bald mountains that have parted with every shred of verdure and stand wrapped in sheets of wrinkled silver rock, over which the sight travels slowly as in delirium; mad, horned mountains, wreathed with dancing mists; low-browed and bent-shouldered faquirs of the wayside, sitting in meditation beneath a burden of glacier-ice that thickens every year; and mountains of fair aspect on one side, but on the other seamed with hollow sunless clefts, where last year's snow is blackened with this year's dirt and smoke of forest-fires. The drip from it seeps away through slopes of unstable gravel and dirt, till, at the appointed season, the whole half-mile of undermined talus slips and roars into the horrified valley.

The railway winds in and out among them with little inexplicable deviations and side-twists, much as a buck walks through a forest-glade, sidling and crossing uneasily in what appears to be a plain way. Only when the track has rounded another shoulder or two, a backward and upward glance at some menacing slope shows why the train did not take the easier-looking road on the other side of the gorge.

From time to time the mountains lean apart, and nurse between them some golden valley of slow streams, fat pastures, and park-like uplands, with a little town, and cow bells tinkling among berry bushes; and children who have never seen the sun rise or set, shouting at the trains; and real gardens round the houses.

At Calgary it was a frost, and the dahlias were dead. A day later nasturtiums bloomed untouched beside the station platforms, and the air was heavy and liquid with the breath of the Pacific. One felt the spirit of the land change with the changing outline of the hills till, on the lower levels by the Fraser, it seemed that even the Sussex Downs must be nearer at heart to the Prairie than British Columbia. The Prairie people notice the difference, and the Hill people, unwisely, I think, insist on it. Perhaps the magic may lie in the scent of strange evergreens and mosses not known outside the ranges: or it may strike from wall to wall of timeless rifts and gorges, but it seemed to me to draw out of the great sea that washes further Asia – the Asia of allied mountains, mines, and forests.

We rested one day high up in the Rockies, to visit a lake carved out of pure jade, whose property is to colour every reflection on its bosom to its own tint. A belt of brown dead timber on a gravel scar, showed, upside down, like sombre cypresses rising from green turf and the reflected snows were pale green. In summer many tourists go there, but we saw nothing except the wonderworking lake lying mute in its circle of forest, where red and orange lichens grew among grey and blue moss, and we heard nothing except the noise of its outfall hurrying through a jam of bone-white logs. The thing might have belonged to Tibet or some unexplored valley behind Kinchinjunga. It had no concern with the West.

[*Letters to the Family*]

✠ ✠ ✠

THE ROCKY MOUNTAINS

THEN WE WENT ACROSS the Rocky Mountains. I can't begin to describe that part of the journey but we were given a set of photographs of all the most wonderful parts and we will show them to you. Just as we began to get into the mountains we saw a party of Red Indians riding along exactly like an illustration in Collier's magazine. The squaw rode behind on a white horse and when they reached the railway she got off and took care of all their bundles. They were the nicest Indians I have ever seen – all dressed in green and red and blue. But they were most filthy dirty.

We passed over a river all crowded with salmon and their black backs Looked like the backs of pigs in a stye. You never imagined such a sight. Our train ran along narrow cuttings over a boiling blue roaring river hundreds of feet below. [. . .] The river roared: the train roared: the rocks threw back the echo and everything round us was rocks and pines and all the tops of the mountains were covered with solid green ice – not merely snow but old unmeltable ice. I had never noticed it before.

But, as I said, I could not begin to describe the wonders of that wonderful snaky twisty-twisty journey. It lasted for a day and a night and a day. In the night I looked out of my window and I could just make out the mountains all black against the stars and below me I could just see a roaring ribbon of ghostly grey and I knew we were still climbing round that terrible river. On the other side of the gorge was an old road which had been made before the railway for men to ride along. It had all gone to pieces and it looked like a road in a bad dream. It all ended in a rude and wrecked old suspension bridge with half the ropes gone. Landslips had carried the road away in some places: and trees had fallen across and blocked it at others but one could only admire the courage of the men who could use it even at its best. Then all of a sudden we dropped into a climate like England. A day before we had seen gardens where the frost had cut down and blackened even the asters. Next morning we saw a garden full of nasturtiums in full bloom. So you see the difference. Then we ran into soft fog and mist and smelt the sea – even the vast North Pacific – and lo and behold we were in Vancouver – 2904 miles from Montreal! Doesn't it sound like a fairy tale.

[Letter to John and Elsie Kipling, 5 October 1907]

♫ 4 ♫

BRITAIN

The Glory of the Garden

Devon – London – Sussex – South Downs – Surrey – Yorkshire – Durham –Torquay – Winchester – Great North Road – Beaufort Castle – Ireland –English Channel.

Through the accident of his birth in Bombay, Kipling was always something of an outsider in Britain, the country his parents saw – and brought him up to regard – as 'home'. Like Conrad at much the same time, he had to work on, to dig deep inside himself, in order to understand the British (though admittedly he did not have to worry about writing in a second language). And the same certainly applied to his observations on Britain. It may have been the land of his fathers and of his culture, but it was not his natural environment. So it always retained a touch of magic for him: a place where both halves of Kipling's head came into play.

Although he had lived with foster parents in Southsea, Hampshire, his first real experience of England was at school at Westward Ho! on the Atlantic coast in Devon. Compare here his recollection of this westerly county in his autobiography with a fictional account from his 'Stalky' stories.

At least he enjoyed the English countryside. Cities were different: as with Calcutta and Chicago, he hated London when he went there on his return from India in October 1889. He initially lived in two unfurnished rooms in Villiers Street, off the Strand – the backdrop for a scene, included here, in his 1891 novel *The Light That Failed*. What really annoyed him about the British capital was, as his poem 'In Partibus' suggests, its whiff of decadence, which left him yearning for the moral certainties of India.

After returning from America for good in 1896, he ended up living in Sussex, a county he loved. In a letter to his friend Charles Eliot Norton, he described England as: 'the most marvellous of all foreign countries that I have ever been in. It is made up of trees and green fields and mud and the Gentry: and at last I'm one of the Gentry!' His passion for Sussex comes out not only in poems but also in his books *Puck of Pook's Hill* and *Rewards and Fairies*, which are historical stories of Sussex people, set in a fairyland framework, and inspired by the evidence of the recent and distant past that he found all around him at 'Bateman's'.

Other counties he liked included Surrey, which evoked fond memories of his daughter Josephine (Taffy in the poem 'Merrow Down', featured here) who died young in 1899, and Yorkshire, the ancestral home of the Kipling family. Although he had only occasionally visited the latter, he evoked it to good effect in his generally humorous Mulvaney stories about three soldiers in India – one of whom, Learoyd, hailed from Yorkshire.

After the early 1900s Kipling moved more freely around Britain by car. His letters are rich sources for observations on the places he visited, such as Durham, Torquay (close to where he lived for a short time) and Winchester. He drew on his experience of driving in stories such as 'The Prophet and the Country', an extract from which is featured here.

As his letter referring to Beaufort Castle, seat of Lord Lovat, shows, he also ventured into Scotland, where he was Rector of St Andrew's University. But when he travelled to Ireland, his strongly Unionist politics obscured his judgement and, despite his mother's Celtic origins, he showed little respect for either the country or its people.

Writing about Britain also meant acknowledging its island heritage. Included here are two homages – one fiction, the other verse – to the 'coastwise lights', or lighthouses, that welcome sailors to Britain's shores. The story 'The Disturber of Traffic' draws on Kipling's love of the Isle of Wight and, in particular, St Catherine's Lighthouse at Niton Undercliffe.

DEVON

OF ALL THINGS IN the world there is nothing, always excepting a good mother, so worthy of honour as a good school. Our School was created for the sons of officers in the Army and Navy, and filled with boys who meant to follow their father's calling.

It stood within two miles of Amyas Leigh's house at Northam, overlooking the Burroughs and the Pebble-ridge, and the mouth of the Torridge whence the Rose sailed in search of Don Guzmán. From the front dormitory windows, across the long rollers of the Atlantic, you could see Lundy Island and the Shutter Rock, where the Santa Catherina galleon cheated Amyas out of his vengeance by going ashore. If you have ever read Kingsley's Westward Ho! you will remember how all these things happened.

Inland lay the rich Devonshire lanes and the fat orchards, and to the west the gorse and the turf ran along the tops of the cliffs in combe after combe till you come to Clovelly and the Hobby and Gallantry Bower, and the homes of the Devonshire people that were old when the Armada was new.

The Burrows, lying between the school and the sea, was a waste of bent rush and grass running out into hundreds of acres of fascinating sandhills called the Bunkers, where a few old people played golf. In the early days of the School there was a small Club-house for golfers close to the Pebble-ridge, but, one wild winter night, the sea got up and drove the Pebble-ridge clean through the Club basement, and the walls fell out, and we rejoiced, for even then golfers wore red coats and did not like us to use the links. We played as a matter of course and thought nothing of it.

[*Something of Myself*]

THEY ALL SWEATED; FOR Stalky led them at a smart trot west away along the cliffs under the furzehills, crossing combe after gorsy combe. They took no heed to flying rabbits or fluttering fritillaries, and all that Turkey said of geology was utterly unquotable.

'Are we going to Clovelly?' he puffed at last, and they flung themselves down on the short, springy turf between the drone of the sea below and the light summer wind among the inland trees. They were looking into a combe half full of old, high furze in gay bloom that ran up to a fringe of brambles and a dense wood of mixed timber and hollies. It was as though one-half the combe were filled with golden fire to the cliff's edge. The side nearest to them was open grass, and fairly bristled with notice-boards.

'Fee—rocious old cove, this,' said Stalky, reading the nearest. '"Prosecuted with the utmost rigour of the law. G.M. Dabney, Col., J.P.," an' all the rest of it. 'Don't seem to me that any chap in his senses would trespass here, does it?'

'You've got to prove damage 'fore you can prosecute for anything! 'Can't prosecute for trespass,' said M'Turk, whose father held many acres in Ireland. 'That's all rot!'

"Glad of that, 'cause this looks like what we wanted. Not straight across, Beetle, you blind lunatic! Any one could spot us half a mile off. This way; and furl up your beastly butterfly-net.'

Beetle disconnected the ring, thrust the net into a pocket, shut up the handle to a two-foot stave, and slid the cane-ring round his waist. Stalky led inland to the wood, which was, perhaps, a quarter of a mile from the sea, and reached the fringe of the brambles.

'Now we can get straight down through the furze, and never show up at all,' said the tactician. 'Beetle, go ahead and explore. Snf! Snf! Beastly stink of fox somewhere!'

On all fours, save when he clung to his spectacles, Beetle wormed into the gorse, and presently announced between grunts of pain that he had found a very fair fox-track. This was well for Beetle, since Stalky pinched him *a tergo*. Down that tunnel they crawled. It was evidently a highway for the inhabitants of the combe; and, to their inexpressible joy, ended, at the very edge of the cliff, in a few square feet of dry turf walled and roofed with impenetrable gorse.

'By gum! There isn't a single thing to do except lie down,' said Stalky, returning a knife to his pocket. 'Look here!'

He parted the tough stems before him, and it was as a window opened on a far view of Lundy, and the deep sea sluggishly nosing the pebbles a couple of hundred feet below. They could hear young jackdaws squawking on the ledges, the hiss and jabber of a nest of hawks somewhere out of sight; and, with great deliberation, Stalky spat on to the back of a young rabbit sunning himself far down where only a cliff-rabbit could have found foot-hold. Great gray and black gulls screamed against the jackdaws; the heavy-scented acres of bloom round them were alive with low-nesting birds, singing or silent as the shadow of the wheeling hawks passed and returned; and on the naked turf across the combe rabbits thumped and frolicked.

'Whew! What a place! Talk of natural history; this is it,' said Stalky, filling himself a pipe. 'Isn't it scrumptious? Good old sea!' He spat again approvingly, and was silent.

['In Ambush', *Stalky & Co.*]

✖ ✖ ✖

LONDON

Nov. 11. An evil-evil day. Rose up in the morn at 9 and found the gloom of the Pit upon the land, a yellow fog through which the engines at Charing Cross whistled agonizedly one to the other and I could see the switch-boxes lit up with cheap and yellow gas when the electric light was manifestly needed. [. . .]

Then there came a fiendish darkness darker than any dust-storm and I had to light my reading lamp before lunch. That about finished me and I did no more but went out to the shop in the basement and got two whopping cherry wood pipes and enfolded myself in the mists of fancy; thinking out subjects to be written and dialogues to be touched up. My thoughts were about as valuable as the baccy smoke.

[Letter to Edmonia Hill, 8–16 November 1889]

✠ ✠ ✠

THE 'BUSES RUN TO Battersea,
    The 'buses run to Bow
The 'buses run to Westbourne Grove
    And Nottinghill also;
But I am sick of London town
    From Shepherd's Bush to Bow.

I see the smut upon my cuff
    And feel him on my nose;
I cannot leave my window wide
    When gentle zephyr blows,
Because he brings disgusting things
    And drops 'em on my 'clo'es'.

The sky, a greasy soup-toureen,
    Shuts down atop my brow.
Yes, I have sighed for London town
    And I have got it now:
And half of it is fog and filth,
    And half is fog and row.

And when I take my nightly prowl
    'Tis passing good to meet
The pious Briton lugging home
    His wife and daughter sweet,
Through four packed miles of seething vice
    Thrust out upon the street.

Earth holds no horror like to this
    In any land displayed,
From Suez unto Sandy Hook,
    From Calais to Port Said;
And 'twas to hide their heathendom
    The beastly fog was made.

I cannot tell when dawn is near,
 Or when the day is done,
Because I always see the gas
 And never see the sun,
And now, methinks, I do not care
 A cuss for either one.

But stay, there was an orange, or
 An aged egg its yolk;
It might have been a Pears' balloon
 Or Barnum's latest joke:
I took it for the sun and wept
 To watch it through the smoke.

It's Oh to see the morn ablaze
 Above the mango-tope,
When homeward through the dewy cane
 The little jackals lope,
And half Bengal heaves into view,
 New-washed – with sunlight soap.

It's Oh for one deep whisky peg
 When Christmas winds are blowing,
When all the men you ever knew,
 And all you've ceased from knowing,
Are 'entered for the Tournament,
 And everything that's going.'

But I consort with long-haired things
 In velvet collar-rolls,
Who talk about the Aims of Art,
 And 'theories' and 'goals,'
And moo and coo with women-folk
 About their blessed souls.

But that they call 'psychology'
 Is lack of liver pill,
And all that blights their tender souls

Is eating till they're ill,
And their chief way of winning goals
    Consists of sitting still.

It's Oh to meet an Army man,
    Set up, and trimmed and taut,
Who does not spout hashed libraries
    Or think the next man's thought,
And walks as though he owned himself,
    And hogs his bristles short.

Hear now, a voice across the seas
    To kin beyond my ken,
If ye have ever filled an hour
    With stories from my pen,
For pity's sake send some one here
    To bring me news of men!

The 'buses run to Islington,
    To Highgate and Soho,
To Hammersmith and Kew therewith
    And Camberwell also,
But I can only murmur ''Bus'
    From Shepherd's Bush to Bow.

['In Partibus', *Abaft the Funnel*]

❊   ❊   ❊

HE LEANED INTO THE darkness, watching the greater darkness
of London below him. The chambers stood much higher than
the other houses, commanding a hundred chimneys – crooked
cowls that looked like sitting cats as they swung round, and
other uncouth brick and zinc mysteries supported by iron
stanchions and clamped by 8-pieces. Northward the lights of
Piccadilly Circus and Leicester Square threw a copper-coloured
glare above the black roofs, and southward by all the orderly
lights of the Thames. A train rolled out across one of the railway

bridges, and its thunder drowned for a minute the dull roar of the streets. The Nilghai looked at his watch and said shortly, 'That's the Paris night-mail. You can book from here to St. Petersburg if you choose.'

[*The Light That Failed*]

✂ ✂ ✂

SUSSEX

God gave all men all earth to love,
    But since our hearts are small,
Ordained for each one spot should prove
    Belovèd over all;
That, as He watched Creation's birth,
    So we, in godlike mood,
May of our love create our earth
    And see that it is good.

So one shall Baltic pines content,
    As one some Surrey glade,
Or one the palm-grove's droned lament
    Before Levuka's Trade.
Each to his choice, and I rejoice
    The lot has fallen to me
In a fair ground – in a fair ground –
    Yea, Sussex by the sea!

No tender-hearted garden crowns,
    No bosomed woods adorn
Our blunt, bow-headed, whale-backed Downs,
    But gnarled and writhen thorn –
Bare slopes where chasing shadows skim,
    And, through the gaps revealed,
Belt upon belt, the wooded, dim,
    Blue goodness of the Weald.

Clean of officious fence or hedge,
    Half-wild and wholly tame,
The wise turf cloaks the white cliff edge
    As when the Romans came.
What sign of those that fought and died
    At shift of sword and sword?
The barrow and the camp abide,
    The sunlight and the sward.

Here leaps ashore the full Sou'west
    All heavy-winged with brine,
Here lies above the folded crest
    The Channel's leaden line;
And here the sea-fogs lap and cling,
    And here, each warning each,
The sheep-bells and the ship-bells ring
    Along the hidden beach.

We have no waters to delight
    Our broad and brookless vales –
Only the dewpond on the height
    Unfed, that never fails –
Whereby no tattered herbage tells
    Which way the season flies –
Only our close-bit thyme that smells
    Like dawn in Paradise.

Here through the strong and shadeless days
    The tinkling silence thrills;
Or little, lost, Down churches praise
    The Lord who made the hills:
But here the Old Gods guard their round,
    And, in her secret heart,
The heathen kingdom Wilfrid found
    Dreams, as she dwells, apart.

Though all the rest were all my share,
    With equal soul I'd see

Her nine-and-thirty sisters fair,
    Yet none more fair than she.
Choose ye your need from Thames to Tweed,
    And I will choose instead
Such lands as lie 'twixt Rake and Rye,
    Black Down and Beachy Head.

I will go out against the sun
    Where the rolled scarp retires,
And the Long Man of Wilmington
    Looks naked toward the shires;
And east till doubling Rother crawls
    To find the fickle tide,
By dry and sea-forgotten walls,
    Our ports of stranded pride.

I will go north about the shaws
    And the deep ghylls that breed
Huge oaks and old, the which we hold
    No more than Sussex weed;
Or south where windy Piddinghoe's
    Begilded dolphin veers
And red beside wide-bankèd Ouse
    Lie down our Sussex steers.

So to the land our hearts we give
    Till the sure magic strike,
And Memory, Use, and Love make live
    Us and our fields alike –
That deeper than our speech and thought,
    Beyond our reason's sway,
Clay of the pit whence we were wrought
    Yearns to its fellow-clay.

God gives all men all earth to love,
    But since man's heart is small,
Ordains for each one spot shall prove
    Beloved over all.

> Each to his choice, and I rejoice
>   The lot has fallen to me
> In a fair ground – in a fair ground –
>   Yea, Sussex by the sea!

[*The Five Nations*]

✷ ✷ ✷

THEY WERE FISHING, A few days later, in the bed of the brook that for centuries had cut deep into the soft valley soil. The trees closing overhead made long tunnels through which the sunshine worked in blobs and patches. Down in the tunnels were bars of sand and gravel, old roots and trunks covered with moss or painted red by the irony water; foxgloves growing lean and pale towards the light; clumps of fern and thirsty shy flowers who could not live away from moisture and shade. In the pools you could see the wave thrown up by the trouts as they charged hither and yon, and the pools were joined to each other – except in flood-time, when all was one brown rush – by sheets of thin broken water that poured themselves chuckling round the darkness of the next bend.

This was one of the children's most secret hunting-grounds, and their particular friend, old Hobden the hedger, had shown them how to use it. Except for the click of a rod hitting a low willow, or a switch and tussle among the young ash leaves as a line hung up for the minute, nobody in the hot pasture could have guessed what game was going on among the trouts below the banks.

['Young Men at the Manor', *Puck of Pook's Hill*]

SOUTH DOWNS

ONE VIEW CALLED ME to another; one hill top to its fellow, half across the county, and since I could answer at no more trouble than the snapping forward of a lever, I let the county flow under my wheels. The orchid-studded flats of the East gave way to the thyme, ilex, and grey grass of the Downs; these again to the rich cornland and fig-trees of the lower coast, where you carry the beat of the tide on your left hand for fifteen level miles; and when at last I turned inland through a huddle of rounded hills and woods I had run myself clean out of my known marks. Beyond that precise hamlet which stands godmother to the capital of the United States, I found hidden villages where bees, the only things awake, boomed in eighty-foot lindens that overhung grey Norman churches; miraculous brooks diving under stone bridges built for heavier traffic than would ever vex them again; tithe-barns larger than their churches, and an old smithy that cried out aloud how it had once been a hall of the Knights of the Temple. Gipsies I found on a common where the gorse, bracken, and heath fought it out together up a mile of Roman road; and a little further on I disturbed a red fox rolling dog-fashion in the naked sunlight.

As the wooded hills closed about me I stood up in the car to take the bearings of that great Down whose ringed head is a landmark for fifty miles across the low countries. I judged that the lie of the country would bring me across some westward running road that went to his feet, but I did not allow for the confusing veils of the woods. A quick turn plunged me first into a green cutting brimful of liquid sunshine, next into a gloomy tunnel where last year's dead leaves whispered and scuffled about my tyres. The strong hazel stuff meeting overhead had not been cut for a couple of generations at least, nor had any axe helped the moss-cankered oak and beech to spring above them. Here the road changed frankly into a carpeted ride on whose brown velvet spent primrose-clumps showed like jade, and a few sickly, white-stalked blue-bells nodded together. As the slope favoured I shut off the power and slid over the whirled leaves, expecting every moment to meet a keeper; but I only

heard a jay, far off, arguing against the silence under the twilight
of the trees.

['They', *Traffics and Discoveries*]

✻ ✻ ✻

SURREY

THERE RUNS A ROAD by Merrow Down –
    A grassy track to-day it is –
An hour out of Guildford town,
    Above the river Wey it is.

Here, when they heard the horse-bells ring,
    The ancient Britons dressed and rode
To watch the dark Phoenicians bring
    Their goods along the Western Road.

Yes, here, or hereabouts, they met
    To hold their racial talks and such –
To barter beads for Whitby jet,
    And tin for gay shell torques and such.

But long and long before that time
    (When bison used to roam on it)
Did Taffy and her Daddy climb
    That Down, and had their home on it.

Then beavers built in Broadstonebrook
    And made a swamp where Bramley stands;
And bears from Shere would come and look
    For Taffimai where Shamley stands.

The Way, that Taffy called Wagai,
    Was more than six times bigger then;
And all the Tribe of Tegumai
    They cut a noble figure then!

[from 'Merrow-Down', *Songs from Books*]

YORKSHIRE

'It's along o' yon hill there,' said Learoyd, watching the bare sub-Himalayan spur that reminded him of his Yorkshire moors. He was speaking more to himself than his fellows. 'Ay,' said he, 'Rumbolds Moor stands up ower Skipton town, an' Greenhow Hill stands up ower Pately Brig. I reckon you've never heeard tell o' Greenhow Hill, but yon bit o' bare stuff if there was nobbut a white road windin' is like ut; strangely like. Moors an' moors an' moors, wi' never a tree for shelter, an' gray houses wi' flagstone rooves, and pewits cryin', an' a windhover goin' to and fro just like these kites. And cold! A wind that cuts you like a knife. You could tell Greenhow Hill folk by the red-apple colour o' their cheeks an' nose tips, and their blue eyes, driven into pin-points by the wind. Miners mostly, burrowin' for lead i' th' hillsides, followin' the trail of th' ore vein same as a field-rat. It was the roughest minin' I ever seen. Yo'd come on a bit o' creakin' wood windlass like a well-head, an' you was let down i' th' bight of a rope, fendin' yoursen off the side wi' one hand, carryin' a candle stuck in a lump o' clay with t'other, an' clickin' hold of a rope with t'other hand.'

'An' that's three of them,' said Mulvaney. 'Must be a good climate in those parts.'

Learoyd took no heed.

'An' then yo' came to a level, where you crept on your hands and knees through a mile o' windin' drift, an' you come out into a cave-place as big as Leeds Townhall, with a engine pumpin' water from workin's 'at went deeper still. It's a queer country, let alone minin', for the hill is full of those natural caves, an' the rivers an' the becks drops into what they call pot-holes, an' come out again miles away.'

['On Greenhow Hill', *The Courting of Dinah Shadd and Other Stories*]

DURHAM

DURHAM HAS ALWAYS HAD schools in its midst but has only been a university for the past 70 years. However the enormous age of town and cathedral make one forget this little accident. Next morning C. and I went over the cathedral, the most impressive to my mind of any I have seen. It is practically all Norman – brute, massive Norman – thick pillars, round headed arches and an air of weight and strength that hits you between the eyes. The tombs of Cuthbert and of the venerable Bede are both there and in the library is a marvellous manuscript supposed to have been written by Bede's own hand. I specially wanted to see it and I did. Also there is a fragment – over a thousand years old – of some gold embroidery on S. Cuthbert's robe, as fresh and dainty as the day it was done. And there is a practical joke of a huge pillar in the transept encised like this. If you look at it from the right, it seems to be falling over to the right; if from the left, to the left. Only seen from directly in front does it appear vertical. The trick is in the V shaped decoration and there were many other marvels beside.

[Letter to Anna Smith Balestier, 30 June 1907]

❖ ❖ ❖

TORQUAY

Now IMAGINE TO YOURSELF, a big stone and stucco Naulakha, long, low with two storeys, stuck on the side of a steep hill falling away almost as sharply as the lower slopes of Wantastiquetz to a hundred foot cliff of pure red soil. Below that is the sea, about two hundred yards from the window. The effect is a delightful mixture of land and sea views. I look straight from my work-table on to the decks of the fishing craft who come in to look after their lobster pots. There isn't another house in sight; there is no harbour or landing place or anything of the kind. We just sit like swallows on a telegraph wire and look across Torbay over

to Portland Bill sixty miles away. Somewhere round the corner,
four miles north, lies Teignmouth (which they naturally call Tin-
muth) and three miles south the rocky nose that covers Torquay
harbour. It is marked by a rocky island called – of all queer names
under heaven – Thatcher Island. If you keep Thatcher Island two
points clear of your port bow on coming out of the harbour you
clear, say the sailing directions, all shoals along the west side of
Torbay. The said 'shoals' take the shape of peculiarly devilish
half-tide rocks round which the whiting and pollack congregate.
Our beach is a tiny cove reached by an almost perpendicular
lane – just the place for smuggling in the old days – and a flight
of rude steps. It isn't a wholesome place to look at because the
cliffs have a knack of falling in huge boulders and there is no way
of getting to the water except by crawling over them. I found out
the peculiarity of the place by going down after a heavy gale:
when I found that the heavy seas had cleaned out most of the
sand between the boulders and utterly changed the lie of the
land. No one seems to go there except myself and the fishers:
for now and then I find footprints in the sand and the mark of a
row boat's keel. Once down in the cove with the cliffs on either
side it is as warm as a conservatory and as lonely as Land's End.
The queerest thing about the place is its rich redness. The grass
and trees come down literally to the water's edge but all the soil
is pure red; and the mixture of red, green foliage and blue sea is
splendid. I never saw such an unEnglish place in my life: though
almost our first introduction to it was a good old equinoctial – a
sou'westerly buster that would have done credit to Vermont.
The glass dropped about an inch and then began pumping up
and down. The wind took about a day to get up and when it
really took hold, it licked the channel up into lather. A big poplar
on our lawn (it was a regular old cotton-wood just the same as
if it had followed us) was the first to go. The wind twisted the
top out of it. Then our back-gate was sent flying: and then a
huge elm came over by the roots and nearly assassinated a hired
yellow cow we keep in the meadow.

[Letter to James M. Conland, 1–6 October 1896]

✠ ✠ ✠

WINCHESTER

WE LEFT – IT seems incredible – Bateman's on Saturday morn
the 3rd and went, in a day that might have come out of July
– to Winchester for lunch and to see the Baker War Memorial
– a four-sided cloister – to the dead Wykehamists. So far as my
knowledge and experience of Memorials goes, this is quite the
most exquisite, beautiful, powerful and moving thing that has
ever been done in that line. I can't describe it in words. You
must, some day, go and look at it for yourself. It's worth a trip
even in a train. And then we went on at evening (having tea by
the wayside on a down) to Salisbury and the White Hart has
been severely modernized, eased of its many and curious smells
and furnished, as the advts say with 'continuous hot water,' in
the rooms. Note also (this is due to the scarcity of labour) one
has gas-metre fires in the rooms now. No calling a maid to light
a fire. Drop in your shilling and you're off. The food on the journey has been continuously bad and of one tough standard. Well,
we went and saw the cathedral both late in the day and early on
Sunday morn. Both lovely.

[Letter to Elsie Bambridge, 5 October 1925]

✠ ✠ ✠

GREAT NORTH ROAD

DAYLIGHT WAS JUST ON the heels of dawn, with the sun following. The icy-blackness of the Great North Road banded itself with
smoking mists that changed from solid pearl to writhing opal,
as they lifted above hedge-row level. The dew-wet leaves of the
upper branches turned suddenly into diamond facets, and that
wind, which runs before the actual upheaval of the sun, swept
out of the fragrant lands to the East, and touched my cheek – as

many times it had touched it before, on the edge, or at the ends, of inconceivable experiences.

My companion breathed deeply, while the low glare searched the folds of his coat and the sags and wrinkles of his face. We heard the far-away pulse of a car through the infinite, clean-born, light-filled stillness. It neared and stole round the bend – a motor-hearse on its way to some early or distant funeral, one side of the bright oak coffin showing beneath the pall, which had slipped a little. Then it vanished in a blaze of wet glory from the sun-drenched road, amid the songs of a thousand birds.

['The Prophet and the Country', *Debits and Credits*]

✠ ✠ ✠

BEAUFORT CASTLE

ON OUR WAY BACK to Inverness we put in for tea at Beaufort Castle. Lord Lovat was out but she was very kind and showed us – perhaps you know it – the amazing herbaceous garden half a mile across the Park surrounded by an old rose-pink wall fifteen feet high. There's a canalized burn runs through it, on a curve, and the whole arena was one pageant of colour – cosmos, clarkias, monthetias, chrysanths, salvia, etc. etc. the whole of the children of the autumn massed and countermassed beside strips of ancient velvet turf, all in order and all waiting for their death. The frost was in the air when we left and she said it was the garden's last day. Next morn, when we got to Inverness (Sunday) the white frost was just melting off the roofs of the city.

[Letter to Mrs E.W. Hussey, 21 September 1921]

IRELAND

THEN DUBLIN IN THE evening – warm, soft and full of black smoke but devil a taxi at the station, only horse-drawn nuisances, with rubber tyres and a smell of horse-dung and stable blankets that took one back to the middle ages. (The car-drivers of Dublin will not permit petrol in any form). So we filed out of the station, which was also a manure pit at, at least, four miles an hour and got to an hotel which (now this is curious) smelt exactly like a U.S. hotel. So did all Dublin and one realized how potent is the Irish esprit de corps. The people in the streets spat joyously (after the manner of the U.S.) and were just as casual and inexact and interested-in-their-own-affairs-at-the-time-they-were-supposed-to-be-on-duty as any citizen of the U.S. Thus we saw the very egg whence the Eastern U.S. was born. [. . .]

And the next day was hot and sunny and soft as a South Irish accent. We loafed into Trinity College quad and spent a couple of hours watching the come and go of students and professors in and out of the soft grey-black buildings: went to the library – unkempt and unswept – saw the Book of Kells and certain other M.S. that I was keen on but it was enough merely to move about the grey quad and the soft green gardens in a sub-tropical atmosphere. Everything outside that limit looked and smelt like a deboshed U.S. (truly a little leaven . . .)

Then next day by automobile from Dublin to Belfast via Balbriggan, Drogheda, Dundalk, Newry, Lisburn through a hand-fed government-aided land of damnably inartistic cottages – for which I am taxed by the way – of expensive make and eye-blistering design. And the only return these fashion-less creatures made for it to me, in a hireling motor halting at four muddy cross roads, was to erect a sign-post in Erse – in Gaelic – or whatever they called it. [. . .] I don't know why it made me so hopping mad – but it did. To waste money on an ingrate and to have him jabber at you in an unknown tongue just when you wanted a simple direction. . . . . And what made me madder was the land's blatant unloveliness wherever man had set his mark on it! They couldn't spoil the green or the sombre superb autumn colouring as we saw it through open and shut mists but their houses – their plantless, gardenless, unkempt workhouse-like cottages and villas – and their own personal aridity of culture! Allah must needs make them poets (and they insist on letting us know that they all are poets) for surely He has deprived them of love of line or knowledge of colour. Again a U.S. trait for village after village was but the Irish patch in a New England town. And most of the folk had new strong red-painted carts and good tools which I would have admired more had I not spent half the evening before with an official of some Govt department or other for 'encouraging agriculture' and I noticed how the man was, so to speak, carried away by the lust of administration, debauched by the people he was hired to help so that it seemed to him right and holy to supply them with good houses, tools, manures and the deuce knows what else, on the easiest terms, because they were incompetent and had been improvident, and he 'hopeth to raise them in the scale'. Maybe I grow harder-hearted in my middle age but it all seemed so false and unsound.

Then we got into the North and the car literally bumped into a new country of decent folk, unadorned by Government cottages and new red carts. [. . .] The talk was familiar and so was the decent, unaccommodating Northern type of face: the modelling of cheek and jaw-bone and by the time we ran into the roar and rush of Belfast I was comforted.

[Letter to Andrew Macphail, 21 October 1911]

🗙 🗙 🗙

ENGLISH CHANNEL

OF THE ENGLISH SOUTH-COAST Lights, that of St. Cecilia-under-the-Cliff is the most powerful, for it guards a very foggy coast. When the sea-mist veils all, St. Cecilia turns a hooded head to the sea and sings a song of two words once every minute. From the land that song resembles the bellowing of a brazen bull; but off-shore they understand, and the steamers grunt gratefully in answer.

Fenwick, who was on duty one night, lent me a pair of black glass spectacles, without which no man can look at the Light unblinded, and busied himself in last touches to the lenses before twilight fell. The width of the English Channel beneath us lay as smooth and as many-coloured as the inside of an oyster shell. A little Sunderland cargoboat had made her signal to Lloyd's Agency, half a mile up the coast, and was lumbering down to the sunset, her wake lying white behind her. One star came out over the cliffs, the waters turned to lead colour, and St. Cecilia's Light shot out across the sea in eight long pencils that wheeled slowly from right to left, melted into one beam of solid light laid down directly in front of the tower, dissolved again into eight, and passed away. The light-frame of the thousand lenses circled on its rollers, and the compressed-air engine that drove it hummed like a bluebottle under a glass. The hand of the indicator on the wall pulsed from mark to mark. Eight pulse-beats timed one half-revolution of the Light; neither more nor less.

['The Disturber of Traffic', *Many Inventions*]

✠ ✠ ✠

OUR BROWS ARE BOUND with spindrift and the weed is on our
   knees;
Our loins are battered 'neath us by the swinging, smoking seas.
From reef and rock and skerry – over headland, ness, and voe –
The Coastwise Lights of England watch the ships of England
   go!

Through the endless summer evenings, on the lineless, level
   floors;
Through the yelling Channel tempest when the siren hoots and
   roars –
By day the dipping house-flag and by night the rocket's trail –
As the sheep that graze behind us so we know them where they
   hail.
We bridge across the dark and bid the helmsman have a care,

The flash that wheeling inland wakes his sleeping wife to
    prayer;
From our vexed eyries, head to gale, we bind in burning chains
The lover from the sea-rim drawn – his love in English lanes.

We greet the clippers wing-and-wing that race the Southern
    wool;
We warn the crawling cargo-tanks of Bremen, Leith, and Hull;
To each and all our equal lamp at peril of the sea –
The white wall-sided war-ships or the whalers of Dundee!

Come up, come in from Eastward, from the guardports of the
    Morn!
Beat up, beat in from Southerly, O gipsies of the Horn!
Swift shuttles of an Empire's loom that weave us, main to main,
The Coastwise Lights of England give you welcome back again!

Go, get you gone up-Channel with the sea-crust on your plates;
Go, get you into London with the burden of your freights!
Haste, for they talk of Empire there, and say, if any seek,
The Lights of England sent you and by silence shall ye speak!

['The Coastwise Lights', *The Seven Seas*]

✺ 5 ✺

EUROPE

Cradle of Good Living

France – French Roads – Rouen – Chartres – Camargue – Vernet-les-Bains – Port-Vendres – Florence – Italian Alps – Belgium – Seville – Gibraltar – Marienbad.

After he became rich, Kipling was able to indulge his passion for Europe. His first love was France – the legacy of a visit to the Paris Exhibition with his father in 1878. As a lifelong Francophile, he later liked to be driven around France in his Rolls Royce, making use of the practical layout of the French road system, originally introduced by Napoleon.

The selections here reflect the places he visited in France and elsewhere on the Continent. Having been to Italy (Venice, Florence and other cities) before the First World War, he returned during the conflict to write forceful propaganda articles about the Italian campaign against the Austrians in the Alps. He came to know Belgium through his work for the War Graves Commission, as recalled in his poignant story 'The Gardener'. Spain and Gibraltar were also post-war points of call, partly because his son-in-law George Bambridge worked at the British Embassy in Madrid. For health reasons, Kipling, late in his life, visited a spa at Marienbad in Czechoslovakia, taking care to avoid spending too long en route in Germany.

FRANCE

In the spring of the Paris Exhibition of 1878 my father was in charge of the Indian Section of Arts and Manufactures there, and it was his duty to arrange them as they arrived. He promised me, then twelve or thirteen years old, that I should accompany him to Paris on condition that I gave no trouble. The democracy of an English School had made that easy.

Our happy expedition crossed the Channel in a steamer, I think, made of two steamers attached to each other side by side. (Was it the old Calais–Douvres designed to prevent seasickness which even the gods themselves cannot do?) And, late at night, we came to a boarding-house full of English people at the back of the Parc Monceau. In the morning, when I had waked to the divine smell of roasting coffee and the bell-like call of the marchand-d'habits, my father said in effect, 'I shall be busy every day for some time. Here is —' I think it was two francs. 'There are lots of restaurants, all called Duval, where you can eat. I will get you a free pass for the Exhibition and you can go where you please.' Then he was swallowed by black-coated officials and workmen in blouses.

Imagine the delight of a child let loose among all the wonders of all the world as they emerged from packing-cases, free to enter every unfinished building that was being raised round an edifice called the Trocadero, and to pass at all times through gates in wooden barricades behind which workmen put up kiosques and pavilions, or set out plants and trees! At first, these genial deep-voiced men asked questions, but after a few days no one looked at my pass, and I considered myself an accepted fly on this great wheel of colour and smells and sights, all revolving to a ceaseless mitraille of hammers and machinery. My father, too, had been entirely correct as to this Monsieur Duval. His restaurants were everywhere in Paris; his satisfying déjeuners cost exactly one franc. There were also, if one had made the necessary economies, celestial gingerbreads to be bought everywhere.

[*Souvenirs of France*]

✠ ✠ ✠

FRENCH ROADS

'The National Roads of France are numbered throughout, and carry their numbers upon each kilometre stone. By following these indications, comprehensible even to strangers, the tourist can see at a glance if he is on the correct road. For example, Route Nationale No.20 conducts from Paris to the Spanish frontier at Bourg-Madame, in the Eastern Pyrenees; and No.10 to the same frontier at Hendaye, on the Bay of Biscay.' – GUIDE BOOK.

NOW PRAISE THE GODS of Time and Chance
    That bring a heart's desire,
And lay the joyous roads of France
    Once more beneath the tyre –
So numbered by Napoleon,
    The veriest ass can spy
How Twenty takes to Bourg-Madame
    And Ten is for Hendaye.

Sixteen hath fed our fighting-line
    From Dunkirk to Péronne,
And Thirty-nine and Twenty-nine
    Can show where it has gone,
Which slant through Arras and Bapaume,
    And join outside Cambrai,
While Twenty takes to Bourg-Madame,
    And Ten is for Hendaye.

The crops and houses spring once more
    Where Thirty-seven ran,
And even ghostly Forty-four

Is all restored to man.
Oh, swift as shell-hole poppies pass
    The blurring years go by,
And Twenty takes to Bourg-Madame,
    And Ten is for Hendaye!

And you desire that sheeted snow
    Where chill Mont Louis stands?
And we the rounder gales that blow
    Full-lunged across the Landes –
So you will use the Orleans Gate,
    While we slip through Versailles;
Since Twenty takes to Bourg-Madame,
    And Ten is for Hendaye.

Sou'-West by South – and South by West –
    On every vine appear
Those four first cautious leaves that test
    The temper of the year;
The dust is white at Angoulême,
    The sun is warm at Blaye;
And Twenty takes to Bourg-Madame,
    And Ten is for Hendaye.

Broad and unbridled, mile on mile,
    The highway drops her line
Past Langon down that grey-walled aisle
    Of resin-scented pine;
And ninety to the lawless hour
    The kilometres fly –
What was your pace to Bourg-Madame?
    We sauntered to Hendaye.

Now Fontarabia marks our goal,
    And Bidassoa shows,
At issue with each whispering shoal
    In violet, pearl and rose,
Ere crimson over ocean's edge

The sunset banners die . . .
Yes – Twenty takes to Bourg-Madame,
But Ten is for Hendaye!

Oh, praise the Gods of Time and Chance
That ease the long control,
And bring the glorious soul of France
Once more to cheer our soul
With beauty, change and valiancy
Of sun and soil and sky,
Where Twenty takes to Bourg-Madame,
And Ten is for Hendaye!

[*Rudyard Kipling's Verse*]

✠ ✠ ✠

ROUEN

AND SO ROUEN IN an hour and a half. My Lord! What a Doré
view of the town and the spires and the looping river from the
hill above! All done with a silver-point in that thin clean air. – All
the hotels of France are under strong reparation and expansion
(this comes of not paying your lawful debts) so that stinks of
paint and petrol mix with the smell of the upright citizen on all
the floors and chased us to our bedroom where, by the way, the
lock stuck till the maid rescued us! 'Tis a prosperous land and
so cheers me when I think how ungodly prosperous the Hun
is. Hotel 9/10th void but the streets busy. Went off at once to
Rouen Cemetery (11,000 graves) and collogued with the Head
Gardener and the contractors. One never gets over the shock
of this Dead Sea of arrested lives – from VC's and Hospital
Nurses to coolies of the Chinese Labour Corps. [. . .] Then the
Cathedral which I can't love as much as I ought to do, except
Joan of Arc's chapel. That Young Lady by the way seems to be
rapidly displacing the Deity throughout France. Do you know
that St Joseph – most accommodating of all spouses – is always
the first of the Saints to be 'demobilized' in favour of the latest

cult. But, all the same, I did my penance, bare-headed, at the Market above the place where Joan was burned. Also, lit my candles to her in the Cathedral – same as I did at Rheims when the Huns were bombarding. And this morn (time always seems long when you travel) the day broke down in foul rain and wet and we went for St Andelys (switchbacking in mist and feature-shrouding rain) across the big hogsbacks and into the wooded valleys 'twixt river and river. A large-boned country – rather like a giant's hunting-field, and fun to take at top-speed. Lunched in the hotellized remnant of a XVIth century chateau (and jolly good grub). Then the Cathedral which has some decent XIV century glass. *Colour, old man, is what, au fond, clinches a creed.* Colour and the light of God behind it. That's as near as Man will ever get. Then by side roads (you ought to have seen me reading the map) and by my faultless guidance we crashed into Evreux whose Cathedral is a wonder – but not *the* wonder; and thence to Dreux – more gothic and sparser; and at last in the tail of a dripping day to Chartres – the great blue-grey bulk of the Cathedral dominating, it seemed, half France. Our old hotel had been modernized, to our immense wrath, and, like Rouen, was full of ouvriers, paint, petrol and noises. Got into the Cathedral – on the very last fading of the twilight and it was as though one moved within the heart of a Jewel of the Faith. You know the inexpressible colour glories of Chartres – all the windows superb and some without flaw or blemish in any aspect. Last time I'd seen it the glass was all out, because of bombings by the Hun. Now all the glories were returned – rose window and all – and in that last few minutes of darkness overcoming day, the windows burned and glowed like the souls of martyrs. Don't know when I've been more touched in the deeps.

[Letter to Sir Henry Rider Haggard, 14 March 1925]

✠ ✠ ✠

CHARTRES

COLOUR FULFILS WHERE MUSIC has no power:
  By each man's light the unjudging glass betrays
All men's surrender, each man's holiest hour
  And all the lit confusion of our days –
Purfled with iron, traced in dusk and fire,
  Challenging ordered Time who, at the last,
  Shall bring it, grozed and leaded and wedged fast,
  To the cold stone that curbs or crowns desire.
Yet on the pavement that all feet have trod –
  Even as the Spirit, in her deeps and heights,
Turns only, and that voiceless, to her God –
  There falls no tincture from those anguished lights.
And Heaven's one light, behind them, striking through
Blazons what each man dreamed no other knew.

['Chartres Windows', *Rudyard Kipling's Verse*]

✠ ✠ ✠

CAMARGUE

WESTWARD FROM A TOWN by the Mouths of the Rhône, runs a road so mathematically straight, so barometrically level, that it ranks among the world's measured miles and motorists use it for records.

I had attacked the distance several times, but always with a Mistral blowing, or the unchancy cattle of those parts on the move. But once, running from the East, into a high-piled, almost Egyptian, sunset, there came a night which it would have been sin to have wasted. It was warm with the breath of summer in advance; moonlit till the shadow of every rounded pebble and pointed cypress wind-break lay solid on that vast flat-floored waste; and my Mr. Leggatt, who had slipped out to make sure, reported that the road surface was unblemished.

['The Bull That Thought', *Debits and Credits*]

✠ ✠ ✠

VERNET-LES-BAINS

WE HAVE HAD RATHER an interesting little trip. Lord Montague of Beaulieu – the great motor man – came here on Monday with a sixty horse power Rolls-Royce 6-cylinder car and took us for a little run to get lunch at a place called Mont Louis. We saw it on the map but did not in the least realize how high it was. It was more than 5400 feet above the sea. Down here, which is only 2000 feet it was warm and dusty. We climbed along a road built on the sides of the mountains [. . .] and at last we found bits of drifted snow on the road and the air got cooler. Then we came to a sheet of ice on the road and got up to a huge stone fort on the top of a mountain. We entered it through a stone gateway (see postcards) and found a tiny little street where the snow was lying swept up 4 feet high. All round us were plains of snow that looked like good ski-ing ground. We had lunch at a funny little hotel and then we went on three miles to a place called Col-du-Perche to get a view into Spain (we weren't eight miles from the frontier). Then, almost in a minute, we ran into deep snow and had to go along roads where the snow was six feet high on each side of us and the car was up to its axles in the drifts. Then we saw people ski-ing, just like Engelberg, and we wanted to take their skis away and play ourselves. The railway line was all snowed up and they said they didn't expect it to be thawed out for weeks. Well, then we ran back to Vernet in a little more than one hour and the sensation as we came down was a very funny one – like dropping in a balloon. Our mouths got dry and our ears popped and sang. But wasn't it queer – to climb into mountains and meet old winter again.

[Letter to John Kipling, 9 March 1910]

✠ ✠ ✠

PORT-VENDRES

THEN THE MEDITERRANEAN HOVE up, all sapphire, with a shark's fin of a lateen sail here and there and a rip or two of white wave tops before the wind, and forty-foot palms (they looked like date palms) waving in the hollows of the hills against the coast. We lunched at Port-Vendres – a large Catalan lunch – but I made my meal chiefly of Bouillabaisse. Never met it before: never knew it could be so perfect – specially the sauce of pale yellow with slices of bread soaked in it. And the fish seemed to have been out of the water less than an hour. I noted the local fishing boats, that they are fully decked and the deck has a camber more steep than that of the old fashioned torpedo boats. Tremendous timbers too for their size, knees and deck beams out of all proportion: so that they can stand unlimited hammering and with the hatches closed should be as tight as the bottle that they resemble in section. The sail stuff very poor – like cotton. I think the system of painting 'em makes it easy for every family to spot its own boat coming in, at the extreme limit of vision. Also the head of the mast with the pulley in it is this shape and painted as gaily as a fishing float. All thoroughly effective and workmanlike and evolved by the attrition of wind, water and rock.

[Letter to Colonel H.W. Feilden, 15–19 March 1911]

✠ ✠ ✠

FLORENCE

YOU ASK WHAT FLORENCE is like. It's beautiful – miles more beautiful than Rome, and we'll send you some postcards to prove it. It lies all among low hills at the foot of the Apennines (kindly consult Dicker to see if I have put in enough n's!) and the hills are covered with white and pink and grey villas and cypress trees and olives, mixed up with vineyards and cultivated fields and here and there an almond tree in blossom from head to foot. You know, the grass does not wither in winter at Florence. It just stops growing for a few weeks but stays as green as before.

February here comes to about the same as April at home. There are great pink and white anemones growing wild in the grass and the rose trees are sprouting, the lilac is in bud and yesterday we saw the first irises in bloom in the English cemetery [. . .] The air is beautifully light and springy and on a fine day with a hot sun shining one feels as though one were drinking champagne that did not give one a head. The River Arno runs through the town and the houses come slap down into the river just like the pictures of Venice.

[Letter to John Kipling, 21 February 1912]

🏵 🏵 🏵

ITALIAN ALPS

WHEN ONE REACHED THE great Venetian plain near Army Headquarters, the Italian fronts were explained with a clearness that made maps unnecessary.

'We have three fronts,' said my informant. 'On the first, the Isonzo front, which is the road to Trieste, our troops can walk, though the walking is not good. On the second, the Trentino, to the north, where the enemy comes nearest to our plains, our troops must climb and mountaineer, you will see.'

He pointed south-east and east across the heat haze to some evil-looking ridges a long way off where there was a sound of guns debating ponderously. 'That is the Carso, where we are going now,' he said; then he turned north-east and north where nearer, higher mountains showed streaks of snow in their wrinkles.

'Those are the Julian Alps,' he went on. 'Tolmino is behind them, north again. Where the snow is thicker – do you see? – are the Carnic Alps; we fight among them. Then to the west of them come the Dolomites, where tourists used to climb and write books. There we fight, also. The Dolomites join on to the Trentino and the Asiago Plateau, and there we fight. And from there we go round north till we meet the Swiss border. All mountains, you see.'

He picked up the peaks one after another with the ease of a man accustomed to pick up landmarks at any angle and any change of light. A stranger's eyes could make out nothing except one sheer rampart of brooding mountains – 'like giants at a hunting' – all along the northern horizon.

The glass split them into tangled cross-chains of worsted hillocks, hollow-flanked peaks cleft by black or grey ravines, stretches of no-coloured rock gashed and nicked with white, savage thumbnails of hard snow thrust up above cockscombs of splinters, and behind everything an agony of tortured crags against the farthest sky. Men must be borne or broke to the mountains to accept them easily. They are too full of their own personal devils.

The plains around Udine are better – the fat, flat plains crowded with crops – wheat and barley patches between trim vineyards, every vine with her best foot forwards and arms spread to welcome spring. Every field hedged with old, strictly pollarded mulberry-trees for the silkworms, and every road flanked with flashing water-channels that talk pleasantly in the heart.

At each few score yards of road there was a neat square of limestone road-metal, with the water-channel led squarely round it. Each few hundred yards, an old man and a young boy worked together, the one with a long spade, the other with a tin pot at the end of a pole. The instant that any wear showed in the surface, the elder padded the hollow with a spoonful of metal, the youth sluiced it, and at once it was ready to bind down beneath the traffic as tight as an inner-tube patch.

There was curiously little traffic by our standards, but all there was moved very swiftly. The perfectly made and tended roads do most of the motor's work. Where there are no bumps there can be no strain, even under maximum loads. The lorries glide from railhead to their destination, return, and are off again without overhaul or delay. On the simple principle that transportation is civilisation, the entire Italian campaign is built, and every stretch of every road proves it.

But on the French front Providence does not supply accommodating river-beds whence the beautiful self-binding stuff can be shovelled ready-made into little narrow-gauge trucks all over the landscape. Nor have we in France solid mountains where man has but to reach out his hand to all the stone of all the pyramids. Neither, anywhere, have we populations expert from birth at masonry. To parody Macaulay, what the axe is to the Canadian, what the bamboo is to the Malay, what the snow-block is to the Esqimaux, stone and cement is to the Italian, as I hope to show later.

They are a hard people habituated to handling hard stuffs, and, I should imagine, with a sense of property as keen as the Frenchman's. The innumerable grey-green troops in the bright fields moved sympathetically among the crops and did not litter their surroundings with rubbish. They have their own pattern of steel helmet, which differs a little from ours, and gives them at a distance a look of Roman Legionaires on a frieze of triumph. The infantry and, to a less extent, other arms are not recruited locally but generally, so that the men from all parts come to know each other, and losses are more evenly spread. But the size, physique, and, above all, the poise of the men struck one at every step. They seem more supple in their collective movements and less loaded down with haberdashery than either French or British troops. But the indescribable difference lay in their tread – the very fall of their feet and the manner in which they seemed to possess the ground they covered. Men whose life runs normally in the open own and are owned by their surroundings more naturally than those whom climate and trade keep housed through most of the year. Space, sunlight, and air, the procession of life under vivid skies, furnish the Italian with a great deal of his mental background, so when, as a soldier, he is bidden to sit down in the clean dust and be still as the hours while the shells pass, he does so as naturally as an Englishman draws a chair to the fire.

'And that is the Isonzo River,' said the officer, when we reached the edge of the Udine plain. It might have come out from Kashmir with its broad sweeps of pale shoals that tailed off downstream into dancing haze. The milky jade waters smelt of snow from the hills as they plucked at the pontoon bridges' moorings which were made to allow for many feet rise and fall. A snow-fed river is as untrustworthy as a drunkard.

The flavour of mules, burning fuels, and a procession of high-wheeled Sicilian carts, their panels painted with Biblical stories, added to the Eastern illusion. But the ridge on the far side of the river that looked so steep, and was in reality only a small flattish mound among mountains, resembled no land on earth. If the Matoppos had married the Karroo they might have begotten some such abortion of stone-speckled, weather-hacked dirt. All along the base of it, indifferent to the thousands of troops around, to the scream of mules, the cough of motors, the whirr of machinery and the jarring carts, lay in endless belts of cemeteries those Italian dead who had first made possible the way to the heights above.

'We brought them down and buried them after each fight,' said the officer. 'There were many fights. Whole regiments lie there – and there – and there. Some of them died in the early days when we made war without roads, some of them died afterwards, when we had the roads but the Austrians had the guns. Some of them died at the last when we beat the Austrians. Look!'

As the poet says, the battle is won by the men who fall. God knows how many mothers' sons sleep along the river before Gradisca in the shadow of the first ridge of the wicked Carso. They can hear their own indomitable people always blasting their way towards the east and Trieste. The valley of the Isonzo multiplies the roar of the heavy pieces around Goritzia and in the mountains to the north, and sometimes enemy aeroplanes scar and rip up their resting-places. They lie, as it were, in a giant smithy where the links of the new Italy are being welded under smoke and flame and heat – heat from the dry shoals of the river-bed before, and heat from the dry ridge behind them.

[*The War in the Mountains*]

✠ ✠ ✠

I'VE JUST RECEIVED YOUR note of the 4th on my return from war among the Alps. An inconceivable trip at the height of 4000 feet, in a country to which the Engelberg valley is tame and of no account, over roads like the creations of giants, and all the while, above us – 3000 feet above us, on the eternal snows one saw the trenches of the Italians on the edge of Monte Nero.

Conceive our Saint Louis trip multiplied by 50 and you'll get some notion of it. We passed miles of ambushed guns and looked out through hidden casements over seas of mountains at villages of Austrians crawling beneath our feet . . . . And all the time guns were booming one against another lazily as they tried trial shots – they were 8′ and 11′ howitzers on our side: and when we climbed (or our car did) up to the very bare tops of mountains behold the grass was all pitted with shell holes. It's a war of giants among mountains. I looked into Tolmino and along 30 mile of Austrian front – wholly different from all I saw yesterday. The immensity of the landscape and the work dwarfs all comparison. I don't know how on earth or in the clouds I can describe it.

[Letter to Elsie Kipling, 11 May 1917]

✠ ✠ ✠

BELGIUM

NEXT MORNING MRS SCARSWORTH left early on her round of commissions, and Helen walked alone to Hagenzeele Third. The place was still in the making, and stood some five or six feet above the metalled road, which it flanked for a hundred yards. Culverts across a deep ditch served for entrances through the unfinished boundary wall. She climbed a few wooden-faced earthen steps and then met the entire crowded level of the thing in one held breath. She did not know Hagenzeele Third counted twenty-one thousand dead already. All she saw was a merciless sea of black crosses, bearing little strips of stamped tin at all angles across their faces. She could distinguish no order or arrangement in their mass; nothing but a waist-high wilderness as of weeds stricken dead, rushing at her. She went forward, moved to the left and the right hopelessly, wondering by what guidance she should ever come to her own. A great distance away there was a line of whiteness. It proved to be a block of some two or three hundred graves whose headstones had already been set, whose flowers planted out, and whose new-sown grass showed green. Here she could see clear-cut letters at the ends of the rows, referring to her slip, realized that it was not here she must look.

['The Gardener', *Debits and Credits*]

SEVILLE

THIS HAPPENED IN SEVILLE, the streets whereof are all cobbles, mostly ten-foot wide and walled in by practically windowless houses, so that every word spoken rings, as in a new plastered bathroom. Fools as we were, we looked out of our balcony into an alley only eight feet wide and said:– 'This is a quiet back-street. We shall sleep untroubled by noise.' We didn't know till late at night that, across that devil's alley was a rich woman, and her daughter and a large varnished motor-car in which the fat and perfumed daughter was howked up and down the gardens of Seville. Nor did we know that if you have a car in Seville 'tis a point of honour to drive with the cut-out wide open. So, when the godly equipage came back from its evening tour and bellowed in that seven foot alley way we thought it was Anarchists and bombs – in our bedroom. Many other things happened – songs, arguments, men and asses colliding with each other, but about 1. a.m. came a pause and we began to sleep. Then came one drunkard in the pious stage of drink, and he, seeing a picture of the madonna and child (mosaic) which that godly household who owned the car had exposed on their outer wall, needs must sing a canticle to Them. Have you ever heard a quavering Spanish canticle? After three or four minutes (Spain is slow to move) windows began to open along the alley and voices, male

and female, urged him to cease. They weren't angry voices
– at all. They were exquisitely modulated, argumentative and
placable. At last, he was convinced that his piety was mis-timed,
grunted and shut up. But the whole thing might have come out
of Gil Blas in its unreason, swiftness, and absurdity.

[Letter to Elizabeth Norton, 22 April 1922]

✖ ✖ ✖

GIBRALTAR

WE GOT AWAY LAST week on the usual hopeless quest of fine
weather in March. Also to show Elsie the Mediterranean. The
result was that we hit Gibraltar in a high, hard, glaringly-lit wind
that cut your liver out, and sent the wife to bed with a chill from
which she is but now recovering. All these here southern cli-
mates north of the Equator are malignant frauds. All the natives
meet you on the beach with the old lie about it being the worst
winter since Hannibal crossed the Alps. As a matter of fact, there
is snow within fifty miles of us, and the unprofitable date-palms
in the garden here are waggling their illustrated-poster leaves in
a climate that demands polar-bears. But, to crown the shame, the
beds are ablaze with iris, heliotrope, rosemary, arums and hibiscus. Where the Devil did they find the sunshine? The wheat is a
foot and a half high, and the beans are in blossom. They do not
farm here with the savage neatness of the French. The taint of the
Moor lies over everything, from the complexion and the teeth of
the women, to the action and gait of the babes in the gutter. And
they are most nobly unconcerned with all the rest of mankind.
Honestly and sincerely ignorant of them, their works, speech and
currencies. After all, if your creed teaches you that all heretics
will assuredly be damned, why worry about them in this present
life? No wonder that, through our War, these people were happy
to see English unbelievers grappling with Lutheran dogs whose
submarines hid in Spanish ports. They made their money out of
both sides alike (and they are rich!) and Holy Mother Church
has Her images in Her temples fresh-gilded throughout.

You must have seen Gib from the sea as you came through. It lies across the view from our windows, changing expression with every shift of the clouds. Just now, it has been saddened by the loss of a submarine which collided with a battle-ship while at practice three or four days ago, and everyone was drowned. I have had to go over twice or thrice about the dead of the War who are buried in that vast, old and most desolate cemetery under the shadow of the vertical Rock. You find the results of all the accidents and chances of soldier and sailor life laid out there through the past two centuries. But they bury them according to their religions, and as I am hunting for some place where we can put up a Cross to the memory of our War dead, it is a bit embarrassing to find that the Church of England are separated by about a quarter of a mile from the RCs and that Presbyterians and Wesleyans lie gloomily apart in another remote corner. And that reminds me, that we are getting on with the War Cemeteries in France, at last. We hope to have quite a quarter of them furnished with their tomb stones, cross and Stone of Remembrance by the year's end, and, in the meantime, all the others are tended and planted and their wooden crosses are looked after till their turn comes. They are worth seeing, and I do think that they are good from the artistic point of view. I expect to go back to France on our return, and inspect some of the latest-made ones.

[Letter to Sir Andrew Macphail, 26 March 1922]

✻ ✻ ✻

MARIENBAD

THIS IS A LAND of huge pine forests and plateaux and a population of fat men and women who sit, by preference, at windows of restaurants eternally gorging chocolate and creams and honey and grease in all forms.

[Letter to Colonel C.E. Hughes, 7 September 1935]

6

MIDDLE EAST AND NORTH AFRICA

A Taste of the Orient

Port Said – Cairo – Valley of the Kings – The Nile – Aswan (Assouan) – Wadi Halfa – Algiers – Jerusalem.

Apart from India, Egypt was the first foreign country Kipling recalled visiting (his memoirs refer to his passing through it en route to England as a small child). Later he delighted in returning to a country which offered him a tantalising glimpse of the East, along with its own ancient civilisation. In early 1913 he spent several weeks in Egypt, travelling up the Nile to Aswan (or Assouan) and Wadi Halfa. His articles about this trip were collected in a book, *Egypt of the Magicians* (1914). Years later, in 1929, he returned to Egypt and also went to Palestine, scene of a visit to the Church of the Holy Sepulchre in Jerusalem. In his regular search for winter sun, he also travelled to Algiers, which reminded him of Bombay.

PORT SAID

THE EAST IS A much larger slice of the world than Europeans care to admit. Some say it begins at St. Gothard, where the smells of two continents meet and fight all through that terrible restaurant-car dinner in the tunnel. Others have found it at Venice on warm April mornings. But the East is wherever one sees the lateen sail – that shark's fin of a rig which for hundreds of years has dogged all white bathers round the Mediterranean. There is still a suggestion of menace, a hint of piracy, in the blood whenever the lateen goes by, fishing or fruiting or coasting.

'This is not my ancestral trade,' she whispers to the accomplice sea. 'If everybody had their rights I should be doing something quite different; for my father, he was the Junk, and my mother, she was the Dhow, and between the two of 'em they made Asia.' Then she tacks, disorderly but deadly quick, and shuffles past the unimaginative steam-packet with her hat over one eye and a knife, as it were, up her baggy sleeves.

Even the stone-boats at Port Said, busied on jetty extensions, show their untamed descent beneath their loaded clumsiness. They are all children of the camel-nosed dhow, who is the mother of mischief; but it was very good to meet them again in raw sunshine, unchanged in any rope and patch.

Old Port Said had disappeared beneath acres of new buildings where one could walk at leisure without being turned back by soldiers.

Two or three landmarks remained; two or three were reported as still in existence, and one Face showed itself after many years – ravaged but respectable – rigidly respectable.

'Yes,' said the Face, 'I have been here all the time. But I have made money, and when I die I am going home to be buried.'

'Why not go home before you are buried, O Face?'

'Because I have lived here so long. Home is only good to be buried in.'

'And what do you do, nowadays?'

'Nothing now. I live on my rentes – my income.'

Think of it! To live icily in a perpetual cinematograph show of excited, uneasy travellers; to watch huge steamers, sliding in and out all day and all night like railway trucks, unknowing and unsought by a single soul aboard; to talk five or six tongues indifferently, but to have no country – no interest in any earth except one reservation in a Continental cemetery.

It was a cold evening after heavy rain and the half-flooded streets reeked. But we undefeated tourists ran about in droves and saw all that could be seen before train-time. We missed, most of us, the Canal Company's garden, which happens to mark a certain dreadful and exact division between East and West.

Up to that point – it is a fringe of palms, stiff against the sky – the impetus of home memories and the echo of home interests carry the young man along very comfortably on his first journey. But at Suez one must face things. People, generally the most sympathetic, leave the boat there; the older men who are going on have discovered each other and begun to talk shop; no newspapers come aboard, only clipped Reuter telegrams; the world seems cruelly large and self-absorbed. One goes for a walk and finds this little bit of kept ground, with comfortable garden-gated houses on either side of the path. Then one begins to wonder – in the twilight, for choice – when one will see those palms again from the other side. Then the black hour of homesickness, vain regrets, foolish promises, and weak despair shuts down with the smell of strange earth and the cadence of strange tongues.

Cross-roads and halting-places in the desert are always favoured by djinns and afrits. The young man will find them waiting for him in the Canal Company's garden at Port Said.

On the other hand, if he is fortunate enough to have won the East by inheritance, as there are families who served her for five or six generations, he will meet no ghouls in that garden, but a free and a friendly and an ample welcome from good spirits of the East that awaits him. The voices of the gardeners and the watchmen will be as the greetings of his father's servants in his father's house; the evening smells and the sight of the hibiscus

and poinsettia will unlock his tongue in words and sentences
that he thought he had clean forgotten, and he will go back to
the ship (I have seen) as a prince entering on his kingdom.

[*Egypt of the Magicians*]

✖ ✖ ✖

CAIRO

CAIRO STRIKES ONE AS unventilated and unsterilised, even
when the sun and wind are scouring it together. The tourist talks
a good deal, as you may see here, but the permanent European
resident does not open his mouth more than is necessary – sound
travels so far across flat water. Besides, the whole position of
things, politically and administratively, is essentially false.

Here is a country which is not a country but a longish strip of
market-garden, nominally in charge of a government which is
not a government but the disconnected satrapy of a half-dead
empire, controlled pecksniffingly by a Power which is not a
Power but an Agency, which Agency has been tied up by years,
custom, and blackmail into all sorts of intimate relations with six
or seven European Powers, all with rights and perquisites, none
of whose subjects seem directly amenable to any Power which at
first, second, or third hand is supposed to be responsible. That is
the barest outline. To fill in the details (if any living man knows
them) would be as easy as to explain baseball to an Englishman
or the Eton Wall game to a citizen of the United States. But it is a
fascinating play. There are Frenchmen in it, whose logical mind
it offends, and they revenge themselves by printing the finance-
reports and the catalogue of the Bulak Museum in pure French.
There are Germans in it, whose demands must be carefully
weighed – not that they can by any means be satisfied, but they
serve to block other people's. There are Russians in it, who do
not very much matter at present but will be heard from later.
There are Italians and Greeks in it (both rather pleased with
themselves just now), full of the higher finance and the finer
emotions. There are Egyptian pashas in it, who come back from

Paris at intervals and ask plaintively to whom they are supposed to belong. There is His Highness, the Khedive, in it, and he must be considered not a little, and there are women in it, up to their eyes. And there are great English cotton and sugar interests, and angry English importers clamouring to know why they cannot do business on rational lines or get into the Sudan, which they hold is ripe for development if the administration there would only see reason. Among these conflicting interests and amusements sits and perspires the English official, whose job is irrigating or draining or reclaiming land on behalf of a trifle of ten million people, and he finds himself tripped up by skeins of intrigue and bafflement which may ramify through half a dozen harems and four consulates. All this makes for suavity, toleration, and the blessed habit of not being surprised at anything whatever.

[. . .]

These modern 'Arabian Nights' are too hectic for quiet folk. I declined upon a more rational Cairo – the Arab city where everything is as it was when Maruf the Cobbler fled from Fatima-el-Orra and met the djinn in the Adelia Musjid. The craftsmen and merchants sat on their shop-boards, a rich mystery of darkness behind them, and the narrow gullies were polished to shoulder-height by the mere flux of people. Shod white men, unless they are agriculturists, touch lightly, with their hands at most, in passing. Easterns lean and loll and squat and sidle against things as they daunder along. When the feet are bare, the whole body thinks. Moreover, it is unseemly to buy or to do aught and be done with it. Only people with tight-fitting clothes that need no attention have time for that. So we of the loose skirt and flowing trousers and slack slipper make full and ample salutations to our friends, and redouble them toward our ill-wishers, and if it be a question of purchase, the stuff must be fingered and appraised with a proverb or so, and if it be a fool-tourist who thinks that he cannot be cheated, O true believers! draw near and witness how we shall loot him.

But I bought nothing. The city thrust more treasure upon me than I could carry away. It came out of dark alleyways on tawny camels loaded with pots; on pattering asses half buried under nets of cut clover; in the exquisitely modelled hands of little

children scurrying home from the cookshop with the evening
meal, chin pressed against the platter's edge and eyes round
with responsibility above the pile; in the broken lights from
jutting rooms overhead, where the women lie, chin between
palms, looking out of windows not a foot from the floor; in
every glimpse into every courtyard, where the men smoke by
the tank; in the heaps of rubbish and rotten bricks that flanked
newly painted houses, waiting to be built, some day, into houses
once more; in the slap and slide or the heelless red-and-yellow
slippers all around, and, above all, in the mixed delicious smells
of frying butter, Mohammedan bread, kababs, leather, cooking-
smoke, assafetida, peppers, and turmeric. Devils cannot abide
the smell of burning turmeric, but the right-minded man loves it.
It stands for evening that brings all home, the evening meal, the
dipping of friendly hands in the dish, the one face, the dropped
veil, and the big, guttering pipe afterward.

Praised be Allah for the diversity of His creatures and for
the Five Advantages of Travel and for the glories of the Cities
of the Earth! Harun-al-Raschid, in roaring Bagdad of old, never
delighted himself to the limits of such a delight as was mine, that
afternoon. It is true that the call to prayer, the cadence of some
of the street-cries, and the cut of some of the garments differed
a little from what I had been brought up to; but for the rest, the
shadow on the dial had turned back twenty degrees for me, and
I found myself saying, as perhaps the dead say when they have
recovered their wits, 'This is my real world again.'

Some men are Mohammedan by birth, some by training, and
some by fate, but I have never met an Englishman yet who hated
Islam and its people as I have met Englishmen who hated some
other faiths. *Musalmani awadani*, as the saying goes – where there
are Mohammedans, there is a comprehensible civilisation.

Then we came upon a deserted mosque of pitted brick
colonnades round a vast courtyard open to the pale sky. It was
utterly empty except for its own proper spirit, and that caught
one by the throat as one entered. Christian churches may
compromise with images and side-chapels where the unworthy
or abashed can traffic with accessible saints. Islam has but one
pulpit and one stark affirmation – living or dying, one only

– and where men have repeated that in red-hot belief through centuries, the air still shakes to it.

Some say now that Islam is dying and that nobody cares; others that, if she withers in Europe and Asia, she will renew herself in Africa and will return – terrible – after certain years, at the head of all the nine sons of Ham; others dream that the English understand Islam as no one else does, and, in years to be, Islam will admit this and the world will be changed. If you go to the mosque Al Azhar – the thousand-year-old University of Cairo – you will be able to decide for yourself. There is nothing to see except many courts, cool in hot weather, surrounded by cliff-like brick walls. Men come and go through dark doorways, giving on to yet darker cloisters, as freely as though the place was a bazaar. There are no aggressive educational appliances. The students sit on the ground, and their teachers instruct them, mostly by word of mouth, in grammar, syntax, logic; *al-hisab*, which is arithmetic; *al-jab'r w'al muqabalah*, which is algebra; *at-tafsir*, commentaries on the Koran, and last and most troublesome, *al-ahadis*, traditions, and yet more commentaries on the law of Islam, which leads back, like everything, to the Koran once again. (For it is written, 'Truly the Koran is none other than a revelation.') It is a very comprehensive curriculum. No man can master it entirely, but any can stay there as long as he pleases. The university provides commons – twenty-five thousand loaves a day, I believe, – and there is always a place to lie down in for such as do not desire a shut room and a bed. Nothing could be more simple or, given certain conditions, more effective. Close upon six hundred professors, who represent officially or unofficially every school or thought, teach ten or twelve thousand students, who draw from every Mohammedan community, west and east between Manila and Morocco, north and south between Kamchatka and the Malay mosque at Cape Town. These drift off to become teachers of little schools, preachers at mosques, students of the Law known to millions (but rarely to Europeans), dreamers, devotees, or miracle-workers in all the ends of the earth. The man who interested me most was a red-bearded, sunk-eyed mullah from the Indian frontier, not likely to be last at any distribution of food, who stood up like a lean wolfhound among collies in a little assembly at a doorway.

And there was another mosque, sumptuously carpeted and lighted (which the Prophet does not approve of), where men prayed in the dull mutter that, at times, mounts and increases under the domes like the boom of drums or the surge of a hot hive before the swarm flings out. And round the corner of it, one almost ran into our inconspicuous and wholly detached Private of Infantry, his tunic open, his cigarette alight, leaning against some railings and considering the city below. Men in forts and citadels and garrisons all the world over go up at twilight as automatically as sheep at sundown, to have a last look round. They say little and return as silently across the crunching gravel, detested by bare feet, to their whitewashed rooms and regulated lives. One of the men told me he thought well of Cairo. It was interesting. 'Take it from me,' he said, 'there's a lot in seeing places, because you can remember 'em afterward.'

He was very right. The purple and lemon-coloured hazes of dusk and reflected day spread over the throbbing, twinkling streets, masked the great outline of the citadel and the desert hills, and conspired to confuse and suggest and evoke memories, till Cairo the Sorceress cast her proper shape and danced before me in the heartbreaking likeness of every city I had known and loved, a little farther up the road.

It was a cruel double-magic. For in the very hour that my homesick soul had surrendered itself to the dream of the shadow that had turned back on the dial, I realised all the desolate days and homesickness of all the men penned in far-off places among strange sounds and smells.

[*Egypt of the Magicians*]

VALLEY OF THE KINGS

THERE IS A VALLEY of rocks and stones in every shade of red and brown, called the Valley of the Kings, where a little oil-engine coughs behind its hand all day long, grinding electricity to light the faces of dead Pharaohs a hundred feet underground. All down the valley, during the tourist season, stand char-a-bancs and donkeys and sand-carts, with here and there exhausted couples who have dropped out of the processions and glisten and fan themselves in some scrap of shade. Along the sides of the valley are the tombs of the kings neatly numbered, as it might be mining adits with concrete steps leading up to them, and iron grilles that lock of nights, and doorkeepers of the Department of Antiquities demanding the proper tickets. One enters, and from deeps below deeps hears the voices of dragomans booming through the names and titles of the illustrious and thrice-puissant dead. Rock-cut steps go down into hot, still darkness, passages twist and are led over blind pits which, men say, the wise builders childishly hoped would be taken for the real tombs by thieves to come. Up and down these alley-ways clatter all the races of Europe with a solid backing of the United States. Their footsteps are suddenly blunted on the floor of a hall paved with immemorial dust that will never dance in any wind. They peer up at the blazoned ceilings, stoop down to the minutely decorated walls, crane and follow the sombre splendours of a cornice, draw in their breaths and climb up again to the fierce sunshine to re-dive into the next adit on their programme. What they think proper to say, they say aloud – and some of it is very interesting. What they feel you can guess from a certain haste in their movements – something between the shrinking modesty of a man under fire and the Hadn't-we-better-be-getting-on attitude of visitors to a mine. After all, it is not natural for man to go underground except for business or for the last time. He is conscious of the weight of mother-earth overhead, and when to her expectant bulk is added the whole beaked, horned, winged, and crowned hierarchy of a lost faith flaming at every turn of his eye, he naturally wishes to move away. Even the sight of a very great king indeed, sarcophagused under electric light in a hall full of most fortifying pictures, does not hold him too long.

Some men assert that the crypt of St. Peter's, with only nineteen centuries bearing down on the groining, and the tombs of early popes and kings all about, is more impressive than the Valley of the Kings because it explains how and out of what an existing creed grew. But the Valley of the Kings explains nothing except that most terrible line in Macbeth:

> To the last syllable of recorded time.
> Earth opens her dry lips and says it.

In one of the tombs there is a little chamber whose ceiling, probably because of a fault in the rock, could not be smoothed off like the others. So the decorator, very cunningly, covered it with a closely designed cloth-pattern – just such a chintz-like piece of stuff as, in real life, one would use to underhang a rough roof with. He did it perfectly, down there in the dark, and went his way. Thousands of years later, there was born a man of my acquaintance who, for good and sufficient reason, had an almost insane horror of anything in the nature of a ceiling-cloth. He used to make excuses for not going into the dry goods shops at Christmas, when hastily enlarged annexes are hidden, roof and sides, with embroideries. Perhaps a snake or a lizard had dropped on his mother from the roof before he was born; perhaps it was the memory of some hideous fever-bout in a tent. At any rate, that man's idea of The Torment was a hot, crowded underground room, underhung with patterned cloths. Once in his life at a city in the far north, where he had to make a speech, he met that perfect combination. They led him up and down narrow, crowded, steam-heated passages, till they planted him at last in a room without visible windows (by which he knew he was, underground), and directly beneath a warm-patterned ceiling-cloth – rather like a tent-lining. And there he had to say his say, while panic terror sat in his throat. The second time was in the Valley of the Kings, where very similar passages, crowded with people, led him into a room cut of rock, fathoms underground, with what looked like a sagging chintz cloth not

three feet above his head. 'The man I'd like to catch,' he said
when he came outside again, 'is that decorator-man. D'you
suppose he meant to produce that effect?'

[*Egypt of the Magicians*]

❖ ❖ ❖

THE NILE

GOING UP THE NILE is like running the gauntlet before Eternity.
Till one has seen it, one does not realise the amazing thinness
of that little damp trickle of life that steals along undefeated
through the jaws of established death. A rifle-shot would cover
the widest limits of cultivation, a bow-shot would reach the
narrower. Once beyond them a man may carry his next drink
with him till he reaches Cape Blanco on the west (where he may
signal for one from a passing Union Castle boat) or the Karachi
Club on the east. Say four thousand dry miles to the left hand
and three thousand to the right.

[*Egypt of the Magicians*]

❖ ❖ ❖

THE NILE AT PRESENT is low and one can't see over the dark
earthen banks – exactly like the banks of the Dudwell when
there has been a slip – but magnified ten thousand times. There
is always a native village of square mud huts and big towers
of mud for pigeon-cots: there is always the solemn fringe of
date palms behind it: there is always the vivid blue-green of
young wheat or onions or the pale goldy-green of sugar cane
and behind everything else, four or five miles away is the pale
pinkish grey of the utterly barren hills of the desert. One feels
that one is sliding down a gutter less than ten miles wide. I had
no notion Egypt was so long and so thin. It's an absolute length-
without-breadth-country. But you never saw such cultivation.
They get three and four crops a year off this amazing Nile mud,

which again is only the silt of the Dudwell: and, on an average after all expenses have been paid, they make £7 (seven pound) profit per acre! At these rates our land at Burwash would fetch us in over £2000 a year. Of course all this cultivation is limited to where the water can be put on the land and where the Nile can deposit its honey-coloured mud. The traffic on the River is incessant. Boats loaded with chopped wheat straw for the beasts to eat when the country is flooded, pots for pigeon-nests; pots for drinking water; lime stone; sugar cane and all that sort of thing are always in sight. They navigate by the grace of God but they don't seem to come to any harm. At least we have only seen one wreck of dahabeah and that looked very ancient.

The rummy thing is the climate. It's – not to put too fine a point on it – rotten cold in the mornings and the evenings and today, within 2 or 3 degrees of the tropic, it hasn't got warm yet at 11: a.m. I have been wearing winter things till today and only wish I'd not taken 'em off. The sky isn't S. African blue but a sort of washed out pale bluish-grey. The river is a pale brown and the banks are dark-brown and the natives are blue black with a smile on 'em like a split water-melon.

[Letter to John Kipling, 17 February 1913]

✖ ✖ ✖

ASWAN (ASSOUAN)

DID I HAPPEN TO tell you anything about the great dam at Assouan? I fancy I alluded to it casually? It is about 100 feet high but it holds back the water for 120 miles! We are now sailing on a Nile without sandbanks, without any shallows – a river that runs brim full slam up to the orange and black rocks of the desert. It's exactly – to compare very wee things with enormously big ones, like the Dudwell when it's full. But the extraordinary thing is to see over a hundred miles of date palms with only their tops sticking out of the water. You see they added sixteen feet more to the height of the dam only a year ago: and as there is less than a foot of fall per mile to this most marvellous river, the effect of that rise is felt all along. [. . .] There is a line of half drowned date palms on both sides of the river showing where the actual banks of the river ran before they built the dam. Of course in the summer when they let out the water to irrigate all the cotton-crop of Lower Egypt the date palms will breathe for a few months but in the long-run they will all die. A palm can only stand being stuck in water for three months at the most – and if water gets into the crown of leaves it dies and turns white like a skeleton.

Meantime the effect of this great river being turned into what looks like a canal half a mile wide is very curious – utterly unlike the straggly shallow sand-banked Nile below Assouan. The people too are different, being black Nubians with flashing teeth – not Egyptians. The costume of the children on the banks is of extreme simplicity. One small maiden whom I saw just now was rather elaborately dressed in a Nubian confection of bootlaces and cowries – not too many of either. [. . .] There were also a few blue beads mixed up with the cowries. From time to time our steamer stops – a bell rings: a plank is let down from the boat and we all troop ashore like a school-treat shepherded by our dragoman (he jaws more than Ibrahim of the Rameses III did) and are taken round a temple. The temples here aren't built in the open like the ones in Lower Egypt but they are cut out from the solid rock with just a portico, and the remains of an avenue of sphinxes in front of 'em. [. . .] They are all awfully impressive in their gloom and darkness (an oxy-hydrogen lamp is employed to light the inner chambers) and they all stink of bats – which is one of the most concentrated stinks that I know.

[Letter to John and Elsie Kipling, 24 February 1913]

WADI HALFA

AT HALFA ONE FEELS the first breath of a frontier. Here the Egyptian Government retires into the background, and even the Cook steamer does not draw up in the exact centre of the postcard. At the telegraph-office, too, there are traces, diluted but quite recognisable, of military administration. Nor does the town, in any way or place whatever, smell – which is proof that it is not looked after on popular lines. There is nothing to see in it any more than there is in Hulk C. 60, late of her Majesty's troopship Himalaya, now a coal-hulk in the Hamoaze at Plymouth. A river front, a narrow terraced river-walk of semi-oriental houses, barracks, a mosque, and half-a-dozen streets at right angles, the Desert racing up to the end of each, make all the town. A mile or so up stream under palm trees are bungalows of what must have been cantonments, some machinery repair-shops, and odds and ends of railway track. It is all as paltry a collection of whitewashed houses, pitiful gardens, dead walls, and trodden waste spaces as one would wish to find anywhere; and every bit of it quivers with the remembered life of armies and river-fleets, as the finger-bowl rings when the rubbing finger is lifted. The most unlikely men have done time there; stores by the thousand ton have been rolled and pushed and hauled up the banks by tens of thousands of scattered hands; hospitals have pitched themselves there, expanded enormously, shrivelled up and drifted away with the drifting regiments; railway sidings by the mile have been laid down and ripped up again, as need changed, and utterly wiped out by the sands.

Halfa has been the rail-head, Army Headquarters, and hub of the universe – the one place where a man could make sure of buying tobacco and sardines, or could hope for letters for himself and medical attendance for his friend. Now she is a little shrunken shell of a town without a proper hotel, where tourists hurry up from the river to buy complete sets of Soudan stamps at the Post Office.

[*Egypt of the Magicians*]

✠ ✠ ✠

ALGIERS

I WISH YOU COULD have seen Marseilles port, as our ship cleared out of it behind the P&O 'China', in hard pale sunshine, under a hard blue sky. There was every breed and variety of ship (and man) on the quays: from a huge French South-American liner down to a blunt-nosed, sow-bellied, sawed-off Boche cargo-boat whose French owners were trying hard to make [it] look a little less like the hereditary bitch that she was. And there was a tramp repainting – her priming-coat of the richest vermillion that ever you saw. She had a bit of a list on and she lay on the green water fairly blazing – like coral – sides, masts and all. The Lord looked after us on the run. We found an oily sea which instantly suggested flying-fish – a regular doldrums sea. And there were porpoises on escort duty and a couple of turtle, which latter I had never seen before. They all added to the joyous sense of escape and change and movement. I had not had much of a time in the train: but the steamer cheered me up in spite of its being chock-full.

[. . .] The hotel has a garden on the slope of a cypress-covered ridge. Directly beneath our windows are orange trees, all studded with ripe fruit and heavy with bridal bloom. There is a twenty foot plantain tree beyond them – the leaves clapping and swording to and fro even as they used to do when I was a small boy at Bombay. Palms run up to the tennis court – date palms and others that I know not. It is very long since I saw dates. Beds of the most violent and deadly mauve and magenta horrors – cinerarias, I should think – lie under the white-washed walls which are blazing with great splashes of bougainvillea. Jasmine is stinking its heart out everywhere, and in place of turf there is that yellow-flowered oxalis – it's a clover ain't it? – that is cut and sold for fodder as in Egypt. Roses, sweet peas, violets with stalks a foot long – pansies, anemones, pig-weed (arum lilies) flowering cacti, like red-hot pokers, are all out in fullest bloom: and behind all their mixed scent is a steady background of comforting, almost camphor-like eucalyptus which has been planted by the French and is now sixty foot timber.

[Letter to Colonel H.W. Feilden, 21–22 February 1921]

✠ ✠ ✠

JERUSALEM

THIS HERE IS A strong keen strenuous British spring climate masked by abundant sunshine, at about the elevation of Madrid. [. . .] Today we lunched with the acting High Commissioner – we dined with him on Sunday – and he took us into new worlds – to see the treasure of the Greek and the Armenian churches. The Greek Church has its share of the Church of the Holy Sepulchre but as soon as we were inside, we were met by strange priests who cut us out of a procession and a congregation pouring into the Church and led us a bit to one side. Then miracles of moving in the 4th dimension happened. Doors opened and we went on in the holy dark into rooms and corridors and reception rooms, all mixed up with inexplicable side-altars: then tapers were served out as tho' it were a mine and we climbed stairs worn to snaily-slimy smoothness and came out on a gallery high above all the congregations and religions. One of 'em, in its screened portion of holiness chanted Latin psalms: so we knew they were R.C.'s.

By this time we were wholly lost in a sort of gigantic stone attic with a steel trap door over the stairs we had crawled up by. Then we sat round a table and the archimandrite gave orders over his shoulder towards an open door, and a monk bore out reliquaries (to begin with) of the True Cross whose value in jewels was beyond count; then mere crosses of diamond and ruby; then Archbishops' mitres of solid gold; then the mitre Peter the Great gave to the Greek church and that topped everything; then a crystal reliquary recently dug up in a crypt, as used on their altars by the Crusaders; then croziers of gold and ivory and then a priceless M.S. illuminated book which the Priest illuminated by means of a bent taper. The Acting High Commissioner tactfully took it from him so that the grease, which was abundant, merely dripped on the table cloth. And so it went on for an hour, while the unseen congregational circus below roared and bawled through its psalms. Then we navigated down the perilous stairs, and through the stinking reeking, putrid, noisome alley ways on foot, till we took car and went to the Armenians. [. . .]

Tomorrow we see a little more of the Holy City. My dear, it is an indescribable muck-heap but it's the most interesting muck-heap in the world and I'll trouble you to find a town where you can see a Nazarene in her native clothes walking with a Bethlehemite, followed by a Bokhara Jew in a bed gown and preceded by three bedouins, the procession closing by a knot of white canvas-dressed prisoners bringing rations to the Arab-Jew-English police! It's unbelievable – and everywhere the donkey and the camel taking far less notice of the motors than they do of them. Do you know that camels on a string are always led by a little donkey? Wise small persons.

[Letter to Elsie Bambridge, 26 March 1929]

⚓ 7 ⚓

SOUTH AFRICA

Winter Warmth

Table Mountain – The Karroo, Cape Province – Simon's Bay – Kimberley and Beyond.

Kipling first visited South Africa in 1891, en route to Australia and Samoa, where he had hoped (unsuccessfully, as it turned out) to see one of his literary heroes, Robert Louis Stevenson. Having come under the influence of Cecil Rhodes, he returned to the Cape with his family in 1898. For the best part of a decade (including a period during the Boer War), he liked to spend part of each winter there, enjoying the sub-tropical climate and the sense of a country being gradually won to the empire. 'The Woolsack' was a house that Rhodes lent to Kipling. It stood beside his own mansion, 'Groote Schuur', on a shoulder of Table Mountain overlooking Cape Town.

Kipling celebrated South Africa in verses such as 'Bridge-Guard in the Karroo' and in the short story 'Mrs Bathurst', with its tableau of Simon's Bay, site of the Royal Navy base on the east side of the Cape of Good Hope.

He also travelled north into Matabeleland (later Rhodesia and Zimbabwe) – a journey that bore literary fruit in his *Just So Stories*, published in 1902.

TABLE MOUNTAIN

INTO THESE SHIFTS AND changes we would descend yearly for five or six months from the peace of England to the deeper peace of 'The Woolsack,' and life under the oak-trees overhanging the patio, where mother-squirrels taught their babies to climb, and in the stillness of hot afternoons the fall of an acorn was almost like a shot. To one side of us was a pine and eucalyptus grove, heavy with mixed scent; in front our garden, where anything one planted out in May became a blossoming bush by December. Behind all tiered the flank of Table Mountain and its copses of silver trees, flanking scarred ravines. To get to Rhodes' house, 'Groote Schuur,' one used a path through a ravine set with hydrangeas, which in autumn (England's spring) were one solid packed blue river.

[*Something of Myself*]

YOUR LETTER REACHES ME in the middle of what might be a perfect cold weather day in India. The plains between Table Mountain which, so to say, rises out of our back yard, and Hottentots Holland are all dancing in the heat mist and the Cape doves are making just the same noise as their Indian sisters among the figs and loquats in the garden. There are hibiscus bushes in full bloom with pomegranates and aloes. It's all like and yet unlike the old country. [. . .] Just behind the house a huge park runs up the slopes of Table Mountain and there a giraffe lives in company with elands, kangaroos and all manner of South African antelope wandering about great fenced fields and all the nations of the earth go and look at them. There is an influx of Sikhs just now – tall silent chaps from Shahpur and Jullundur way come over to the Cape on the rumour of wonderful wages to be had for working for the White Men. They go to the fruit farms and vineyards or on to the railway line and occasionally I am able to interpret between them and some excited foreman who can't make them understand.

[Letter to Edmonia Hill, 8 March 1905]

✵ ✵ ✵

THE KARROO, CAPE PROVINCE

SUDDEN THE DESERT CHANGES,
   The raw glare softens and clings,
Till the aching Oudtshoorn ranges
   Stand up like the thrones of Kings –

Ramparts of slaughter and peril –
   Blazing, amazing, aglow –
'Twixt the sky-line's belting beryl
   And the wine-dark flats below.

Royal the pageant closes,
   Lit by the last of the sun –
Opal and ash-of-roses,
   Cinnamon, umber, and dun.

The twilight swallows the thicket,
   The starlight reveals the ridge.
The whistle shrills to the picket –
   We are changing guard on the bridge.

(Few, forgotten and lonely,
   Where the empty metals shine –
No, not combatants – only
   Details guarding the line.)

We slip through the broken panel
   Of fence by the ganger's shed;

We drop to the waterless channel
   And the lean track overhead;

We stumble on refuse of rations,
   The beef and the biscuit-tins;
We take our appointed stations,
   And the endless night begins.

We hear the Hottentot herders
   As the sheep click past to the fold –
And the click of the restless girders
   As the steel contracts in the cold –

Voices of jackals calling
   And, loud in the hush between,
A morsel of dry earth falling
   From the flanks of the scarred ravine.

And the solemn firmament marches,
   And the hosts of heaven rise
Framed through the iron arches –
   Banded and barred by the ties,

Till we feel the far track humming,
   And we see her headlight plain,
And we gather and wait her coming –
   The wonderful north-bound train.

[from 'Bridge-Guard in the Karroo', *The Five Nations*]

SIMON'S BAY

THE DAY THAT I chose to visit H.M.S. *Peridot* in Simon's Bay was the day that the Admiral had chosen to send her up the coast. She was just steaming out to sea as my train came in, and since the rest of the Fleet were either coaling or busy at the rifle-ranges a thousand feet up the hill, I found myself stranded, lunchless, on the sea-front with no hope of return to Cape Town before 5 p.m. At this crisis I had the luck to come across my friend Inspector Hooper, Cape Government Railways, in command of an engine and a brake-van chalked for repair.

'If you get something to eat,' he said, 'I'll run you down to Glengariff siding till the goods comes along. It's cooler there than here, you see.

I got food and drink from the Greeks who sell all things at a price, and the engine trotted us a couple of miles up the line to a bay of drifted sand and a plank-platform half buried in sand not a hundred yards from the edge of the surf. Moulded dunes, whiter than any snow, rolled far inland up a brown and purple valley of splintered rocks and dry scrub. A crowd of Malays hauled at a net beside two blue and green boats on the beach; a picnic party danced and shouted barefoot where a tiny river trickled across the flat, and a circle of dry hills, whose feet were set in sands of silver, locked us in against a seven-coloured sea. At either horn of the bay the railway line, cut just above highwater mark, ran round a shoulder of piled rocks, and disappeared.

'You see, there's always a breeze here,' said Hooper, opening the door as the engine left us in the siding on the sand, and the strong south-easter buffeting under Elsie's Peak dusted sand into our tickey beer. Presently he sat down to a file full of spiked documents. He had returned from a long trip up-country, where he had been reporting on damaged rolling-stock, as far away as Rhodesia. The weight of the bland wind on my eyelids; the song of it under the car-roof, and high up among the rocks; the drift of fine grains chasing each other musically ashore; the tramp of the surf; the voices of the picnickers; the rustle of Hooper's file, and the presence of the assured sun, joined with the beer to cast me into magical slumber. The hills of False Bay were just dissolving into those of fairyland when I heard footsteps on the sand outside, and the clink of our couplings.

['Mrs Bathurst', *Traffics and Discoveries*]

✖ ✖ ✖

KIMBERLEY AND BEYOND

I HAVE SEEN DIAMOND mining at Kimberley where the diamonds come out by hundreds from the washed gravel. They gave me a beauty of 3 1/2 carats which, as you may believe, the wife has annexed. I have seen every type and breed of native south of the Zambesi in the huge guarded enclosures where the native labour is kept. Kaffirs steal diamonds (chiefly by swallowing them) and that is why they are put through a five days' course of purging before they leave the service of the mines (one chap put away 35 carats of diamonds valued at $5,000 and his stomach didn't seem any the worse for it). Then I went a thousand miles north into Matabele land, over a new-laid railroad across dry rivers, till I came to the city of Bulawayo, a town of 5,000 white men. They treated me like a prince. Then I went on into the Matoppos – a wilderness of tumbled rocks, granite boulders and caves where the white men fought the Matabele in '96. You never dreamed of such a country. [. . .] The land is shot full of gold and prospectors are coming in and going out every day with bags of samples. It's like a cross between a Kansas town, Cripple Creek and a bit of London. Ice is a scarce commodity up there. I left Kimberley with 200 lbs of it which the Diamond Fields Company had given me and it was rather more valuable than diamonds. On the banks of the Macloutsi river – 300 miles from anywhere in particular – I saw a prospector with a pack on his back chucking up green bile under a tree. He was pretty dead with fever and he had an Abra'm Lincoln beard. I stepped out of the train and gave him 20 grains of quinine. Then, like a fool, I offered him whiskey and that set him vomiting worse than ever. Then I thought of the ice: and got out a bottle of soda-water that had been froze into the ice for two days. That fetched him. 'My God,' he said, 'you're as good as an uncle,' and he put it down in a minute. 'Where do you come from?' says I. 'Boston, Mass'chussetts' was the amazing answer. 'And what are you doing here?' says I. 'Pegging out claims an' dyin',' says he. Then the train went on.

[Letter to James M. Conland, early April 1898]

⊠   ⊠   ⊠

HE WENT FROM GRAHAM'S Town to Kimberley, and from Kimberley to Khama's Country, and from Khama's Country he went east by north, eating melons all the time, till at last he came to the banks of the great grey-green, greasy Limpopo River, all set about with fever-trees, precisely as the Kolokolo Bird had said.

['The Elephant's Child', *Just So Stories*]

꒰ 8 ꒱
THE SEA
On the Long Trail

The Pacific – Grand Bank, Atlantic Ocean – Big Steamers – Merchant Shipping – Submarines –The Deep-Sea Cables.

The sea touched on so many of Kipling's passions – from the spirit of adventure, through the traffic of empire to everyday communication between peoples. Although rarely a hands-on sailor himself, he learnt about seafaring from watching ships in ports such as Bombay, Portsmouth and Gloucester, Massachusetts, and from pacing the decks on lengthy ocean voyages. In an extract here he recalls crossing the Pacific in 1889. He also used his experiences of the Atlantic in his novel, *Captains Courageous.*

Although his attachment to the sea was generally romantic, it could also be both practical and didactic. 'Big Steamers' is a poem designed to inform school-children about the importance of the ocean-going vessels that kept Britain provided with food. (This theme was taken up in his talk to the Chamber of Shipping, also featured here.) The 'Harwich Ladies' is another, rather different piece of propaganda that appeared as part of 'The Fringes of the Fleet', a series of articles he wrote for the *Daily Telegraph* in 1915 to remind people that the Royal Navy was active in British coastal waters.

Not exactly shipping, but certainly related, was the subject of his poem 'The Deep-Sea Cables' – about the laying of telegraph cables on the bottom of oceans, allowing instant communication between continents.

THE PACIFIC

THIS IS AMERICA. THEY call her the *City of Peking*, and she belongs to the Pacific Mail Company, but for all practical purposes she is the United States. We are divided between missionaries and generals – generals who were at Vicksburg and Shiloh, and German by birth, but more American than the Americans, who in confidence tell you that they are not generals at all, but only brevet majors of militia corps. The missionaries are perhaps the queerest portion of the cargo. Did you ever hear an English minister lecture for half an hour on the freight-traffic receipts and general working of, let us say, the Midland? The Professor has been sitting at the feet of a keen-eyed, close-bearded, swarthy man who expounded unto him kindred mysteries with a fluency and precision that a city leader-writer might have envied. 'Who's your financial friend with the figures at his fingers' ends?' I asked. 'Missionary – Presbyterian Mission to the Japs,' said the Professor. I laid my hand upon my mouth and was dumb.

As a counterpoise to the missionaries, we carry men from Manila – lean Scotchmen who gamble once a month in the Manila State lottery and occasionally turn up trumps. One, at least, drew a ten-thousand-dollar prize last December and is away to make merry in the New World. Everybody on the staff of an American steamer this side the continent seems to gamble steadily in that lottery, and the talk of the smoking-room runs almost entirely on prizes won by accident or lost through a moment's delay. The tickets are sold more or less openly at Yokohama and Hong-Kong, and the drawings – losers and winners both agree here – are above reproach.

We have resigned ourselves to the infinite monotony of a twenty days' voyage. The Pacific Mail advertises falsely. Only under the most favourable circumstances of wind and steam can their under-engined boats cover the distance in fifteen days. Our

City of Peking, for instance, had been jogging along at a gentle ten knots an hour, a pace out of all proportion to her bulk. 'When we get a wind,' says the Captain, 'we shall do better.' She is a four-master and can carry any amount of canvas. It is not safe to run steamers across this void under the poles of Atlantic liners. The monotony of the sea is paralysing. We have passed the wreck of a little sealing-schooner lying bottom up and covered with gulls. She weltered by in the chill dawn, unlovely as the corpse of a man; and the wild birds piped thinly at us as they steered her across the surges. The pulse of the Pacific is no little thing even in the quieter moods of the sea. It set our bows swinging and nosing and ducking ere we were a day clear of Yokohama, and yet there was never swell nor crested wave in sight. 'We ride very high,' said the Captain, 'and she's a dry boat. She has a knack of crawling over things somehow; but we shan't need to put her to the test this journey.'

[*From Sea to Sea*]

✶ ✶ ✶

GRAND BANK, ATLANTIC OCEAN

But Disko's board was the Grand Bank – a triangle two hundred and fifty miles on each side a waste of wallowing sea, cloaked with dank fog, vexed with gales, harried with drifting ice, scored by the tracks of the reckless liners, and dotted with the sails of the fishing-fleet. – For days they worked in fog – Harvey at the bell – till, grown familiar with the thick airs, he went out with Tom Platt, his heart rather in his mouth. But the fog would not lift, and the fish were biting, and no one can stay helplessly afraid for six hours at a time. Harvey devoted himself to his lines and the gaff or gob-stick as Tom Platt called for them; and they rowed back to the schooner guided by the bell and Tom's instinct; Manuel's conch sounding thin and faint beside them. But it was an unearthly experience, and, for the first time in a month, Harvey dreamed of the shifting, smoking floors of water round the dory, the lines that strayed away into nothing, and the air above that melted on the sea below ten feet from his straining eyes. A few days later he was out with Manuel on what should have been forty-fathom bottom, but the whole length of the roding ran out, and still the anchor found nothing, and Harvey grew mortally afraid, for that his last touch with earth was lost. 'Whale-hole,' said Manuel, hauling in. 'That is good joke on Disko. Come!' and he rowed to the schooner to find Tom Platt and the others jeering at the skipper because, for once, he had led them to the edge of the barren Whale-deep, the blank hole of the Grand Bank. They made another berth through the fog, and that time the hair of Harvey's head stood up when he went out in Manuel's dory. A whiteness moved in the whiteness of the fog with a breath like the breath of the grave, and there was a roaring, a plunging, and spouting. It was his first introduction to the dread summer berg of the Banks, and he cowered in the bottom of the boat while Manuel laughed.

[*Captains Courageous*]

✠ ✠ ✠

BIG STEAMERS

'OH, WHERE ARE YOU going to, all you Big Steamers,
  With England's own coal, up and down the salt seas?'
'We are going to fetch you your bread and your butter,
  Your beef, pork, and mutton, eggs, apples, and cheese.'

'And where will you fetch it from, all you Big Steamers,
  And where shall I write you when you are away?'
'We fetch it from Melbourne, Quebec, and Vancouver –
  Address us at Hobart, Hong-Kong, and Bombay.'

'But if anything happened to all you Big Steamers,
  And suppose you were wrecked up and down the salt sea?'
'Why, you'd have no coffee or bacon for breakfast,
  And you'd have no muffins or toast for your tea.'

'Then I'll pray for fine weather for all you Big Steamers,
  For little blue billows and breezes so soft.'
'Oh, billows and breezes don't bother Big Steamers:
  We're iron below and steel-rigging aloft.'

'Then I'll build a new lighthouse for all you Big Steamers,
  With plenty wise pilots to pilot you through.'
'Oh, the Channel's as bright as a ball-room already,
  And pilots are thicker than pilchards at Looe.'

'Then what can I do for you, all you Big Steamers,
  Oh, what can I do for your comfort and good?'
'Send out your big warships to watch your big waters,
  That no one may stop us from bringing you food.'

'For the bread that you eat and the biscuits you nibble,
  The sweets that you suck and the joints that you carve,
They are brought to you daily by all us Big Steamers –
  And if any one hinders our coming you'll starve!'

['Big Steamers', *A History of England*]

❊   ❊   ❊

MERCHANT SHIPPING

THIS MAY BE A confession of weakness, but it is a lucky man, not to say ship, that has only one weakness; and among my many weaknesses has been an early, acute, and abiding interest in the Mercantile Marine. I have seen its work. I have watched some of its performances from various craft, including gilt-edged liners, where every effort is made to persuade passengers that they are not at sea, but in a much safer place. I am unworthy of those efforts. For when I embark on such a vessel I know I have only to leave the Tudor grill-room, take the electric lift upstairs, and look out of the window of the more or less Perpendicular library on the top floor, and I shall see that same old grey wolf, the Ocean that harried our forefathers, waiting outside. It is not for me to teach you your business, but believe me, gentlemen, a ship is a ship, and you cannot get away from it.

In the same way this island of ours is a ship, as much as H.M.S. *Ascension*, with the additional disadvantage of being moored between two Continents, so that we can enjoy the weather, political and otherwise, from both. Furthermore, H.M.S. *Great Britain* carries a passenger list, including stowaways, of forty-five millions, and, owing to peculiarities of her construction, there are never more than six weeks' supplies of consumable stores aboard her at one time. The balance must come by ship, and if the shipping does not come, a fortnight would deliver us to panic indescribable, and three months would see us embarked on the gallant adventure of cannibalism. These are the facts which underlie the camouflage of our existence on H.M.S. *Great Britain*. Naturally, they do not trouble the passengers aboard her, any more than the sight of the sea worries the passengers on your floating palaces.

[From a speech to the Chamber of Shipping Annual Dinner,
February 1925, *Book of Words*]

✠ ✠ ✠

SUBMARINES

Farewell and adieu to you, Harwich Ladies,
Farewell and adieu to you, ladies ashore!
For we've received orders to work to the eastward
Where we hope in a short time to strafe 'em some more.

We'll duck and we'll dive like little tin turtles,
We'll duck and we'll dive underneath the North Seas,
Until we strike something that doesn't expect us,
From here to Cuxhaven it's go as you please!

The first thing we did was to dock in a minefield,
Which isn't a place where repairs should be done;

And there we lay doggo in twelve-fathom water
With tri-nitro-toluol hogging our run.

The next thing we did, we rose under a Zeppelin,
With his shiny big belly half blocking the sky.
But what in the – Heavens can you do with six-pounders?
So we fired what we had and we bade him good-bye.
Farewell and adieu, &c.

['Harwich Ladies', *The Fringes of the Fleet*]

❀ ❀ ❀

THE DEEP-SEA CABLES

THE WRECKS DISSOLVE ABOVE us; their dust drops down from
   afar –
Down to the dark, to the utter dark, where the blind white
   sea-snakes are.
There is no sound, no echo of sound, in the deserts of the deep,
Or the great gray level plains of ooze where the shell-burred
   cables creep.

Here in the womb of the world – here on the tie-ribs of earth
Words, and the words of men, flicker and flutter and beat –
Warning, sorrow and gain, salutation and mirth –
For a Power troubles the Still that has neither voice nor feet.

They have wakened the timeless Things; they have killed their
   father Time;
Joining hands in the gloom, a league from the last of the sun.
Hush! Men talk to-day o'er the waste of the ultimate slime,
And a new Word runs between: whispering, 'Let us be one!'

[from 'A Song of the English', *The Seven Seas*]

SOUTH AMERICA AND THE CARIBBEAN

Rolling Down to Rio

Sailing to Rio – Brazil – Jamaica – Bermuda.

South America was merely a dream when Kipling wrote the verses 'Rolling Down to Rio' as an upbeat accompaniment to his *Just So* story, 'The Beginning of the Armadillos'. He was able to measure this fantasy against the real thing when he journeyed to Brazil in 1927.

Three years later, in his search for winter sun, he visited Jamaica in 1930, where his wife Carrie fell ill, forcing the Kiplings to move to Bermuda – cue for his latest diatribe about (American) tourists.

SAILING TO RIO

I'VE NEVER SAILED THE Amazon,
I've never reached Brazil;
But the Don and Magdalena,
They can go there when they will!

Yes, weekly from Southampton
Great steamers, white and gold,
Go rolling down to Rio
(Roll down – roll down to Rio!).
And I'd like to roll to Rio
Some day before I'm old!

I've never seen a Jaguar,
Nor yet an Armadill-
O dilloing in his armour,
And I s'pose I never will,

Unless I go to Rio
These wonders to behold –
Roll down – roll down to Rio –
Roll really down to Rio!
Oh, I'd love to roll to Rio
Some day before I'm old!

['The Beginning of the Armadillos', *Just So Stories*]

BRAZIL

THE BRAZILIANS I MET were interested in and entirely abreast of outside concerns, but these did not make their vital world. Their God – they jested – was a Brazilian. He gave them all they wanted and more at a pinch. For instance, once when their coffee-crop exceeded bounds, He sent a frost at the right moment, which cut it down a quarter and comfortably steadied the markets. And the vast inland countries were full of everything that anyone wanted, all waiting to be used in due time. During the War, when they were driven in upon themselves for metals, fibres, and such, they would show a sample to an Indian and ask him: 'Where does one find more of this?' Then he would lead them there. But, possessing these things, they gave one to understand, does not imply their immediate development by concessionaires. Brazil was a huge country, a half or third of which was still untapped. It would attend to itself in time. After a while, one fancied that, somewhere at the back of the scenes, there was the land-owning breed's dislike of the mere buyer and seller of commodities, which suggested an aristocratic foundation to the national fabric. The elaborate rituals of greeting and parting among ordinary folk pointed the same way. Life being large, and the hours easy-winged they expatiate in ceremonial. On the other hand, widespread national courtesy is generally due to some cogent reason. I asked if that reason existed here. Oh yes. Naturally. Their people resented above all things rudeness, lack of consideration, and injury to their 'face.' It annoyed them. Sometimes it made them see red. Then there would be trouble. Therefore, mutual accommodation from highest to humblest was the rule.

I had proof of this later at Carnival time, when the city of Rio went stark crazy. They dressed themselves in every sort of fancy-kit; they crowded into motors; they bought unlimited paper serpentines, which, properly thrown, unroll five fathoms at a flick; and for three days and three nights did nothing except circulate and congregate and bombard their neighbours with these papers and squirts of direful scent. (I made good practice against five angels in orange and black; a car-load of small boys not very disguised as young devils; and a lone, coroneted divinity in turquoise and silver.) The pavements were blocked with foot-folk all bearing serpentines, and wearing their fancy in clothes. City organisations and guilds assembled and poured out of their quarters, in charge of huge floats and figures, which were guarded by amateur cavalry; and companies of negro men and women fenced themselves inside a rope which all held, formed barbaric cohorts and platoons of red, green and yellow, and so advanced, shaking earth and air with the stamp and boom of immemorial tunes as they Charlestoned through the crowds. It was Africa – essential and unabated. The forty-foot floats that cruised high above the raging sea dealt raw-handedly with matters that the Press might have been too shy to discuss – such as a certain State railway, which is said to be casual in its traffic. Hence it was represented by twin locomotives butting like rams. To all appearance, the populace was utterly in charge of everything, and one bored one's way, a yard at a time, into it, while it shouted whatever came into its well-informed head, and plastered everybody with confetti. The serpentines hung like wreckage after flood on the branches of trees in the avenues; lay in rolls and fringes on the streets like seaweed on a beach; and were tangled and heaped over the bows of the cars till these resembled hay-carts of the operatic stage. But at no time, and in no place, was there anything approaching disorder, nor any smell of liquor. At two o'clock of the last night I saw a forty-foot avenue masked from kerb to kerb with serpentines and confetti. At five that same morning they were utterly gone – with the costumes and the revellers. There wasn't even a headache hanging over in the clean air!

Talking of this, people told me that drink was not a Brazilian failing, nor, as the state of the streets after Carnival proved, did men normally throw litter about. For one thing, they were racially neat-handed, as those are who deal in strong sunlight with wood, fibres, cane and rattan; and their fight against fever in the past had most practically taught them tidiness. Unpleasant things happen to the householder to-day if his cisterns and rubbish-heaps attract mosquitos in the city, and hard-handed

Municipal chiefs see that he pays up. And that is the reason why it is so hard to find a bad smell in Rio.

[*Brazilian Sketches*]

🌐 🌐 🌐

JAMAICA

HERE WE FINISH UP the day with a bang. No silly twilight performances. Just – sun-down, stars up and all the world of palm trees and bananas pushed back into the night in five minutes. But Dawn (I have seen some) seems to take longer: but it's a marvellous sight, and is purer and clearer than anything imaginable. Our rooms [in the Titchfield Hotel, Port Antonio] are all windows, overlooking a winding harbour – unimaginable blues and greens – with poinsettias and hibiscus rampant in the gardens which naturally put any palm-house at Kew to shame. Outside everything is the sea that takes to Cuba and the Spanish Main. We are in an annexe – about 200 yards from the huge main building which is all doors and openings. The dining room – like that at Kingston – is practically one vast open verandah – not a shred of glass anywhere: and what milky warm winds there are, roam about at large everywhere. Two monkeys (chained I grieve to say) inhabit a palm tree opposite our sitting room. He is an expert catcher of sugar, with a prehensile tail. She keeps house somewhere at the foot of the tree and grabs everything that he misses. Hence, brawls among the foliage. We came here by car, along the coast – a four hour run last Friday and had tea in a weird house of horror tho' it looked pretty enough, half way along. The manager of a big banana plantation, wasted with fever, and his equally ravaged wife, lived there – 200 feet up – looking down on creeks and bayous and mangrove swamps – the smell of which brought back all my old memories of fever. A little railway went to a little pier where steamers could lie. The railway delivered bananas – raw green bananas – into dark sheds. That was its business – to send bananas to the U.S.: somehow, vivid tho' the colour was, it was all indescribably forlorn.

[Letter to Elsie Bambridge, 5 March 1930]

✠ ✠ ✠

BERMUDA

THIS HOTEL [HOTEL BERMUDIANA] is 100% American. Oh God! They come in vast steamers to drink, and stay about three days – to be succeeded by the identical duplicates who drink more. By the way – if you can get it – try a 'Bacari'. [sic] It's a cocktail that lifts roofs. These folk however are so benighted that they do not know 'gin, tonic and bitters' as a drink. I have asked for it. The barman now dispenses it as a 'Kipling'. I have met no one worth talking to but I have signed 1,780,000 autographs and 78,542 books as far as I can remember. The flowers here are unbelievable. Mrs Kipling's room is finer than any florist's shop in Piccadilly. All flowers grow all together regardless of the seasons – all by the road and in the ditches and Easter lilies by the field-full. There isn't much to do except to watch them growing because the lower part of the hotel is uninhabitable. [. . .]

PS. The Bermudas are *not* the West Indies and they don't like being compared with 'em. Their pride is that they were *not* discovered by the late C[hristopher] C[olumbus].

[Letter to George Bambridge, 31 March 1930]

ᕼ 10 ᕽ

UBIQUE

Further Aspects of Travel

The Exiles' Line – The Lure of Foreign Lands – Benefits of Travel – East and West – Overseas Clubs – Some Aspects of Travel – With the Night Mail – As Easy as ABC – Envoi.

Kipling liked considering the wider implications of travel, and that meant not just its history, but also its psychological consequences and even its future. So in his poem 'The Exile's Line' he clearly enjoyed reflecting on the part the P&O steamship company played in the logistics of empire.

He recognised that, as a result of easier travel, Britons were starting to think and act differently. Like the discharged irregular in his poem 'Chant-Pagan', they had gained a certain 'attitude' as a result of exposure to foreign lands. Their independence of mind and dissatisfaction with conventional niceties were rather welcomed by Kipling.

More personally, he credited his own basic tolerance to his experience of different cultures and religions, which gave him 'two separate sides' to his head. It was certainly no use being too dogmatic – the theme of his lines about the dangers of attempting to 'hustle the East'.

Not all travellers want to mix with foreigners, however. Sometimes they prefer to socialise with their fellow countrymen in institutions such as the Overseas Club, which Kipling observed in Japan.

He elaborated on his more general ideas about travel in a lecture to the Royal Geographical Society in 1914, when he talked about the distinctive smells of places, the ideal attributes of an expedition leader, and the shrinking of the globe that came with easier and quicker movement. Under cover of fiction, he speculated on the future of travel in a couple of powerful stories – 'With the Night Mail' and the more disturbing 'As Easy as ABC' – both of which foresee an authoritarian world where 'transport is civilisation'.

In conclusion I reproduce Kipling's poem 'A Song of the Cities' from his 1896 collection *The Seven Seas*, which ranges widely on the interrelationship between seafaring, travel, empire and Britishness. These short verses about different cities he knew and loved are not great descriptive pieces, but they are testimony to the reverence he felt for the spirit of place.

THE EXILES' LINE

Now the new year reviving old desires,
The restless soul to open sea aspires,
  Where the Blue Peter flickers from the fore,
And the grimed stoker feeds the engine-fires.

Coupons, alas, depart with all their rows,
And last year's sea-met loves where Grindley knows;
  But still the wild wind wakes off Gardafui,
And hearts turn eastward with the P&Os.

Twelve knots an hour, be they more or less –
Oh slothful mother of much idleness,
  Whom neither rivals spur nor contracts speed!
Nay, bear us gently! Wherefore need we press?

The Tragedy of all our East is laid
On those white decks beneath the awning shade –
  Birth, absence, longing, laughter, love and tears,
And death unmaking ere the land is made.

And midnight madnesses of souls distraught
Whom the cool seas call through the open port,
  So that the table lacks one place next morn,
And for one forenoon men forego their sport.

The shadow of the rigging to and fro
Sways, shifts, and flickers on the spar-deck's snow,
  And like a giant trampling in his chains,
The screw-blades gasp and thunder deep below;

And, leagued to watch one flying-fish's wings,
Heaven stoops to sea, and sea to Heaven clings;

While, bent upon the ending of his toil,
The hot sun strides, regarding not these things:

For the same wave that meets our stem in spray
Bore Smith of Asia eastward yesterday,
    And Delhi Jones and Brown of Midnapore
To-morrow follow on the self-same way.

Linked in the chain of Empire one by one,
Flushed with long leave, or tanned with many a sun,
    The Exiles' Line brings out the exiles' line
And ships them homeward when their work is done.

Yea, heedless of the shuttle through the loom,
The flying keels fulfil the web of doom.
    Sorrow or shouting – what is that to them?
Make out the cheque that pays for cabin room!

And how so many score of times ye flit
With wife and babe and caravan of kit,
    Not all thy travels past shall lower one fare,
Not all thy tears abate one pound of it.

And how so high throe earth-born dignity,
Honour and state, go sink it in the sea,
    Till that great one upon the quarter deck,
Brow-bound with gold, shall give thee leave to be.

Indeed, indeed from that same line we swear
Off for all time, and mean it when we swear;
    And then, and then we meet the Quartered Flag,
And, surely for the last time, pay the fare.

And Green of Kensington, estrayed to view
In three short months the world he never knew,
    Stares with blind eyes upon the Quartered Flag
And sees no more than yellow, red and blue.

But we, the gypsies of the East, but we –
Waifs of the land and wastrels of the sea –
    Come nearer home beneath the Quartered Flag
Than ever home shall come to such as we.

The camp is struck, the bungalow decays,
Dead friends and houses desert mark our ways,
    Till sickness send us down to Prince's Dock
To meet the changeless use of many days.

Bound in the wheel of Empire, one by one,
The chain-gangs of the East from sire to son,
    The Exiles' Line takes out the exiles' line
And ships them homeward when their work is done.

How runs the old indictment? 'Dear and slow,'
So much and twice so much. We gird, but go.
    For all the soul of our sad East is there,
Beneath the house-flag of the P&O.

[Rudyard Kipling's Verse]

❂ ❂ ❂

THE LURE OF FOREIGN LANDS

Me that 'ave been what I've been –
    Me that 'ave gone where I've gone –
Me that 'ave seen what I've seen –
    'Ow can I ever take on
With awful old England again,
An' 'ouses both sides of the street,
And 'edges two sides of the lane,
And the parson an' gentry between,
An' touchin' my 'at when we meet –
Me that 'ave been what I've been?

Me that 'ave watched 'arf a world
'Eave up all shiny with dew,
Kopje on kop to the sun,
An' as soon as the mist let 'em through
Our 'elios winkin' like fun –
Three sides of a ninety-mile square,
Over valleys as big as a shire –
Are ye there? Are ye there? Are ye there?
An' then the blind drum of our fire . . .
An' I'm rollin' 'is lawns for the Squire,
                                        Me!

Me that 'ave rode through the dark
Forty mile, often, on end,
Along the Ma'ollisberg Range,
With only the stars for my mark
An' only the night for my friend,
An' things runnin' off as you pass,
An' things jumpin' up in the grass,
An' the silence, the shine an' the size
Of the 'igh, unexpressible skies –
I am takin' some letters almost
As much as a mile to the post,
An' 'mind you come back with the change'!
                                        Me!

Me that saw Barberton took
When we dropped through the clouds on their 'ead,
An' they 'ove the guns over and fled
Me that was through Di'mond 'ill,
An' Pieters an' Springs an' Belfast –
From Dundee to Vereeniging all –
Me that stuck out to the last
(An' five bloomin' bars on my chest) –
I am doin' my Sunday-school best,
By the 'elp of the Squire an' 'is wife
(Not to mention the 'ousemaid an' cook),
To come in an' 'ands up an' be still,

An' honestly work for my bread,
My livin' in that state of life
To which it shall please God to call
                              Me!

Me that 'ave followed my trade
In the place where the Lightnin's are made,
'Twixt the Rains and the Sun and the Moon –
Me that lay down an' got up
Three years with the sky for my roof –
That 'ave ridden my 'unger an' thirst
Six thousand raw mile on the hoof,
With the Vaal and the Orange for cup,
An' the Brandwater Basin for dish, –
Oh! it's 'ard to be'ave as they wish
(Too 'ard, an' a little too soon),
I'll 'ave to think over it first –
                              Me!

I will arise an' get 'ence; –
I will trek South and make sure
If it's only my fancy or not
That the sunshine of England is pale,
And the breezes of England are stale,
An' there's somethin' gone small with the lot;
For I know of a sun an' a wind,
An' some plains and a mountain be'ind,
An' some graves by a barb-wire fence;
An' a Dutchman I've fought 'oo might give
Me a job were I ever inclined,
To look in an' offsaddle an' live
Where there's neither a road nor a tree –
But only my Maker an' me,
And I think it will kill me or cure,
So I think I will go there an' see.
                              Me!

['Chant-Pagan', *The Five Nations*]

✖ ✖ ✖

BENEFITS OF TRAVEL

Much I owe to the Lands that grew –
More to the Lives that fed –
But most to Allah Who gave me two
Separate sides to my head.

Much I reflect on the Good and the True
In the Faiths beneath the sun,
But most upon Allah Who gave me two
Sides to my head, not one.

Wesley's following, Calvin's flock,
White or yellow or bronze,
Shaman, Juju or Angekok,
Minister, Mukamuk, Bonze –

Here is a health, my brothers, to you,
However your prayers are said,
And praised be Allah Who gave me two
Separate sides to my head!

I would go without shirt or shoe,
Friend, tobacco or bread,
Sooner than lose for a minute the two
Separate sides of my head!

['The Two-Sided Man', *Kim*]

EAST AND WEST

Now it is not good for the Christian's health to hustle the
Aryan brown,
For the Christian riles, and the Aryan smiles and he weareth the
Christian down;
And the end of the fight is a tombstone white with the name of
the late deceased,
And the epitaph drear: 'A Fool lies here who tried to hustle the
East.'

[*The Naulakha*]

✖   ✖   ✖

OVERSEAS CLUBS

All things considered, there are only two kinds of men in
the world – those that stay at home and those that do not. The
second are the most interesting. Some day a man will bethink
himself and write a book about the breed in a book called 'The
Book of the Overseas Club,' for it is at the clubhouses all the way
from Aden to Yokohama that the life of the Outside Men is best
seen and their talk is best heard. A strong family likeness runs
through both buildings and members, and a large and careless
hospitality is the note. There is always the same open-doored,
high-ceiled house, with matting on the floors; the same come
and go of dark-skinned servants, and the same assembly of
men talking horse or business, in raiment that would fatally
scandalise a London committee, among files of newspapers
from a fortnight to five weeks old. The life of the Outside Men
includes plenty of sunshine, and as much air as may be stirring.
At the Cape, where the Dutch housewives distil and sell the very
potent Vanderhum, and the absurd home-made hansom cabs
waddle up and down the yellow dust of Adderley Street, are
the members of the big import and export firms, the shipping
and insurance offices, inventors of mines, and exploiters of new
territories with now and then an officer strayed from India to

buy mules for the Government, a Government House aide-de-camp, a sprinkling of the officers of the garrison, tanned skippers of the Union and Castle Lines, and naval men from the squadron at Simon's Town. Here they talk of the sins of Cecil Rhodes, the insolence of Natal, the beauties or otherwise of the solid Boer vote, and the dates of the steamers. The argot is Dutch and Kaffir, and every one can hum the national anthem that begins 'Pack your kit and trek, Johnny Bowlegs.' In the stately Hongkong Clubhouse, which is to the further what the Bengal Club is to the nearer East, you meet much the same gathering, minus the mining speculators and plus men whose talk is of tea, silk, shortings, and Shanghai ponies. The speech of the Outside Men at this point becomes fearfully mixed with pidgin-English and local Chinese terms, rounded with corrupt Portuguese. At Melbourne, in a long verandah giving on a grass plot, where laughing-jackasses laugh very horribly, sit wool-kings, premiers, and breeders of horses after their kind. The older men talk of the days of the Eureka Stockade and the younger of 'shearing wars' in North Queensland, while the traveller moves timidly among them wondering what under the world every third word means. At Wellington, overlooking the harbour (all right-minded clubs should command the sea), another, and yet a like, sort of men speak of sheep, the rabbits, the land-courts, and the ancient heresies of Sir Julius Vogel; and their more expressive sentences borrow from the Maori. And elsewhere, and elsewhere, and elsewhere among the Outside Men it is the same – the same mixture of every trade, calling, and profession under the sun; the same clash of conflicting interests touching the uttermost parts of the earth; the same intimate, and sometimes appalling knowledge of your neighbour's business and shortcomings; the same large-palmed hospitality, and the same interest on the part of the younger men in the legs of a horse. Decidedly, it is at the Overseas Club all the world over that you get to know some little of the life of the community. London is egoistical, and the world for her ends with the four-mile cab radius. There is no provincialism like the provincialism of London. That big slack-water coated with the drift and rubbish of a thousand men's thoughts esteems itself the open sea because the waves of all the oceans break on her borders. To those in her midst she is terribly imposing, but they forget that there is more than one kind of imposition. Look back upon her from ten thousand miles, when the mail is just in at the Overseas Club, and she is wondrous tiny. Nine-tenths of her news – so vital, so epoch-making over there – loses its significance, and the rest is as the scuffling of ghosts in a back-attic.

Here in Yokohama the Overseas Club has two mails and four sets of papers – English, French, German, and American, as suits the variety of its constitution – and the verandah by the sea, where the big telescope stands, is a perpetual feast of the Pentecost. The population of the club changes with each steamer in harbour, for the sea-captains swing in, are met with 'Hello! where did you come from?' and mix at the bar and billiard-tables for their appointed time and go to sea again. The white-painted warships supply their contingent of members also, and there are wonderful men, mines of most fascinating adventure, who have an interest in sealing-brigs that go to the Kurile Islands, and somehow get into trouble with the Russian authorities. Consuls and judges of the Consular Courts meet men over on leave from the China ports, or it may be Manila, and they all talk tea, silk, banking, and exchange with its fixed residents. Everything is always as bad as it can possibly be, and everybody is on the verge of ruin. That is why, when they have decided that life is no longer worth living, they go down to the skittle-alley – to commit suicide. From the outside, when a cool wind blows among the papers and there is a sound of smashing ice in an inner apartment, and every third man is talking about the approaching races, the life seems to be a desirable one. 'What more could a man need to make him happy?' says the passer-by. A perfect climate, a lovely country, plenty of pleasant society, and the politest people on earth to deal with.

[*From Tideway to Tideway*]

❊　❊　❊

SOME ASPECTS OF TRAVEL

[. . .] LET US LEAVE it there, and consider for a while the illimitable, the fascinating subject of smells in their relation to the traveller. We shall soon have to exchange them for blasts of petrol and atomised castor-oil. Have you noticed wherever a few travellers gather together, one or the other is sure to say: 'Do you remember that smell at such and such a place?' Then he may go on to speak of camel – pure camel – one whiff of which is all Arabia; or of the smell of rotten eggs at Hitt on the Euphrates, where Noah got the pitch for the Ark; or of the flavour of drying fish in Burma. Then the company begin to purr like cats at valerian, and, as the books say, 'conversation becomes general'.

I suggest, subject to correction – there are only two elementary smells of universal appeal – the smell of burning fuel and the smell of melting grease. The smell, that is, of what man cooks his food over and what he cooks his food in. Fuel ranges from coal to cowdung – specially cowdung – and coco-nut husk; grease from butter through ghi to palm and coco-nut oil; and these two, either singly or in combination, make the background and furnish the active poison of nearly all the smells which assault and perturb the mind of the wayfaring man returned to civilisation. I rank wood-smoke first, since it calls up more, more intimate and varied memories, over a wider geographical range, to a larger number of individuals, than any other agent that we know. My powers are limited, but I think I would undertake to transport a quarter of a million Englishmen to any point in South Africa, from the Zambezi to Cape Agulhas, with no more elaborate vehicle than a box of matches, a string or two of rifle cordite, a broken-up biscuit-box, some chips of a creosoted railway sleeper, and a handful of dried cowdung, and to land each man in the precise spot he had in his mind. And that is only a small part of the world that wood-smoke controls. A whiff of it can take us back to forgotten marches over unnamed mountains with disreputable companions; to day-long halts beside flooded rivers in the rain; wonderful mornings of youth in brilliantly lighted lands where everything was possible – and generally done; to uneasy wakings under the low desert moon and on top of cruel, hard pebbles; and, above all, to that God's own hour, all the world over, when the stars have gone out and it is too dark to see clear, and one lies with the fumes of last night's embers in one's nostrils – lies and waits for a new horizon to heave itself up against a new dawn. Wood-smoke magic works on everyone according to his experience. I live in a wood-smoke country, and I know how men, otherwise silent, become suddenly and surprisingly eloquent under its influence.

And next to wood-smoke for waking rampant 'wanderlust' comes the smell of melting grease – such a smell or bouquet of smells as one may gather outside a London fried-fish shop. It is less sentimental and vague in its appeal than wood-smoke, but it hits harder. Where grease is melting, something is being cooked, and that means a change from tinned food for one night at any rate. It is an opulent, a kaleidoscopic, a semitic smell of immense range and variety of colour. Sometimes it reconstructs big covered bazaars of well-stocked cities with the blue haze hanging in the domes; or it resurrects little Heaven-sent single stalls picked up by the roadside, where one can buy penny bottles of sauce or a paper of badly needed buttons. It implies camels kneeling to unload; belts and straps being loosened; contented camp-followers dodging off to buy supplies – turmeric assafœtida, currystuffs; men washing their hands in sand before dipping them into the greasy pewter platters. And the next gust or surge of it may be pure Central Asia – thick, and choking as butter-lamps before a Tibetan shrine – a Tibetan shrine, with frost in the air, one star on the tip of a mountain, and a brown-cloaked Bhotyali rustling up through dry maize-stalks to sell a chicken. Or it may thin out to a mere echo of an appeal that calls up all the pulse and thrill and clamour of the true tropic night-blazing moonlight, black shadow, the roar of the tree-toads, a touch of Chinese matting, a gust of jasmine or champak, and the languid puff of a warm phosphorescent sea.

To me, as to others, a fried-fish shop can speak multitudinously for all the East from Cairo to Singapore; and I have heard West Coast men say that, when the smell turns bitter, it will sometimes duplicate the smell of their palm-oil chop, and cause them to re-live horrible depressing evenings by the light of kerosene lamps, hung under corrugated iron roofs of factories beside brown rivers that bubble. It does not cover the South Seas, that wonderful fifth quarter of the world, where, I believe, the smell of first appeal is burning coco-nut husk, a heavy loading of coco-nut oil, and a dash of salt coral-reef. But it is no mean magician, as we all know.

And so much for universals. Coming now to smells of particular appeal, what would most vividly remind a Polar explorer of past experiences? I suggest that ether-like smell given off by the flame of a big spirit-lamp when it is flattened out against the heated metal cooking-plate above – an unmixed smell, simple of itself, like Falstaff's sack. I should put the limits of this appeal roughly as from the Seventies to either pole. From the Seventies to the Sixties runs that belt of unsanctified latitudes which are the stamping-ground of the winds, the wilderness and the fringes of the restless ice, all linked together, in the minds of men who know it, by the desolate smell of the stranded berg as it piles up reeking with ooze gouged off the sea-floors. Melville, of the *Jeannette*, once told me that it would 'send your heart into your boots – if you hadn't eaten them already'. At the Sixties and down to Labrador, it seems to me we reach kindly timber and a suggestion of meat on the hoof. The smell of stranded ice is mixed with the clear breath of seas that are not always frozen, and the acrid tang of a raw moose-hide being passed back and forth through wood-smoke to cure it – this last as characteristic as the smell of home-made rimpje on a Dutch farm at the other side of the world. A little lower, the appeals thicken and become more complex. I suggest evergreens sweating in the sun; birchwood smoke; the oily bark itself; pinegums, resin and tallow melted together; the cleanswept smell of milky-green snow-water pouring over pebble bars; and not so far in the background, a suspicion, or a camp-shifting certainty, of skunk. Here – say 50°N. and 65°W. – we meet our friend the horse, or rather he pushes his way into the rotten-wood smudge (that is an awakening smell, too) beside us. He keeps us company west through the grass-scented prairie air till we are more conscious of him and his saddlery than any other flavour in the landscape.

There is a heart-searching little motif of five notes – horse; old saddlery; coffee; fried bacon; and tobacco (from cut plug to maize-leaf cigarettes) – that can carry a man down from high dry camps in the Selkirks, or wet ones in Oregon, down and down over red spicy dust and dead white dust, through the scent of sage-brush and sharp peppery euphorbias, down to the torrid goat-scented South where fried beans, incense, and the abominable brassy smell of pulque will pass him on to all the forlorn brood of mangrove, foreshore and yellow-fever stinks, until he leaves his horse on the beach, and the Tropics lift up his heart with the wholesome rasp of sunbaked coral and dried fish.

Forgive me, ladies and gentlemen! I will not go on with the catalogue, though I feel like the commercial traveller in the story, who said: 'If you don't care to look at my samples, d'you mind my having a look at 'em. It's so long since I've seen them.'

It is probable that the future will have no place for these links with past delights and labours – that they will be forgotten like the labours themselves – as we have forgotten the smell of homemade soap or the whistle and rap of the flails on a threshing-floor. Only a little while ago a man wrote me from Northern Canada: 'We have broken into a new belt of wheat 40 miles wide – and we have left the horse behind!' Even now one can charge by rail in less than a week through the exquisitely graduated and significant series of smells, that lie like iridescence on an oyster-shell, over the last 2500 miles of South Africa, and one can return with no more than a general impression of sunshine and coal-smoke. And, as people always say in the middle of a revolution: 'We are only at the beginning of things.'

Conceive for a moment a generation wholly divorced from all known smells of land and sea-travel – a generation which will climb into and drop down from the utterly odourless upper airs, unprepared in any one of its senses for the flavour, which is the spirit, of the country it descends upon! Everything that we have used till now has allowed us time for a little mental adjustment of horizons – time and contact with the changing earth and waters under us. In the future, there will be neither mental adjustment nor horizons as we have understood them: not any more of the long days that prove and prepare, nor the nights that terrify and make sane again, neither sweat nor suffering, nor the panic knowledge of isolation beyond help – none, so far as we can guess, of the checks that have hitherto conditioned all our travels.

And hitherto our life has only taught us to love what we have suffered for or with. One loves a stray dog after one has had to sit up with him for a night or two. How much more that corner of the Earth to which we have given our very hide and health and reputation!

And it is the same on the human side. Men like a man who has shown himself a pleasant companion through a week's walking-tour. They worship the man, who over thousands of miles for hundreds of days, through renewed difficulties and efforts, has brought them without friction, arrogance, or dishonour, to the victory proposed, or to the higher glory of unshaken defeat. Anything like a man can bustle hounds after a sinking fox, but it takes something like a man to bring them home with their sterns up after they have lost him, or – seen him run into by another pack! It is one of the mysteries of personality that virtue should go out of certain men to uphold – literally to ennoble – their companions even while their own nerves are like live wire, and their own mouths are full of the taste of fever and fatigue. There is no headmark by which we can recognise such men before they have proved themselves. Their secret is incommunicable. One man, apparently without effort, inspires the human equivalent of 'three blind 'uns and a bolter' and makes them do miracles. Another, working hard all the time, scientifically reduces half a dozen picked men to the level of sulky, disloyal schoolboys. And everybody wonders how it happened.

The explanations are as bewildering as the facts. A man was asked some time ago why he invariably followed a well-known man into most uncomfortable situations. He replied: 'All the years I have known So-and-so, I've never known him to say whether he was cold or hot, wet or dry, sick or well; but I've never known him forget a man who was.' Here is another reply to a similar question about another leader, who was notoriously a little difficult to get on with. One of his followers wrote: 'So-

and-so is all you say and more, and he grows worse as he grows older; but he will take the blame of any mistake any man of his makes, and he doesn't care what lie he tells to save him.' And when I wrote to find out why a man whom I knew preferred not to go out with another man whom I also knew, I got this illuminating diagnosis: 'So-and-so is not afraid of anything on earth except the newspapers. So I have a previous engagement.' In the face of these documents, it looks as though self-sacrifice, loyalty, and a robust view of moral obligations go far to make a leader, the capacity to live alone and inside himself being taken for granted.

But then come the accidents for which no allowance is made – or can be made. A good man, who has held a disorganised crowd together at the expense of his own vitality, may be tried, slowly or suddenly, beyond his limit, till he breaks down, and, as Hakluyt says, is either 'ignominiously reported or exceedingly condemned'. There is a limit for every man, an edge beyond which he must not go. But here at home only the doctor, the nurses, and the clergymen see what happens next – not the caravan, not the grinning coolies, and the whole naked landscape – and afterwards all the world!

However, these things, and worse, are part of the rule of the road. They have never hindered men from leading or following. Even in these days a man has but to announce he is going to gamble against death for a few months on totally inadequate cover, and thousands of hitherto honest Englishmen will fawn and intrigue and, if necessary, lie like anyone you choose to think of – in order to be allotted one life-share in the venture.

But what of the future? Into what terms will this world-old, foot-pound energy of travel translate itself under the new conditions? Here is our position. Up to the present we have been forced to move in two dimensions by the help of the Three Beasts of Burden and a few live coals in a pot. Now we perceive that we can move in three dimensions, and the possibilities of our new freedom distract and disturb us in all relations. This is because our minds are still hobbled and knee-haltered by inherited memories of what were held to be immutable facts – distance, height and depth, separation, homesickness, the fear of accident and foul weather. The sea, in spite of our attacks, is still unplumbed, salt, and estranging; a mountain-range means so many days' delay or détour; so many extra rations, sure changes of heat and cold. The desert and the wilderness have still to be approached by cautious sap and mine – depôt and cache. Where there is no water for 200 miles, we shake our head and limp round it. A little while ago we should have done so, humbly, glad to be excused. Now we step out of our path grudgingly, resentfully, resolute to come back again and take no refusal.

Presently – very presently – we shall come back and convert 200 miles across any part of the Earth into its standardised time equivalent, precisely as we convert 5 miles with infantry in column, 10 with cavalry on the march, 12 in a Cape cart, or 50 in a car – that is to say, into two hours. And whether there be one desert or a dozen mountain-ranges in that 200 miles will not affect our time-table by five minutes.

Month by month the Earth shrinks actually, and, what is more important, in imagination. We know it by the slide and crash of unstable material all around us. For the moment, but only for the moment, the new machines are outstripping mankind. We have cut down enormously – we shall cut down inconceivably – the world-conception of time and space, which is the big flywheel of the world's progress. What wonder that the great world-engine, which we call Civilisation, should race and heat a little; or that the onlookers who see it take charge should be a little excited, and, therefore, inclined to scold? You could witness precisely the same flurry in any engine-room on the Atlantic this evening, where a liner happens to be pitching her propellers out of water. For the moment the machines are developing more power than has been required for their duties. But just as soon as humanity can get its breath, the machines' load will be increased and they will settle smoothly to their load and most marvellous output.

Frankly, one is not so much interested in the achievements of the future as in the men of the present who are already scouting and reporting along its fantastic skyline. All, or nearly all, that can be accomplished by the old means has been won and put to general account. The old mechanism is scrapped: the moods and emotions that went with it follow. Only the spirit of man carries on, unaltered and unappeasable. There will arise – they are shaping themselves even now – risks to be met as cruel as any that Hudson or Scott faced; dreams as world-wide as Columbus or Cecil Rhodes dreamed, to be made good or to die for; and decisions to be taken as splendidly terrible as that which Drake clinched by Magellan, or Oates a little farther south. There is no break in the line, no loads are missing; the men of the present have begun the discovery of the New World with the same devoutly careless passion as their predecessors completed the discovery of the Old.

[From a talk to the Royal Geographical Society, 7 February 1914,
Book of Words]

✠　✠　✠

WITH THE NIGHT MAIL

'FIVE THOUSAND-SIX, SIX THOUSAND eight hundred' – the dip-dial reads ere we find the easterly drift, heralded by a flurry of snow at the thousand fathom level. Captain Purnall rings up the engines and keys down the governor on the switch before him. There is no sense in urging machinery when Eolus himself gives you good knots for nothing. We are away in earnest now – our nose notched home on our chosen star. At this level the lower clouds are laid out, all neatly combed by the dry fingers of the East. Below that again is the strong westerly blow through which we rose. Overhead, a film of southerly drifting mist draws a theatrical gauze across the firmament. The moonlight turns the lower strata to silver without a stain except where our shadow underruns us. Bristol and Cardiff Double Lights (those statelily inclined beams over Severnmouth) are dead ahead of us; for we keep the Southern Winter Route. Coventry Central, the pivot of the English system, stabs upward once in ten seconds its spear of diamond light to the north; and a point or two off our starboard bow The Leek, the great cloud-breaker of Saint David's Head, swings its unmistakable green beam twenty-five degrees each way. There must be half a mile of fluff over it in this weather, but it does not affect The Leek.

'Our planet's over-lighted if anything,' says Captain Purnall at the wheel, as Cardiff–Bristol slides under. 'I remember the old days of common white verticals that 'ud show two or three hundred feet up in a mist, if you knew where to look for 'em. In really fluffy weather they might as well have been under your hat. One could get lost coming home then, an' have some fun. Now, it's like driving down Piccadilly.'

He points to the pillars of light where the cloud-breakers bore through the cloud-floor. We see nothing of England's outlines: only a white pavement pierced in all directions by these manholes of variously coloured fire – Holy Island's white and red – St. Bee's interrupted white, and so on as far as the eye can reach. Blessed be Sargent, Ahrens, and the Dubois brothers, who invented the cloud-breakers of the world whereby we travel in security!

'Are you going to lift for The Shamrock?' asks Captain Hodgson. Cork Light (green, fixed) enlarges as we rush to it. Captain Purnall nods. There is heavy traffic hereabouts – the cloud-bank beneath us is streaked. with running fissures of flame where the Atlantic boats are hurrying Londonward just clear of the fluff. Mail-packets are supposed, under the Conference rules, to have the five-thousand-foot lanes to themselves, but the foreigner in a hurry is apt to take liberties with English air. 'No. 162' lifts to a long-drawn wail of the breeze in the fore-flange of the rudder and we make Valencia (white, green, white) at a safe 7000 feet, dipping our beam to an incoming Washington packet.

[*Actions and Reactions*]

AS EASY AS ABC

By TEN O'CLOCK WE were over Lake Michigan. The west shore was lightless, except for a dull ground-glare at Chicago, and a single traffic-directing light – its leading beam pointing north – at Waukegan on our starboard bow. None of the Lake villages gave any sign of life; and inland, westward, so far as we could see, blackness lay unbroken on the level earth. We swooped down and skimmed low across the dark, throwing calls county by county. Now and again we picked up the faint glimmer of a house-light, or heard the rasp and rend of a cultivator being played across the fields, but Northern Illinois as a whole was one inky, apparently uninhabited, waste of high, forced woods. Only our illuminated map, with its little pointer switching from county to county, as we wheeled and twisted, gave us any idea of our position. Our calls, urgent, pleading, coaxing or commanding, through the General Communicator brought no answer. Illinois strictly maintained her own privacy in the timber which she grew for that purpose.

'Oh, this is absurd!' said De Forest. 'We're like an owl trying to work a wheat-field. Is this Bureau Creek? Let's land, Arnott, and get hold of someone.'

We brushed over a belt of forced woodland – fifteen-year-old maple sixty feet high – grounded on a private meadow-dock, none too big, where we moored to our own grapnels, and hurried out through the warm dark night towards a light in a verandah. As we neared the garden gate I could have sworn we had stepped knee-deep in quicksand, for we could scarcely drag our feet against the prickling currents that clogged them. After five paces we stopped, wiping our foreheads, as hopelessly stuck on dry smooth turf as so many cows in a bog.

['As Easy as ABC', *A Diversity of Creatures*]

✖ ✖ ✖

ENVOI

BOMBAY

ROYAL AND DOWER-ROYAL, I the Queen
    Fronting thy richest sea with richer hands –
A thousand mills roar through me where I glean
    All races from all lands.

CALCUTTA

Me the Sea-captain loved, the River built,
    Wealth sought and Kings adventured life to hold.
Hail, England! I am Asia – Power on silt,
    Death in my hands, but Gold!

MADRAS

Clive kissed me on the mouth and eyes and brow,
    Wonderful kisses, so that I became
Crowned above Queens – a withered beldame now,
    Brooding on ancient fame.

RANGOON

Hail, Mother! Do they call me rich in trade?
    Little care I, but hear the shorn priest drone,
And watch my silk-clad lovers, man by maid,
    Laugh 'neath my Shwe Dagon.

SINGAPORE

Hail, Mother! East and West must seek my aid
    Ere the spent gear may dare the ports afar.
The second doorway of the wide world's trade
    Is mine to loose or bar.

HONG-KONG

Hail, Mother! Hold me fast; my Praya sleeps
    Under innumerable keels to-day.
Yet guard (and landward), or to-morrow sweeps
    Thy war-ships down the bay!

HALIFAX

Into the mist my guardian prows put forth,
  Behind the mist my virgin ramparts lie,
The Warden of the Honour of the North,
  Sleepless and veiled am I!

QUEBEC AND MONTREAL

Peace is our portion. Yet a whisper rose,
  Foolish and causeless, half in jest, half hate.
Now wake we and remember mighty blows,
  And, fearing no man, wait!

VICTORIA

From East to West the circling word has passed,
  Till West is East beside our land-locked blue;
From East to West the tested chain holds fast,
  The well-forged link rings true!

CAPE TOWN

Hail! Snatched and bartered oft from hand to hand,
  I dream my dream, by rock and heath and pine,
Of Empire to the northward. Ay, one land
  From Lion's Head to Line!

MELBOURNE

Greeting! Nor fear nor favour won us place,
  Got between greed of gold and dread of drouth,
Loud-voiced and reckless as the wild tide-race
  That whips our harbour-mouth!

SYDNEY

Greeting! My birth-stain have I turned to good;
  Forcing strong wills perverse to steadfastness:
The first flush of the tropics in my blood,
  And at my feet Success!

BRISBANE

The northern stock beneath the southern skies –
I build a Nation for an Empire's need,
Suffer a little, and my land shall rise,
Queen over lands indeed!

HOBART

Man's love first found me; man's hate made me Hell;
For my babes' sake I cleansed those infamies.
Earnest for leave to live and labour well,
God flung me peace and ease.

AUCKLAND

Last, loneliest, loveliest, exquisite, apart –
On us, on us the unswerving season smiles,
Who wonder 'mid our fern why men depart
To seek the Happy Isles!

['The Song of the Cities', from 'A Song of the English', *The Seven Seas*]

BIBLIOGRAPHY

Works by Kipling

Abaft the Funnel, 1909
Actions and Reactions, 1909
Barrack-Room Ballads and Other Verses, 1892
Book of Words, 1928
Brazilian Sketches, 1940
Captains Courageous, 1897
The City of Dreadful Night and Other Places, 1891
The Courting of Dinah Shadd and Other Stories, 1890
Debits and Credits, 1926
Departmental Ditties and Other Verses, 1886
A Diversity of Creatures, 1917
Egypt of the Magicians, 1914
The Five Nations, 1903
The Fringes of the Fleet, 1915
From Sea to Sea, 1900
From Tideway to Tideway, 1892
A History of England, 1911
Just So Stories, 1902
Kim, 1901
Letters of Marque, 1891
Letters to the Family, 1908
Life's Handicap, 1891
The Light That Failed, 1890
Many Inventions, 1893
The Muse Among the Motors, 1904
The Naulahka, 1892

The Phantom Rickshaw and Other Stories, 1890
Plain Tales from the Hills, 1888
Puck of Pook's Hill, 1906
Rewards and Fairies, 1910
Rudyard Kipling's Verse, inclusive edition, 1919, 1927, 1933
The Seven Seas, 1896
Songs from Books, 1913
Something of Myself, 1937
Souvenirs of France, 1933
Stalky & Co, 1899
Traffic and Discoveries, 1904
The War in the Mountains, 1917

Works by Others or Special Editions

Kemp, Sandra and Lisa Lewis (eds), *Rudyard Kipling: Writings on Writing,* Cambridge University Press, 1996

Kipling, Rudyard, *Something of Myself and Other Autobiographical Writings,* ed. Thomas Pinney, Cambridge University Press, 1990

Lycett, Andrew, *Rudyard Kipling,* Weidenfeld & Nicolson, 1999

McAveeney, David C., *Kipling in Gloucester,* Curious Traveller Press, 1996

Cortazzi, Hugh and George Webb (eds), *Kipling's Japan,* Athlone Press, 1988

Macdonald, Meryl, *The Long Trail: Kipling Round the World,* Tideway House, 2000

Pinney, Thomas (ed.), *Kipling's India,* Macmillan, 1986

——, *The Letters of Rudyard Kipling,* 6 volumes, Macmillan, 1990–2004

Smith, Michael, *Kipling's Sussex,* Brownleaf, 2008

INDEX